D0240012

Dorothy,

My soul is between these covers.

Enjoy!

Susan

Sulayman

Sulayman

A Journey To Love and Truth

A novel

Susan Gabori

Library of Congress Control Number:		2011910149
ISBN:	Hardcover	978-1-4628-9037-8
	Softcover	978-1-4653-5035-0
	Ebook	978-1-4628-9038-5

Cover photograph:
"Mosque in Córdoba, Spain, completed in 987"

This book was printed in the United States of America.

To order additional copies of this book, contact:
Xlibris Corporation
1-888-795-4274
www.Xlibris.com
Orders@Xlibris.com
98428

Contents

Preface

In the name of Allah, the Compassionate,
the Merciful, whose aid I implore.

It is my sincere wish that this manuscript be read not only by people of my own religion but other monotheists, as well as polytheists, who have not yet discovered the Way of Allah, the Absolute, the All Knowing.

In these pages, I have attempted to outline my spiritual quest from the time it was a dormant seed to its final bloom. I hope my personal struggles will serve those already on the path, as well as those about to wake to the possibility of the Absolute. My experiences have shown that once people, no matter of what religion, embark upon the spiritual road, they are all searching for the same Truth, the same God.

This preface predominantly addresses the three monotheistic religions: Islam, Christianity, and Judaism. I fully understand that we all put a different date on our years; we all have a different way of counting the passing of time. For Islam, year one is marked by the Hijra, Muhammad's flight from Mecca to Medina. For Christians, year one begins with the birth of Christ. For the Jews, year one represents God's first words to Abraham.

According to Muslim calculations, my story opens in 349, when I am twenty-one years old. For the Christians, the time is 960. The Jews write 4721. To show my respect toward the people of the Qur'an, as well as the people of the Old and New Testament, I originally wanted to include all three dates in this manuscript. This has proven to be a more cumbersome task than I had anticipated. Finally, I chose to indicate only the Muslim and Christian dates; the reason being that, at present, these two religions share the power on earth.

I do hope the Jews will forgive me for having excluded their calendar years. I would like to assure them it was not done as a sign of disrespect. On the contrary, we well know that the roots of both Christianity and Islam reach back to Judaism. Judaism and the Jewish people are the spiritual ancestors of us all. They were the first to hear and record the words of God, the Absolute. In addition, their book, the Torah, gave both the Christians and the Muslims the beginning of their spiritual, monotheistic history.

Sulayman ibn Ahmed ibn Idris
392/1002

I. Family

Before me, slaves on horseback are leading mules laden with carpets. Since our small caravan left the city of Fez three weeks ago, we have been traveling through Morocco, across the Strait of Gibraltar, and over the hills of al-Andalus. The endless rolling in the saddle has exhausted our bodies and inflamed our desire to reach home. It has been six months since we last saw Cordoba. It is springtime now; the blossoming of nature welcomes us. Myriad colors burst from the branches of trees proclaiming the generosity of Allah.

Once more, I survey the hazy distance before me and at last catch sight of the Great Mosque's proud minaret. Its gold and silver elliptical spheres glisten in the setting sun, a magnificent jewel against the clear blue sky. Soon I will be within the walls of Cordoba, breathing in the musk of its throbbing life!

With renewed energy, I kick my horse to join my father and Isaac at the lead.

I glance behind me, at the rolling hills in the mist. One behind the other they rise and fall toward the sky, so smooth and gentle God must have formed them with His own hands. Their curves bring to mind a woman's body. I sigh heavily, hopefully I am almost of age, and surely, my father will offer to buy me a concubine when we get home. Perhaps he'll suggest I go with him to choose one at the slave market. My brother, Husan, has teased me about this upcoming possibility, and my father has hinted at it in Fez. *Soon,* I think, longingly.

The last rays of the sun clothe the hills in slashes of transparent gold and silver. We move between the geometrically planted olive groves, rising and dipping with the curves of the road. Cordoba disappears and reappears, each time closer than the last.

From the distance, floating on air, the call of the muezzin reaches us, "God is Great. God is Great. God is Unique and his prophet is Muhammad . . ." At first, one clear voice enjoins all to prayer. Then the lone tenor is magnified by a rippling chorus of chants from all the minarets of all the mosques in the city. The rich sonorous wave urges all to bow to the grace of Allah.

"Sulayman," my father quickly turns to me. "A prayer before we cross the bridge. God has favored us on this trip."

He puts up his hand and the thundering sound of hooves calms down. The horses and mules come to a stop around us. I get off by the side of the road and pull my prayer rug from the saddle.

"You will excuse us, Isaac," my father says to his partner.

"Of course, of course." Waves Isaac. "We'll ride ahead to our synagogue. We'll reach it in time for the first star in the sky."

"I'll leave the goods in the warehouse, and we'll meet tomorrow." My father waves back.

"As usual." Nods Isaac. Accompanied by his two sons and four slaves, he continues toward the Roman bridge.

My father, brothers, and the slaves, who have converted to Islam, dismount. I face east and clear my mind in an effort to feel God's presence. My forehead bends to the ground in total submission to the Absolute.

Refreshed, we continue on our way, impatient to be home. The numerous suburbs of Cordoba spread before us. Shortly I will be within those walls! We cross the Roman bridge stretching over the Guadalquivir toward the open bronze doors of the walled city. Freshly pickled heads impaled atop the walls gape into the distance: probably the usual lot of Christians from the latest Holy War and a few Muslim heretics. One head catches my attention. As we approach, I look at it more carefully and shudder. I see the head of a man with long red hair, the same color as my own. I quickly look away.

When I was young, the children at school always teased me about my red hair, telling me I looked like a Christian. For years, I was very lonely and refused any attempts at friendship. I hated my mother for being a Christian, for having given me this hair color; I blamed her for my youthful shame. What kind of Arab am I with freckles and light skin! No amount of consolation could soothe the pain of my difference. Only prayer gave me comfort. Only when addressing God did I feel I belonged.

My father turns left before the main gate, which is now swarming with people fresh from the Great Mosque, after prayer. We follow the road outside the city walls, beside the river. Archers and cavalrymen ride past us. We overtake mules slowly pulling carts laden with stone or marble. Across the river, the animal market is just closing. A mad clucking of chickens bursts through the air. Berbers lead away their sheep and goats. A drover gathers his camels. The familiarity of the scene delights me. I have missed Cordoba.

We enter the Merchants' gate, passing through a thick stone corridor into a large open square swelling with noise and activity. The usual cluster of beggars confronts us. My father reaches into his purse and distributes a few coins to grateful faces. In the middle of the square, people crowd around booths selling multicolored sweets, fried fish, spicy meatballs, and countless exotic delicacies to soothe hunger. Merchants, dressed in the styles of their homeland, are engaged in animated discussions. Fortune-tellers in glittering outfits predict the outcome of business ventures, while nearby, the playful rhythm of the tambourine accompanies a Qur'an chanter. By the side of a wall, a passionate storyteller enacts his lore to a captivated audience. After the solitude of the hills, my eyes shift from group to group, enchanted by the contrast of this swirling activity.

Soon, our caravan turns into a narrow street shaded by high stonewalls. We stop before the familiar green metal door and wait for my father to unlock it. He motions the slaves to unpack the animals and take the merchandise inside. With four small rugs under my arms, I enter the dark passageway of the warehouse and emerge into the courtyard bathed in the orange glow of the transparent roof covering. My brother, Ali, sits by a table just inside the entrance, noting down the rugs in a book. My father is lovingly examining the carpets as they are laid down in neat rows on the pale green marble floor of the courtyard. He sorts them according to tribe and geographic origin and then, one by one, hauls them into the various rooms off the portico, muttering that he should let the servants do this work. My father has a rather obsessive nature; once inside the warehouse, an extreme need to organize takes hold of him.

"Father, we'll do all that tomorrow," Ali firmly announces, pulling a heavy carpet from his hands.

"I can't help myself," replies my father as he picks up a lighter rug.

At last, all the merchandise is unloaded. I sit down on a bench in the portico.

"Sulayman," my oldest brother, Husan, shouts at me, "as the youngest, you should be working the hardest."

"I'm learning the trade by watching."

"No need to watch. You are going to be a judge, not a merchant. Now come here and give us some muscle."

Reluctantly I abandon my peaceful spot. I pick up one end of a large rolled-up rug. Husan and I carry it into one of the rooms off the courtyard, leaving behind a trail of sand on the floor. After several tries, we manage to heave it atop a high pile containing rugs of a similar size.

"Done," exhales Husan.

My father is kneeling in the courtyard before a particularly beautiful red and blue carpet. He is gently caressing its nap. The servants lead the pack donkeys to the far end of the courtyard, into their stables. Finally, we all gather outside, ready to leave. My father is not among us. I poke my head back in and see him intently bent over another carpet. I shake my head in amazement. He shows the same loving care to the carpets as he does to his wives and children. He is a man with a capacity to fully focus on whatever requires his attention. I have never seen him impatient or angry. I hope that one day, I too will learn patience. I whistle. He looks up, as if aroused from a dream, and lets out a deep, reluctant sigh.

"This is my favorite time, you know," he says mounting his horse. "The merchandise we have spent months collecting is at last all in one place."

"That large Berber rug is a treasure," says Husan.

"Rugs are like people, each has its own character," my father says softly as we make our way through the narrow curving streets, the hooves of the animals reverberating between the stonewalls.

I recognize our house, at last; the thick cedar door at the end of the street, we knock, and a servant opens it. The animals go around to the back. We enter.

Freshly bathed and dressed, I cross the first courtyard and see my father hurrying toward me, clearly with something important to announce. Immediately my hopes rise. Now is the time, he will offer to buy me a concubine. He puts a firm hand on my shoulder and leads me around the central fountain. The gentle spray of the water dances on my face and I cannot suppress an expectant smile. Most of my friends already have concubines. Soon it will be my turn.

"Your grandfather has just died," comes my father's hoarse whisper.

"My grandfather . . . ?" In my disappointment, it takes me a few seconds to grasp his meaning. My mind rushes to my paternal grandfather, then remember he had died several years ago. He must mean my mother's father.

Finally, realizing the seriousness of the news, I ask, "How is mother?"

"She is grieving, of course." His arm still around my shoulder, he continues to lead me around the fountain.

The last time I saw my maternal grandfather was about a year ago. He was always very kind to me despite his reputation of tyranny in his peach groves.

"The funeral is tomorrow," my father continues gently. "You and Aishah should accompany your mother to the ceremony."

"Of course," I quickly reply, resenting my father for such instructions.

"Good. I have said nothing to your mother. You make your offer at the proper moment."

"Of course," I repeat, trying to hold back my rising anger.

Disengaging myself from his arm, I make a sudden move toward the dining area. My father's strong grip stops me.

"I know you would have offered to go with your mother, without my suggestion. I know that. But you must understand, I can't help feeling protective toward her."

My anger dissipates into a smile, and I kiss him on both cheeks.

In the dining room, the whole family greets us. My father's three wives are here, most of my half-brothers and half-sisters as well as my full sister Aishah, and Husan's wife and two-year-old daughter, Leila. They have arranged themselves on large cushions around several low brass tables laden with bowls of stuffed vine leaves, eggplant puree, avocado marinated in herbs, giant green and black olives. The somber atmosphere mutes the normally vivid colors of the room. My eyes immediately search out my mother. She is delicately wiping her nose with a handkerchief. Her femininity belies a surprisingly strong will. Only recently have I recognized the strength behind her grace. I have not seen her since our arrival and am now taken aback by her swollen, bloodshot eyes. Still, her fine lips hold a welcoming smile. I rush over to gather her in my arms. I can feel by the heaving of her shoulders that she has once more begun to cry.

"Cry, Catherine, cry," chants Saida in her deep throaty voice that can sound so comforting at such times. Saida is the oldest of my father's three wives, and, since all her children are now married, she often plays mother to the other two. Being mother for Saida means firm compassion. However, being a grandmother is altogether another matter. Leila can reduce Saida to contented giggling jelly. Now Saida's focus is not on her granddaughter but on my mother.

"You must let your tears flow freely, Catherine. Let the fountain run till there is no more water. Water held in, festers," she coos.

My mother sits back down dabbing her eyes on the sleeve of her blouse. My sister Aishah moves over on the cushion to make room for me between herself and mother.

"You'll sleep in my arms tonight, Catherine." My father offers gently as he sits down between Saida and Ali.

My mother nods a meek assent as my father hits the brass gong for the hot course to be brought in.

I have difficulty understanding this extreme sadness since my grandfather was not such a loved man. I lean over to Aishah and whisper, "How did he die?"

"Murdered by one of his employees who ran off with a cart full of valuables."

I put a hand over my eyes in shock. My poor mother!

"Your grandfather was not the most honest of men, but life is in the hands of God," says Lobua, my father's second wife's daughter. "Any man trying to emulate God should be dealt with in the harshest of ways." Lobua, twenty-eight, an exotically beautiful and intelligent woman, is never shy to express her opinion. I have always admired her honest, outspoken attitudes.

"If we punish a man by killing him, are we not also playing God?" asks Husan with a little smile. He enjoys teasing Lobua. Husan likes nothing better than a satisfying argument. He is a firm believer that cultured people must know how to debate in a clear and logical manner. Since I am the youngest in the family and he is nine years my senior, he has always taken great interest in my education and has spent whole afternoons teaching me how to defend a point of view in a logical manner. He has greatly influenced my decision to become a judge.

"The Qur'an clearly states: a death deserves death," Lobua insists.

How could it be otherwise? I think.

"Perhaps God is simply testing us," Husan gives her a mischievous wink.

I long to take Lobua's side, if only for the sake of winning an argument against Husan. But I am too aware of my mother's grief and tell myself to maintain silent respect.

In a low voice I ask my mother, "When is the funeral?"

"Tomorrow," she replies quietly.

"I will accompany you."

"Thank you, Sulayman." My mother flashes me a grateful smile.

After breakfast, my mother, my sister Aishah, and I make our way through the bustling activity of the streets. In the Christian quarter, we finally find an imposing building with a large metal cross atop a conical roof. Inside the church, the air is thick with incense. Amid the dark gloom, daylight pokes through a few small windows near the ceiling. Innumerable candles cast an ocher glow upon life-size statues of suffering saints in the side aisles. Between the statues, frescoes depict an emaciated Christ with a vacant look in his eyes and drops of bright red blood on his white body. Muhammad was known to be strong and virile. He was a soldier of God. Christ looks incapable of fighting a pigeon. The saints around him fare no better. My face tightens in disgust.

The cries and whispers of mourners reverberate in the macabre coolness. Near the altar, a white marble statue of a ghostly Virgin Mary welcomes the assembled. I shudder and fight against the morbidity beginning to seep into my soul. When I was younger, I was ashamed of my mother's Christianity and tried hard to convert her to Islam. My father often took me aside and explained I should allow my mother to practice her beliefs. He told me to be generous; "After all," he patiently repeated, "the Muslims rule al-Andalus." When I was older, I saw that numerous prominent Muslims had wives of different religions, and I became more comfortable with my mother's Christianity. Or, perhaps as I grew older, I was no longer teased about my red hair and I could allow myself more tolerance.

An open coffin lies before a pinioned Christ on a large wooden cross. People kneel by the coffin to pay their respects and then move on.

"You two can stay at the back while I go up front," my mother whispers to Aishah and me.

We sit in the last pew and watch. Up front my mother throws her arms around the priest. They hold each other for a surprisingly long time before kneeling side by side to pray.

Later she proudly leads him to the back.

"Sulayman, Aishah, this is my favorite brother, Sebastian," she announces.

"At last," Sebastian greets us with a warm smile and scrutinizing eyes.

I had often heard my mother speak of Sebastian, a priest in the northern Christian territories. Before me stands a handsome man with the same color of hair as my own.

"Father Sebastian, then," I say.

"To you, Uncle Sebastian."

The church ceremony is followed by a procession through the streets. The carved wooden coffin, balanced on a cart, is pulled by a donkey. Ahead of the donkey walk several altar boys and Sebastian waving incense. A choir, accompanied by a horn, drum, and cymbals, follows the coffin. After the choir walk family and friends, at times singing, at other times blowing their noses.

The procession heads outside the city walls, past a number of Muslim cemeteries surrounded by tall cypresses. In contrast, the Christian cemetery is only marked off by a metal fence. Inside, I notice the same heretical motifs reappear on the tombs as in the church: marble or stone angels, the Virgin Mary, saints, Christ. I glance at Aishah. She too is trying to mask her distaste.

Sebastian stands by the dugout hole, directing proceedings. I put my arms around my mother who is no longer crying. Having seen her brother must have revived her. I listen to Sebastian's speech till the echoing call of the muezzin floats through the air. "God is Great. God is Great . . ." The familiar repetitions calm my indignation and soothe my spirit. I refuse to let this call to prayer pass unnoticed. I will teach these Christians about purity.

I gently remove my arm from mother's shoulder. Aishah gives me a suppressed smile as I head toward a secluded corner of the cemetery.

After the ritual ablutions with the earth, I face east and begin to pray. Disapproving stares swell my pride. I infuse my movements with conscious grace. I want to show these infidels how a Muslim prays; how little a Muslim needs to reach out to God.

After the funeral, Sebastian asks me, "How did it feel to pray in a Christian cemetery?"

"Your statues did not distract me," I reply.

"The statues are there to help, not distract," Sebastian points out.

"Muslims do not need frozen representations to lead them to the Divine," I challenge.

"I understand saint worship is very popular among poorer Muslims," he counters with a smile.

"But we do not need statues of our saints."

"But their sanctuaries are of key importance."

"As a more concrete contact . . ." I gesture toward the sky.

"As the statues of our saints."

People crowd around us to claim Sebastian's attention. My mother takes my elbow to lead me away. Sebastian calls out, "I'm staying at the monastery in the hills, to the east of Medina al-Zahra. Do come by for a chat."

Outside the closed green door of the warehouse, retailers are already lining up to examine our stock. Husan, Ali, my father, and I enter the courtyard. Isaac's slaves are unrolling the rugs. Yusuf, his son, is checking the pattern and tribe names in the book. Isaac and my father confer in one corner. An interesting design catches my attention, and I kneel beside a large rug with a magnificent multicolored border design of floral arabesque.

"You once told me about a friend dealing in slaves," I hear my father say. "Is he still in the business?"

"Naturally"—Isaac laughs—"and doing very well. Your Holy Wars are providing him with plenty of merchandise."

"I want to buy Sulayman a concubine. It's time. He's already twenty-one."

I am suddenly alert. *Will it finally happen?*

"My dear Ahmed, your timing is impeccable. My friend just returned with a fresh cargo of slaves."

"Could Sulayman and I look at them before they go to market?"

"Let me have a word with him. Come to my house for lunch in two days time, and I will have an answer for you."

"I am opening the doors to the retailers," Husan yells from the front.

I pretend to remain absorbed in the pattern of the rug and feel a strong arm tighten around my shoulders. My father leans toward me, his closely cropped beard touches my ear. "Soon you'll be sleeping in the arms of a beautiful girl," he whispers.

I feel myself blush. My father laughs and pats my cheeks with the palm of his hand.

"I must go to the mosque for a lecture," I say meekly, standing up.

"Go! Take care of your mind and soon your body too will be satisfied."

I meet Shihab, a good friend, in the courtyard of the Great Mosque.

"The lecture is cancelled," he tells me. "Come back to the house for a game of chess."

A game of chess does not sound appealing, at present. I look around me, vaguely searching. White pigeons flit about the round marble bowl of the fountain. People, deep in discussion, are gathered under the shade of the cypress trees. Judges listen to cases in the portico. What should I do?

"What happened to you on the trip? You look disconnected," Shihab comments.

"Disconnected . . . that's a good word," I reply. "But it has nothing to do with the trip. My father wants to buy me a concubine."

"It's about time," comes a gleeful reply. "She will give you great pleasure. You must choose her yourself. Don't let your father do it for you."

Shihab is two years elder than me. His advice in these matters should be heeded since he already has a concubine. I remember his utter delight upon receiving her. I had never seen him in such a carefree and good-natured mood as the first few months of her arrival.

"Did you choose yours?" I ask.

"Naturally. But I know someone whose father just gave him one as a present. Though she was beautiful, he still fell in love with a slave girl at the market soon after."

"That could happen to anyone, whether you choose your concubine or not."

"I suppose, affairs of the heart are very unpredictable." Shihab thinks for a second. "I've never really been in love."

"Let's leave chess for another day," I suggest.

I aimlessly wander through the covered market near the mosque. I move through the thick smell of freshly butchered goat and am assailed by the cloying sweetness of almonds in boiled honey. Vendors, competing for attention, shout at the bustling crowd. I turn into a cool residential lane and down a narrow winding street between high stonewalls. In the distance, the hills rise in a haze. I pass under several thick stone arches; walk through a small plaza, and up wide steps narrowing at the top. Making a right-hand turn into a dead-end street, I bang on our thick cedar door. A slave opens, and I quickly head for the stables.

I find one remaining donkey, saddle it, and lead it out into the streets. I head north, away from the river, following the stone-lined road toward the mountains, past the suburbs. Soon I reach Medina al-Zahra, the walled city of our Caliph, Abd al-Rahman III. I continue climbing and turn in at a small dirt road. The ascent grows steeper. Finally, I reach the monastery at the top.

At the gate, I ask for Father Sebastian. The monk nods and leads me into the courtyard where peach and quince trees are growing in a haphazard arrangement. I tie my donkey to a tree trunk. Nearby, a monk is carving something out of wood. At the far end of the courtyard, near the stairs, I see a well. At last, Sebastian comes down the old wooden stairs. Upon seeing me, his face bursts into a wide smile. His openness is disarming. I had expected to meet curious reservation. Despite any logic, an inner affection quickly blossoms for this stranger.

"I was just about to have lunch, come join me," he offers.

He leads me into a room with long wooden tables. A number of monks dressed in their brown habit are already eating with jugs of wine and baskets of bread before them. An enormous wooden cross hangs on one wall. Fortunately, there is no statue of Christ impaled upon it. The aroma of freshly baked bread and stewed cinnamon apples permeate the room. We choose an empty table and sit down facing each other. Sebastian offers me a thick slice of bread from the earthenware platter. It is still warm to the touch. I decline his offer of wine.

"Muslims do not drink wine," I announce, unable to suppress a tone of self-righteousness. I chide myself, knowing innumerable Muslim families drink wine, including my own. Only during the month of Ramadan do we fully abstain.

"Will you allow me a few glasses?" he asks.

"Of course." I smile, in spite of myself.

"We have before us the blood and body of Christ, you know," he says merrily, as he pours himself a large cup of red wine.

"Does your profession help you deal with death better than the average person?" To my surprise, the question rolls out, void of premeditation.

"You mean my father's death?" He smiles.

"Yes."

"In my profession, as you call it, we learn to accept death as the will of God. Therefore, I have not lost a father. My father has simply been called to God."

"That is the way we Muslims see death as well. But it does not always help the pain of the living."

A young monk, about my age, comes to our table. I play with a crust of bread and turn my face away from him. For some unknown reason, I find his look of utter servitude embarrassing.

"Bring us some water and two meals," Sebastian says to him.

"Prayer helps human pain," he adds after the young monk has left.

"Prayer . . ." I begin and immediately lapse into silence, thinking of the difference between the prayer of a Muslim and the prayer of a Christian.

Reading my thoughts, Sebastian smiles. "We all pray to God differently, yet we share the same God."

"But the Christians have committed a grave sin by deifying Jesus," I burst out.

"Jesus is the Son of God . . ."

"Jesus was His prophet, as Muhammad . . ."

"Was Muhammad also a virgin birth?" Sebastian asks with a trace of sarcasm.

"Jesus was a virgin birth as proof that nothing is impossible for God," I point out. "When Jesus called himself the Son of God, he meant that God's Fatherhood was all embracing, that every human being was a child of God, not only him." How often I have used this argument with my mother when I was young!

A hot steaming bowl of soup is placed before us, along with a jug of water.

"I agree, every human being is a child of God. Nevertheless, Jesus was not a man like you and me. The miracles he performed attest to his

Divine quality." Sebastian blows on the surface of the soup, sending a cloud of steam in my direction.

I dip a crust of bread into the brown liquid. Thinking this could be a good opportunity to practice my debating skills, I begin to gear up for a good argument. "Deifying Jesus and creating the Trinity merely negates the Absoluteness of God. By making Jesus divine, you have made God's divinity relative."

"Our Trinity represents the One. It simply gives people a more accessible route to God."

"Knowing God's laws is the best way to reach Him," I insist.

"Is that why you are studying law?"

"The knowledge of Divine Law will lead me to Divine Truth."

"That is why I am a priest." Sebastian smiles. "You see, we do have something in common after all."

The young monk brings two new heaping dishes to replace our empty soup bowls. I look at the various shades of brown before me; it must be meat with vegetables and potatoes.

"Is this pork?" I ask cautiously.

"No. It's veal," Sebastian replies after careful inspection.

He begins to eat with great relish, clearly enjoying the food. I take a careful taste. Just as I thought, it is simplistic and bland, like all Christian cooking. In Arab cooking, fruits and nuts are used with meats, fish, vegetables, and lentils. In addition, the variety of our spices renders each dish distinct to the palate. It seems that just as our approach to food is different, so is our approach to God.

"Muslims accept Jesus as a prophet. Why can the Christians not accept Muhammad?" I ask.

"Well . . ." Sebastian looks slightly confused. "Do you really accept Jesus?"

Clearly, he does not know our Holy Book. "Yes," I say emphatically, enjoying a surge of exhilaration at the possibility of winning. "But as I said before, not the Trinity because there you are dividing the Absoluteness of God."

"The Muslims give different attributes to God. You call him Merciful, Compassionate, Just, as well as numerous other things. These attributes also divide His Absolute nature."

I take a spoonful of meat and vegetables. It is quite tasteless. "The Mu'tazila would certainly agree with you . . ."

"Who?"

"The Mu'tazila were a group of rationalists, influenced by Greek thought. They too felt that the different names of God splintered His Oneness. But today's thinking does not agree with them."

Sebastian stops eating. "Why must various interpretations quarrel with each other? Jesus gave the word to Christianity, Moses gave the word to Judaism, and Muhammad gave the word to Islam. Why must each religion presume that it, and no one else, has the right prophet?"

Can he truly believe his words? If he does, then he must accept Muhammad. Islam believes in the words of Jesus, Moses, and all the other prophets of the Bible. The Qur'an tells us the people had misinterpreted their words and refused to follow Divine Law. This is why Muhammad was sent, to once more deliver the Word of God. Could Sebastian be a Muslim without realizing it?

He exhales a breath of heavy sadness. "The older I get, the more confusing religion becomes. I carry on my work as a priest without much trouble because my work often has so little to do with religion. Of course, I must claim that my actions are in the name of Christ, Our Lord."

"Christ is not our Lord."

Sebastian tears off a crust of bread and dips it into the stew. A look of fatigue washes over his face.

"Sulayman, we must not discuss religion. We will never agree. What starts as being amusing becomes tiresome. You're an intelligent young man. We must be able to discuss something other than God."

"Medicine?" I venture.

Sebastian considers this. "No," he replies at last. "The art of healing comes from God."

I search for another topic. The art of carpet weaving would also eventually lead to God. Astrology? I know so little about it. Poetry? Music?

"My father is buying me a concubine," I finally say.

"That is interesting!" he exclaims with sudden enthusiasm.

"Concubinage is an old and established institution in the church."

"I never understood why priests were not allowed to marry."

Sebastian laughs and takes a big gulp of wine, swirling the liquid around in his mouth before swallowing it. "They did marry at one time. Then the Church decided the servants of God should be more mysterious, less earthly. And they removed us from carnal knowledge."

"I don't agree . . ."

"I am not certain I do either. Did God not bestow us with sexual desire?" He drinks some more wine. "But then some say sexual desire is the work of the devil."

"No. We need the sexual act to procreate, and procreation is the work of God." Silently, I wonder what my future concubine will look like.

"I sometimes ask myself what kind of world the church envisions if it is so bent on eliminating earthly desires?"

"You do not sound satisfied with Christianity." I put my hand on his arm. "Why not become a Muslim?"

"My dear Sulayman, I was born a Christian. I have dedicated my life to Christianity. There is a lot I can find to criticize about the institution of the Church. No institution is perfect. But I speak with God in the language of Christianity."

I respect his integrity: begrudgingly. It would have been wonderful to convert a priest. "You see"—I smile—"even concubinage leads us to God."

"Perhaps all roads lead to God, Sulayman."

The dining room has emptied out. A warm, moist stillness surrounds us.

II. Esther

By the time my father and I go to his partner Isaac's house, all spiritual questions have been replaced by concerns of a more carnal nature. We settle down on comfortable cushions in front of a large brass table. The sun-filled room is replete with color. The wooden doors have been folded back to allow a view of the porticoed courtyard, carefully planted with lemon trees and rose bushes. A hint of fresh lavender is in the air. I survey my surroundings at leisure while Isaac tells my father about the poems of *Chalaf ibn Ayub ibn Ferag*. Just last night he had heard them recited at the home of a friend and was much impressed by their musical rhythm. Fantasies of a concubine play in my head.

Two women enter, casting their shadows onto the mosaic wall. They place ceramic dishes of salads on the table. A delicate white hand with silver bracelets and rings puts a plate before me. I look up with a smile and am surprised to see a strikingly beautiful girl of about my age. Her black hair is a magnificent contrast to her porcelain skin. I watch her move gracefully around the table, astounded that my fantasies have come to life.

"This is my daughter, Esther," Isaac says as the girl stands by his side. Her deep brown eyes sparkle and a shy smile plays around full, sensuous lips.

As soon as she leaves, her father tells us that she is a girl of exceptional intelligence and should have been born a boy. Against the wishes of his wife and his rabbi, he has been secretly teaching her Jewish laws.

As we begin to eat, the conversation drifts back to poetry. I long to hear more about Esther, but Isaac shows no inclination to return to this subject. Once sated and slowly sipping mint tea, he tells my father that a new shipment of slaves will be presented tomorrow. He advises us to go early in the morning before the market opens to make our choice.

Back in my room, I look at my reflection on a plate of silver. Tomorrow, I must wear my smartest clothes, and I should do something about my red hair. This color is annoying; I will never get used to it. Why must I look like a Christian! Why could I not have inherited my father's coloring? Even Shihab teases me about my hair; nature has been generous with him. He is exceptionally handsome with jet-black hair and light olive skin. Women are always sending him love notes. I jump up and rush to the market in search of a woman to dye my hair as I am certain the concubine will prefer someone who looks more like an Arab.

The change in my hair color brings great mirth to the women of the household. They find the combination of black hair and freckles extremely amusing. Their laughter distresses me.

At night, as I am trying to fall asleep, I wonder if I had been right in trying to change my appearance. Allah has given me auburn hair. Why should I want to interfere with His creation?

A mixture of anxiety, tension, and anticipation keep me from sleep. The early morning call of the muezzin is a grateful relief as the rhythm of prayer will give me calm.

The slave market is quiet in the morning, and most of the doors are still locked. My father and I easily locate Isaac's friend. He takes us into a large courtyard where girls of various ages, colors, and shapes linger around the fountain or in the portico. There are also a few boys among them, probably eunuchs. Fragrances of different perfumes float in the air. Isaac's friend and my father are quick to engage in an animated discussion. I watch the girls talking to each other, obviously waiting for the market to open. Standing in the portico, knowing I can have one of these girls for myself, gives me a wonderful sense of maturity. Have I reached manhood? Is this what it takes? My glance rests on a girl with black hair and deep olive skin, dressed in a brilliant gold, red, and green outfit. She is quite tall with generous hips and full breasts.

I point her out to my father. He nods in approval but warns me that this girl will have to last me a long time, I should make my choice with care. My eyes continue their search. Suddenly I notice a Nubian girl looking at me. I feel myself blush and quickly avert my eyes in embarrassment. My eyes drift back to her. Now ignoring me, she stands by the fountain, playing with the water in the bowl. Her hair is black and wavy. Her skin is a light, silky brown. She too is tall, about my height. Her limbs are strong; her hips tight with small buttocks rising upward. Her breasts are firm and pointed. With a quick movement of her head, she turns in my direction again.

"She was captured in mid-Africa, a member of a ruling family," Isaac's friend whispers in my ear. "She is said to have some white blood."

Her large, dark brown eyes hold a flicker of curiosity mixed with daring. I sense impetuousness underneath her contained exterior. My palms grow sweaty; I swallow my excess saliva. After a quick decision, I casually lean over to Isaac's friend. "Keep her for me."

"She is a good choice," he replies. "She would have been the first to go."

"What's her name?"

"Naziha."

I leave my father behind to negotiate the price and take her home, while I rush to the Great Mosque to catch a lecture.

The lecturer cannot hold my attention. During a discourse on the differences between revealed and not revealed knowledge, the image of Naziha plays in my mind, and I imagine her breasts, her thighs, and the feel of her skin. The lecturer's deep voice rises and falls in the background. By the time he finishes, I have sunk into such a deep daydream that I wake to Shihab shaking me back to my senses.

In the public courtyard, the bright sunshine revives me. I walk over to the shadowed portico and join a group of people listening to a judge hearing a case of adultery. The claimant, defendant, and witnesses plead their positions as the scribes diligently record their words. The crowd murmurs their opinion as all are completely absorbed in the drama knowing that, whatever the outcome of the case, they will soon witness a flogging. Again, my attention wanders. I casually glance around. I notice a very familiar face standing next to me. From where do I know this person? I look more carefully. Of course, it is Esther, Isaac's daughter!

"Esther," I quietly whisper in her direction. She does not hear. "Esther!"

She turns, clearly not recognizing me. Though I remind her who I am, she still looks confused. "Is your hair a different color?" she asks hesitantly.

I laugh. Of course, the black hair! "It was auburn when you saw me yesterday."

"That's right," she replies with a quick smile.

People standing close by flash annoyed looks in our direction so we quietly leave the crowd.

"I preferred the auburn," she tells me.

I am surprised. "I thought everyone prefers the typical Arab coloring."

"I don't like people who are typical. I like people who are different."

I too prefer people with unique qualities, people not necessarily part of a group, though I have never thought of my red hair as signaling me out in a positive way.

"Can you come for a walk?" I ask. Women of aristocratic families, with a good education, have a fair amount of freedom in Cordoba. However, perhaps Isaac puts restrictions on Esther.

"Of course," she quickly replies. "My father thinks I am at the mosque for lectures. But I am certain he would not object to a walk with you, he knows your family well."

We walk through the street of woodworkers. Bamboo matting, stretched across the roofs of the houses, cast ribbed shadows on the stone pavement. The smell of sawdust and freshly cut wood permeate the narrow street lined with workshops. Men are carving or staining in silent concentration; others are talking to customers.

"Come, inspect this box!" bellows a vendor.

We continue to a nearby garden and sit on a tiled bench facing the central fountain. Around the fountain stand plum trees, their branches bursting with delicate pale pink flowers. My fantasies have evaporated, replaced by the soft, tingling presence.

"I understand your father is teaching you law," I say, rubbing the leaves of the southernwood between my fingers to coax out their scent.

"Yes. I cannot study openly with my brothers."

"Isaac thinks you should have been a boy."

"So do I."

"But you're a beautiful girl," I protest.

"Perhaps I would have been a beautiful boy!" Her laughter joins the falling water of the fountain.

"If you were a man, would you practice law?"

"I am not certain," she replies, suddenly contemplative. "I love law because it teaches me the story of our people."

"I'm studying law at the Great Mosque . . ."

"Of course, my father mentioned that," she says, turning to me with quick enthusiasm.

"Muslim law is Divine. It helps me understand God."

"The laws of Moses are as well. But I also think the body of Jewish law reflects human logic."

"In Muslim law, there is no place for human logic—Divine knowledge guides our actions and judgments," I point out.

"But reason and revelation complement each other," she says.

"Human reason often borders on heresy!" It so annoys me that both Christians and Jews consider human logic a strong part of their law. They do not understand that Divine Law is the only law man should follow as we do not have sufficient knowledge to create our own laws. In all humility, we must turn to the laws of God.

"But definition of heresy changes with time," she says.

Our discussion rises to a passionate debate that is interrupted by a rather loud groan of my empty stomach. Esther immediately remembers her own hunger and jumps up laughing.

"We must go eat something," she announces.

On our way to the food market, noisy crowds near the Great Mosque blocks our way. Eager anticipation hangs in the air. Everyone's heads are turned the same direction. Our necks crane to catch a glimpse of the attraction, and finally I spot a wooden podium in the center of the crowd with a man kneeling on top. His hands are tied behind his back; his head is bent toward a wide copper bowl. Three large men tower over him. One is wielding an enormous sword, its edge glinting in the rays of the sun. Another holds a rough sack, while the third bellows out to the spectators, "Take note! Let this be an example to you all!"

The first man lifts his sword high into the air, gripping it with both hands as the commotion of the crowd fades to silence. With a quick, swooshing slice, the sword descends on the neck of the kneeling man. The truncated head clanks into the metal bowl. The third man grabs it with oversized hands, holding it high in the air for all to see the bulging whiteness of the staring eyes and the oozing blood. Then the head is carelessly dropped into the sack. The crowd reluctantly disperses.

"Why did he die?" I ask the person closest to me.

"A heretic." Esther and I exchange a quick glance.

"What was his heresy?"

"A Christian who denounced Muhammad."

"No!" yells someone else. "He was a Muslim who falsely denounced a cadi."

"No, he converted to Judaism!" shouts a disembodied voice.

The movement of the crowd carries us.

"I'm glad we didn't eat before witnessing that," says Esther.

"It is one thing to see a head already desiccated, but I've never enjoyed executions," I say.

The food market is overflowing with people. Everyone is crowding the stalls. The beheading must have stirred appetites! At last, Esther and I manage to buy some skewered lamb balls with apricots. I pick up fresh figs at another stall. When I look around, Esther has disappeared, and my eyes search the crowd until I finally catch sight of her waving arms high in the air. As I get close, I find she has saved two seats for us on a slab of stone jutting from the wall.

"This is luck!" I say, happily settling down.

"Two old men were ready to leave, and I ran to get their place." She gives me a satisfied smile.

Finally, we begin to eat. Esther drops an oily apricot onto her violet pants and does not seem to notice. I pick up the apricot sitting on her knees and want to put it in her mouth but decide that would be too intimate a gesture. I glance at her lips. They are full and firm; they must be soft to the touch. Reluctantly I hand her the juicy apricot.

"You eat it." She laughs. "You found it!"

She tries, unsuccessfully, to rub the remaining oil from the pants. I gather the hem of my shirt and rub the spot. The oil is now gone, but the spot remains.

"I am sure it can be washed out with an herb," she says.

Our stomachs sated. We wander through the covered streets of the book market. The sun streams down in pools of light from the square skylights. We stop at shops, leafing through the pages of old and new manuscripts.

"If you find anything on Jewish philosophy, let me know," says Esther.

I think that I myself would like to read something on Jewish philosophy. To date, I have only studied Islam. The slow, rhythmic chant of the muezzin fills the air, "Allah is Great. Allah is Great . . ."

Esther notices my look of confusion. "You go to the mosque. I'll stay here a little while longer before returning home."

Reluctantly I start to leave and then turn back toward her. "When will I see you again?"

"Soon. Probably at the mosque."

After prayer, I take a slow walk by the river, under the fig trees. I sit on a bench along the paved road below the pleasure gardens and enjoy the silvery ripples playing on the surface of the water.

By the time I arrive home, lanterns already lit the first courtyard. My father and two slaves are putting the summer brocade covering around the trunk of the palm trees.

"Sulayman, where have you been? I expected you here a long time ago," my father cries.

In a sudden flash, I remember Naziha.

"You forgot, didn't you? I don't understand you. How could you have forgotten?"

"Is she here?" I whisper.

"Of course, she is here." My father puts his arm around my shoulder. "Harith," he calls out. "Sulayman and I will eat in the library. Ask one of the servants to bring the food."

Suddenly he stops and claps his hands together in great excitement. "First, I want to show you something I bought after your concubine. It's a treasure!"

He leads me to the fig tree near the stairs. "Look. Do you see something unusual?"

I look at the small green figs growing on branches with firm fan-like leaves. Then my eyes catch a glitter. Sitting next to a plump fig is a bird with wings, tail, and beak of finely worked gold. Its head and breast are silver; its eyes a deep ruby. It is a magnificent, life-size sculpture of a lark!

"Where is it from?" I ask, impressed.

"Baghdad, I'm told. But wait. This is not an idle bird. Watch closely."

My father pulls aside a branch, stands behind the bird, and blows at its head. Its beak separates and a short flute-like song emerges.

"In the wind, the bird merrily sings the whole day," my father explains proudly.

"How can it sing?" I ask hardly believing what I just heard.

"You see the tiny holes in its neck?"

I look closer and nod.

"There are plates of silver inside its throat with more holes. As the wind blows through those holes, the song of a lark emerges," my father explains.

"Are there different types of birds?"

"Yes. And they all make their own specific sound. Some people have ten different birds in their garden." He laughs.

"Can you imagine the racket of sounds in a strong wind?" I laugh.

Even exquisite beauty can turn distasteful when overabundant.

We finish the meal in the library. My father wipes his beard, leans back against the wall, and says, "Remember everything I have told you about women. They do not like to rush. The slower, the longer, the better. Above all, patience. Patience, even if you feel agony in holding back. Remember"—my father smiles to himself in silence—"that agony can create delicious pleasure."

He languidly bites into a plump date. I pick up a sugared pear to soothe my nervousness.

"Do not rush her. Speak to her gently. You have all the time you desire. Your life stretches before you. Don't get it over and done with in the time it takes to recite one line of poetry."

I nod. A part of the pear goes down the wrong way. I burst into a coughing fit.

"Now, go to her. She is in the middle courtyard, upstairs, next to Aishah's room."

Wiping my cool, perspiring hands on my trousers, I cross the passageway between the first and second courtyards, walk past the lemon trees, and ascend the cedar staircase. My knees feel weak. I walk along the inner gallery and find the door of her room open. She is trying on rings that my father's wives must have given her. As soon as she sees me, a look of challenge flashes in her eyes.

"May I come in?"

"This is your house," she replies in surprisingly good Arabic.

I close the door behind me. A bronze oil lamp burns by the bed giving the room a warm glow. At first Naziha is reserved. To try to put her at ease and calm my nervousness, I ask her questions about herself. I learn that she comes from a tribe of polytheists, from the heart of Africa. She proudly tells me that dancing is a favorite activity of her tribe. Singing and dancing mark every celebration or mourning. She has always danced with her tribe, since she was a small girl.

"Why don't I show you?" she offers.

"Please."

I settle into the soft red and yellow cushions of the bed, leaning my back against the tapestry hanging on the wall. I watch Naziha move in the amber glow of the light. Her agile body sways slowly; her feet move with small light steps. The wide pants, gathered at the ankles, quiver with their own rhythm. The hips, adorned by a jeweled leather belt, begin to gyrate. The waist, contained in a royal blue brocade vest, remains steady. The arms move up and down, at first slowly, and then the movements speed up. She turns around in circles, arms reaching high. Her face holds a look of inner concentration as she keeps rhythm to an inner music. The speed increases, building to frenzy. Her body sways; her breasts bounce with independent energy. In despair, I wonder how I will be able to take my time. Beads of sweat spot her blouse. I wipe the moisture from the back of my neck.

She suddenly stops, leaving a throbbing silence. My cheeks are burning.

I reach my hand toward her, and she comes to lie down beside me. I caress her face, her arms, and watch her eyes slowly close. I feel her brown skin under my fingers and see my own whiteness in contrast. My father's advice rings in my ears.

"Go slowly," I tell myself, "go slowly."

However, time becomes meaningless. I lose all awareness. My movements are dictated by nature, by an inner force, a primordial rhythm.

When I once more become conscious of time, I feel surrounded by gentle peace and soft exhaustion. For a long time I lie beside her, watching her sleep. Her flawless, sculptural breasts glow with sweat. The dark nipples are relaxed. There is an exotic elegance to her curves. I thank Allah for guiding me in my choice. Carefully, I pull my arm out from under her head and get dressed.

Standing in the coolness of the gallery, I become aware of distant voices. I amble to the end of the gallery and down the stairs leading to the portico.

Downstairs I pass through the arched passageway into the main courtyard. The pink marble floor sparkles in the glow of the lanterns. Naziha's naked body flashes before me. Soon I will return to her.

Laughter, music, and clapping mix with the falling water of the fountain. A crowd of people lounge in the reception room, listening to the recitation of a poet accompanied by the lute. My father notices my presence by the door and waves me over. Surrounded by his three wives, he caresses my mother's hair, showing me his affection for her. The room is filled with visiting scholars, poets, and musicians. Two people are playing chess in one corner.

There are bowls of fruit and sweets on various small tables scattered about the room. A large silver kettle of tea is kept warm by the oil flame underneath. I find a place on the carpet near my sister Aishah who pushes a cushion over to me and offers a bowl of fresh figs. I bite into the plump purple fruit. Its moist softness caresses my tongue and incredible pleasure flows through my body bringing to mind the texture of Naziha's skin, the taste of her mouth.

The chords of the lute rise and fall to the poet's voice.

Laughter curls around the room. A sense of total well-being envelops me. I watch the delicate movement of the girl's wrist as she plucks the strings. The poet's eyes burn at the vision of an inner land.

My concentration fades. The poet's words grow hazy. I settle deeper into the cushion and close my eyes. The rich sounds lazily recede into the distance.

In one corner of the Great Mosque, 'Abdallah ibn 'Ali al-Sarraj sits on his small stool before his captivated students. He holds forth in sonorous tones on the topic of his passion: philosophy.

"Knowledge is a Divine quality," announces 'Abdallah with a great flourish of his arms. "Therefore, the acquisition of knowledge is the obligation of all believers. Since Allah is Infinite, it stands to reason that Divine Knowledge is also infinite. We all know that man has a finite nature. This finite nature must learn from the Sacred, must reach toward infinite knowledge. My dear students, you may take comfort in knowing that you will never understand everything. There will always be knowledge for you to discover. Since knowledge is infinite and we human beings are finite, no individual can ever know everything. Only Allah knows all."

I have followed 'Abdallah's lectures with keen interest for two years now. A man of integrity, he accepts no new information without first putting it through a rigorous set of questions. He is so well known for his keen mind and astute scholarship that even the Caliph invites him to Medina al-Zahra to debate visiting Christian, Jewish, or Muslim scholars.

He is also reputed to make many a heart flutter. I can well believe it. 'Abdallah is a classically proportioned, an elegant-looking man in his late thirties, with straight, thick black hair, burnished skin, and deep black eyes that can immediately change from languorous ease to sharp curiosity. At different times, both my sisters have tried to capture his heart. Although 'Abdallah is gallant, almost seductive in his gallantry, he maintains his distance. Marriage is of no interest to him. He is a man of the mind.

Without doubt, 'Abdallah is my most challenging teacher. He encourages discussion, unlike other teachers who expect their students to simply learn what has been written without questioning. Of course, it is important to accept some knowledge. To question everything that has gone before would be a waste of time; it would allow no progress. Personally, I am more interested in questions. The search, the spirit of inquiry, excites me.

"Allah has eternal knowledge," 'Abdallah continues. "Allah is also omniscient and omnipotent. In the face of these attributes, is free will possible for man?" He stops for a dramatic pause. "This question has plagued man through the ages. Within the confines of Islam, the Jabrites believed in strict predeterminism. The Mu'tazilites and Qadarites believed in free will. Then the Asharites came along and tried to steer a middle course. They said that Allah is the creator of every action, but He also created in man the power of free choice. In other words, Allah has granted man the freedom to make the right choice or the wrong choice." 'Abdallah beams mischievously. "Do any of you have opinions on the question of free will or destiny?"

A hesitant discussion gradually builds to an argument that breaks into a furious shouting match. My friend Shihab and I jump in on the side of free will, liberally quoting from the Qur'an to support our position.

"Allah does not impose upon any soul a duty but to the extent of its ability," I proudly yell out. To me it is clear that the Qur'an has ample evidence to support man's potential to make the right or wrong choice. The choice is man's responsibility. The power to recognize right from wrong is a God-given gift. However, this gift often proves very sublime. How difficult it is sometimes to make the correct decision!

Shihab shouts above the commotion, "Allah has never changed a favor which He has conferred upon a people until they change their own condition."

Another loudly counters in support of predetermation, "Allah makes whom He pleases err and He guides whom He pleases.'"

'Abdallah puts up a hand to quiet the commotion. "Would you say that Allah is filled with contradictions?" he asks, widely smiling.

We fall silent, shocked at his comment. It seems the Qur'an provides for numerous possibilities. Certainly, Allah's creation contains everything. It is up to man to find the right path. This is what my father has always taught me. Whenever children from school teased me and beat me up because of my red hair, my father comforted me by saying, in time, they will recognize that they have been unjust. Naturally, I was in a hurry to grow up and see justice done.

After the lecture, 'Abdallah's servants roll up the carpet, upon which we have all been sitting, and ceremoniously carry it out of the mosque. Shihab and I go into the courtyard to sit beside the white pigeons at the edge of the fountain. Soon 'Abdallah joins us, clearly satisfied with the lecture.

"Once you boys are judges, you're going to have fewer discussions like this," he announces.

"Why do you say that?" I ask.

"As a judge, you work with concrete, immutable rules, especially since ijtihad, original reasoning, has been recently ruled out."

"Surely one can apply philosophy to law," I insist.

"No, in law, there is no philosophy. The al-faqih likes to think of law as a solid, unquestionable entity. All cases must fit under the laws of the Qur'an, the Hadith, or the written consensus of the community. Nothing more can be added."

"That makes no sense," I protest.

"Personal opinion must play a role in the administration of the law," Shihab adds, equally upset.

'Abdallah laughs and throws his arms around us. "Well, one thing that can never be solidified is thinking. And no theologian can argue with that." He turns to me. "By the way, Sulayman, your father tells me he is preparing for another trip. Are you going with him again?"

"Probably. We haven't yet discussed it." I have not even begun to think about the next trip.

"Is it a good idea to leave off your studies for six months at a time?"

"I take my books with me and go to lectures wherever I am."

"I think you are at a stage in your studies where you need continuity."

"What do you mean?" I ask.

"You should continue with the same professors, especially if you are studying to be a judge."

"You're suggesting I not go with my father the next time?"

"Yes. There will be plenty of other trips. You should focus on your studies now."

Perhaps he is right. As much as I enjoy accompanying my father on his travels, I do not intend to become a merchant.

My half-brothers Jamal, Husan, and Ali are already following my father's trade. My future beckons toward another direction. As well, I do not want to leave Naziha for six months. She gives me such pleasure.

At the warehouse, I am surprised to find Esther pleading with her father to be allowed on the next trip. With persuasive logic, she lists the various chores she could perform: write his letters, do the accounting. She paints a colorful picture where her presence would be invaluable. Isaac looks doubtful.

"You should trust your daughter, Isaac," I advise. "You educated her."

"She is stubborn—stubborn and intelligent. The worst combination in a girl." Isaac shakes his head in feigned exasperation. "All right. All right." He takes her hands in his. "I'll have difficulty explaining this to your mother."

Esther throws her arms around her father's neck.

In a room off the courtyard, I find my father sitting on a carpet, before a bronze writing table. I tell him that 'Abdallah had suggested I stay behind to concentrate on my studies. My father is all in favor of doing everything necessary to help my scholastic life.

"You know how much I respect 'Abdallah. You should follow his suggestion."

Unexpected sadness infuses my heart. Now it seems I will not see Fez again for several years. I will have no more reason to be involved in carpet buying; no reason to visit distant tribes. I will miss these experiences. I have accompanied my father on these trading trips since I was a small boy. Has a part of my life ended? Does entering adulthood mean I must sacrifice the pleasures of my youth?

My sister Aishah tells me Naziha has settled into the household with ease. She likes Naziha and approves of my choice. I playfully propose that she herself should ask my father to buy her a slave. We both laugh imagining my father's reaction to such a suggestion. Unknown to my father, Aishah, now twenty-four, has already told me she never wants to get married. I think Lobua, four years elder and extremely strong-minded and independent, has been a great influence on her. Ever since I can remember, Lobua has been studying, and she had turned the house upside down with joy when she was hired to write official letters for the Caliph.

I once overheard my mother talking to Kinza, my father's second wife and Lobua's mother. They were discussing how lucky their daughters were to live in a society that allows them freedom to follow their ambitions. Then I heard my mother say she herself had longed to sing and perform but her father hit her every time she even hummed to herself. Kinza, after making sympathetic clucking sounds, asked my mother to sing. My mother, at first shyly and then with building force, broke into a very sad and moving Christian song that had brought tears to my eyes as I stood hiding behind the closed door. Since overhearing their conversation, I have quietly encouraged Aishah to follow her heart, as opposed to expected custom.

I pass through the pink marble courtyard. My father's gold and silver lark is chirping in the breeze. As I am about to leave the house, Aishah comes running after me, hastily putting her purple and pink veil around her neck. She insists on accompanying me to the book market.

We make our way along the pleasantly cool narrow streets. Gradually the noise from the market penetrates the silence of the stonewalls. We turn into the wider road of the spice vendors. In front of the stalls stand large copper bowls filled with the spices of the world. The individual aromas mingle in the air to create a thick, rich scent guaranteed to make the passerby light-headed.

"See the future. See Allah's designs. The present heralds coming joys and sorrows," invokes a gaily dressed fortune-teller at the bend of the street.

The rhythmic roll of a kettledrum drowns her litany out. Everyone looks around for the source of the sound. Soon a herald turns into the main street followed by a donkey drawing a cart. On the cart stands a shirtless, fat man, his head bent in shame.

"This is Ibn Umar," yells the herald to the drum beat. "He is a thief and a criminal. His cheating and overcharging consumes the wealth of honest Muslims. Recognize him so you may avoid him!"

The drum continues its threatening roll. After a pause, the herald continues his chant. People press to the side of the street, giving the small procession room to pass. The inspector of police walks behind the cart turning his head from side to side, scowling at the crowd.

"The shame of such an exhibition will make an honest man of him," I say to Aishah.

"Dishonesty is not easy to convert," comes a gruff answer from beside me. I look over to see a fat man with an enormous oily, bulbous face and a complexion of eruptions smiling at me. *He must be talking from experience*, I think. I wonder if he himself has difficulty in finding the road to honesty.

We continue to the street of booksellers. The book auction has attracted a sizeable crowd to the small square. We arrive in time to hear a man bid an enormous sum for a book on the history of al-Andalus, by Ahmed ibn Muhammad al-Razi. I stand on my toes to catch sight of the man offering so many dinars.

"I know him," I whisper to Aishah with growing indignation. "A pompous government official said to have a magnificent library. Nevertheless, the man is ignorant! Only buys books for decoration."

"He's not alone," Aishah answers. "Lobua has seen manuscripts she was desperate to obtain disappear to the rich."

I cannot understand why people hoard books they will never read. They are hoarding knowledge they are totally unaware of possessing.

"Sulayman, look!" Aishah yells, pointing to someone in the crowd.

My eyes follow her fingers. With a cry of surprised pleasure, I immediately push through the crowd.

"Mustafa!" I yell. "Is it really you?" Turning to me, his face lights up with recognition. We hold each other in a long, tight embrace.

"Aishah," Mustafa says, looking over my shoulder as we finally separate, "you have grown more beautiful than I remember."

Aishah covers her deep blush with her violet veil.

"You know, the further north one goes, the more Muslim women wear the veil," Mustafa comments.

"What has happened since we last saw you?" I ask.

"What were you doing in the north?" inquires Aishah as we move away from the auction.

"After leaving your father's house, I went to fight in Navarre, in the Caliph's Holy War. Then I settled in Toledo for a year."

"When did you get back?"

"A few days ago. I was planning to visit your family soon." Mustafa is looking at Aishah whose blushing cheeks are just visible over the veil.

I leave the two of them alone and duck into a nearby stall to buy a book for Esther. As I pay, I keep glancing through the door at Mustafa. He looks in exceptionally good health. Fighting has swelled his muscles. My father had bought Mustafa in the slave market when he was fourteen years old. He is a Slav who not only converted to Islam but also took on an Arabic name. When Mustafa was twenty, my father offered him his freedom. At the time, he was not yet ready to leave and asked my father's permission to stay. Three years later, he finally took his leave. I was sad to see him go; he had become part of our family. Also, he was my only true friend as I was growing up. He always told me that having red hair meant strength. It was simply ignorance on the part of the other boys not to know this. I begged him to stay on and join my father in the material and carpet business. I even took the liberty to suggest he could travel the cities of al-Andalus to buy the silks and brocades my father sells in Fez. He told me he first had to learn to stand in the world alone. He had to learn to be a man. I respected his decision. After he left, Aishah was in a state of inconsolable distress. They have always liked each other. It was after Mustafa had gone that Aishah started talking about never marrying.

"What are you doing with yourself now?" I ask, once more joining them.

"I was thinking of asking your father for some work," Mustafa answers.

"Go see him quickly. He'll have a place for you on his next trip to Fez."

III. Love

For days, I carry the book I had bought for Esther to the mosque. Each morning I go to my lectures certain she will be by the fountain when I come out. Each day I return home disappointed. Even the sight of Naziha's enticing nudity cannot wipe Esther from my mind. I aimlessly walk the narrow streets in solitude. Just as I begin to despair, she appears by the fountain. I can barely contain my exuberance. It is a brilliant day, and we decide to walk to the zoo through the pleasure gardens lining the river. After a lengthy stroll in the sun, we are relieved to find ourselves in the shade of tall poplar trees lining the main road of the zoo. As we discuss subjects ranging from aesthetics to religion, we laugh at the lion lazily sleeping on his back. Esther asks about my lecturers and the books I have read. She energetically enters into discussions regarding the minutest points. She stimulates my reason, questions my beliefs, and pushes the limits of my established thought. My mind tingles with new possibilities.

We stop to watch the leopard pacing back and forth in his cage. I challenge the basis of her ideas and demand logic to back up her observations. We sit on a bench and admire the Persian prune tree, its pink flowers in full bloom upon the bare branches. We both fall silent at the exquisite sight of a pond filled with tall, elegant calla lilies. Nature seems so much more radiant in her company.

In front of the parrot cages, I finally hand Esther the book. "A present for your trip to Fez," I explain shyly.

She lowers her eyes, and color floods her cheeks. She opens the first page. "You remembered!" she cries, eyes sparkling with delight. "This will bring me such pleasure. Whenever I read it, I will think of you."

"That was my intention." I force myself to overcome my sudden timidity.

It is late afternoon, and the heat of the sun sits heavy in the air. By the time we return to the mosque, we must take leave of each other. Both of us are reluctant to separate. Time passes as we sit by the fountain near the mosque, our fingers playing close to each other in the water. How difficult it is to part! I will not see her for six or seven months. I should not have listened to 'Abdallah. I should have accompanied my father on this trip. I could have been together with Esther all the time.

At last, we tear away from each other, a wrenching break. I am furious with 'Abdallah. I pass a fountain in a square, its thin spray of water playing like a sorrowful lute. I hate myself for this illogical longing. I force myself to think of Naziha; the glow of her brown skin, the rise of her buttocks. I bend over the bowl of the fountain to splash cool water on my face.

Near the portico of the Great Mosque, 'Abdallah, Shihab, and I try to maintain our distance from the crowd yet still hear the proceedings. I crane my neck to keep the accused in view.

"Al-Kashani says there is no difference between Islam, Christianity, and Judaism," cries an appalled witness standing before the judge and a crowd of curious onlookers.

"And why do you say this, al-Kashani?" the judge, sitting in the shade with his scribes, turns to a humble, elderly man.

"Because Allah told me this is so," al-Kashani replies softly.

"You have talked with Allah?"

"Yes."

A unanimous gasp rises from the crowd.

"Yes?" echoes the judge, eyebrows rising heavenward.

"Sufis talk to Allah." al-Kashani smiles.

"And Allah tells you a man may believe in either Abraham, Jesus, or Muhammad?"

"All are Allah's prophets. And all three monotheistic religions believe in Allah. That is the unifying principle."

"But they do not all accept Muhammad as their Prophet." The judge's forehead is tightly knitted in vertical lines. The long gray hairs of his eyebrows rigidly point toward the accused man before him.

Al-Kashani, a professed Sufi, remains silent.

"If they do not accept Muhammad," continues the judge, "they cannot accept Allah."

A murmur of concurrence ripples through the crowd.

"Allah is Allah, no matter what else they believe," the Sufi insists gently.

The hairs rise on my forearms.

"But he does not accept the importance of Muhammad," cries the witness.

"I do accept Muhammad," the Sufi replies slowly. "I only say that one does not need to accept Muhammad in order to accept Allah. And you must agree that Allah is the highest, the all-important."

Involuntarily, I find myself nodding and quickly stop. The crowd shifts in discomfort.

"That man is going to die," my friend Shihab predicts in a whisper.

"Once a Sufi is brought to trial, few walk away free," 'Abdallah says sadly. "They refuse to defend themselves. They believe they are in the care of Allah."

"You disagree?" I turn to him. The trial has created a strange disturbance in me. I feel drawn to al-Kashani's gentle smile and sense he possesses an inner wisdom. Such a man could not be a traitor to Islam.

"Allah does take care of them, but they must help Him. If a man jumps into the fire, chances are he will burn," 'Abdallah replies.

"Sufis must know that," I say.

"Divine ecstasy sometimes makes you lose touch with the physical world of less enlightened souls," 'Abdallah adds with a trace of sarcasm.

"I've spoken to Sufis in Baghdad," Shihab quickly offers. "They were more interested in the intellectual exploration of the Divine than in spiritual ecstasy."

"Some think Islamic society sets tight limits on their philosophizing. They turn to Sufism for scholastic freedom," 'Abdallah explains.

"What exactly is Sufism?" I ask. I have never been absolutely clear about what they represent.

"Sufis call themselves Ahl al-Haqq, the followers of the Truth." 'Abdallah smiles at me.

"Are judges not also followers of the Truth?" I pursue.

"If you were to speak to all the people who claim to seek the Truth, you would have to conclude there are innumerable paths to the Truth, not just one."

There is only one Truth, I logically tell myself. Are there different ways to approach it and still arrive at the same Truth? Can the various roads really lead in the same direction?

"Do you know Sufis here in Cordoba?" asks Shihab.

"Yes. I sometimes attend their meetings."

I am surprised to hear this. 'Abdallah has never mentioned Sufism to us.

A roar of approval rises from the crowd. I turn back to the judge in time to see the Sufi being led away by a burly guard. The peaceful expression on the Sufi's face, and his subtle inward smile, fills me with amazement. I have never seen anyone radiate such peace, especially someone just accused of heresy and surely on his way to death. Beyond any reason, I feel an overwhelming empathy for the man. He must be saved! He does not deserve to die! I am astonished at such thoughts; from where have they come?

The crowd disperses. We walk out of the courtyard into the street alive with the throbbing noise of city life. I turn to 'Abdallah and am surprised to hear myself ask, "Would you take me to a Sufi meeting?"

Laughing, he puts his arm around my shoulders. "So, Sulayman, you are curious?"

A fresh breeze strokes the warm night. The scent of jasmine mingles with the sweet aroma of night flowers opening to the darkness. With the first hint of light, they will close once more, leaving behind a faint trail of their nightly existence.

'Abdallah and I cross the Roman bridge to the south bank of the Guadalquivir. We walk along the river road. At last, we arrive at a white stucco summer villa: the Sufi hermitage. The house has been donated to the Sheykh by one of his followers. Its magnificence is astonishing. I am uncertain what I had expected but certainly not such opulence. Inside, in the main courtyard, the focal point is a three-tiered central fountain of ocher and white marble surrounded by a large, round pool containing yellow and white water lilies. Off the portico is the reception room where numerous followers, both men and women, sit on the green-tiled floors spread with cushions and bronze oil lamps. Some disciples are dressed in simple beige robes, as the Sheykh himself; others are sporting the latest style of the day.

The Sheykh, a man with graying hair, beard, and an angelic smile, is the image of infinite benevolence. I am mesmerized by the scene, the atmosphere. Humility, a most foreign sensation, rises from my abdomen, to my chest, filling my throat and head. The Sheykh is explaining that a Sufi must serve two masters if he or she does not want to be left vulnerable to possible heretical charges. A Sufi must meditate and look within to reach the Divine Truth; also, a Sufi must worship and look without to the laws of Islam and the world of his fellow Muslims. The first is to satisfy inner needs; the second is to satisfy society's needs. Neither can be neglected unless one is prepared to step outside of society.

One man points out that persecution can happen to anyone who does not hold accepted beliefs. He identifies himself as a Mu'tazila follower in his thinking and explains he had to flee Baghdad because the orthodox are determined to wipe out rational thought.

In a soft, deep voice the Sheykh discusses the soul, the sun, spiritual transmutation. There is talk of symbolism, the thousand veils, the movement toward the Divine within all. The undercurrents of the words, the smell of mystical intentions, are enchanting, though strangely bewildering.

Refined, focused tautness pulls me upward, above the quotidian physical world. I hardly understand the words; their meaning is hidden from my limited awareness. Yet I sense the lightness, the purity. I sense that these minds travel elevated territories without borders; territories not available to most, not even sought by most. Unable to contribute anything to the meeting, I sit in quiet and wonder as a thin layer of dust lifts from my mind allowing me to breathe deeper. How can I maintain this feeling of open lightness?

It is late night when 'Abdallah and I recross the bridge in silence. The mood of enchantment is still with me. I want to hold onto this magical state. I fear that as soon as I enter the narrow streets, within the city walls, my mind will once more be confined; the dust will once more settle. I suggest a short stroll.

We walk down to the river and along the path paved with large square stones. We stop under an old willow tree, and I gaze out at the ripples on the surface of the water reflecting the moon. What lies beyond, below, above?

"This meeting has had more of an effect on you than I had anticipated," comments 'Abdallah.

I nod my head, not wishing to disturb the air with my words. 'Abdallah puts his hand on my shoulder. I nod my head again, still lost in the ripples.

"First study the law before you graduate to the spirit," he advises.

The spirit, I repeat to myself. *Is it the spirit that flies freer once the dust is lifted?*

'Abdallah caresses my cheeks. I continue to gaze at the flecks of light on the water. He steps before me, blocking my view of fluidity and takes my face in his hands. There is a small sparkle in the darkness of his eyes. I make an effort to look deeper into the sparkle, to sense something beyond the body, to touch something invisible to the eye. 'Abdallah leans close. The sparkle approaches. His lips brush mine. Their physicality surprises me and evokes a longing to reach out. I feel the weight of 'Abdallah's body. My back is pressed against the trunk of the tree. His lips urgently open and the wetness of his tongue enters my mouth. I reach out in thirsty response. 'Abdallah's lips search out my ear, and I hear a whisper thick and breathless with desire, "I love you, love you, Sulayman. I have wanted to say these words to you for such a long time. Love . . ."

Suddenly the longing shatters and I pull away violently. Filled with sudden anger, I rush away from him. I make my way to the nearest city gate. The guard, his oil lamp in one hand and a leashed watchdog in the other, opens the heavy door for me. I hurry through the winding lantern-lit streets. Soon I must pass through another gate with another guard.

By the time I reach home, perspiration flows down my body. I stop in the courtyard to calm my emotions and find the terrible longing once more surging forth. I walk through the passageway to the women's courtyard and upstairs to Naziha's bedroom. The light cover is pulled up to her waist. The firm mounds of her breasts reach toward the ceiling, as she lies calmly asleep on her back. I hear my short, quick breaths whisper into the silence. I quickly bend down to kiss the soft nipples, my palms caressing the mounds, my tongue licking until I feel the emerging hardness. She stirs, rustling the cotton cover. My hands rush down her body, her thighs, around her buttocks, traveling restlessly, urgently. My hands are aflame. My tongue seeks out the innermost crevices, hungry to devour the whole body, to make her a part of me. I move suspended in timelessness, furious desire throbbing within, rising to a higher and higher plane, rushing toward the light; at last, bursting into oblivion.

I fall to the bed beside her, suddenly chilled with the wetness of my need. I open my eyes to darkness, trying to recall the point of orgasm, trying to recall the feeling: total abandonment, absolute surrender. Is that how one should feel in the presence of God? But now I am left empty, drained. Is it because I was so close to the Absolute? That infinite space without borders, going on forever. Now I have fallen back into consciousness. Is it possible to maintain a level of ecstasy for a long time? An eternal orgasm?

Now I understand why Sufis write love poems, poems of passionate desire, addressed to the beloved. They are after that eternal orgasm of physical oblivion, that most focused and highest pitch of existence. They desire Allah as their lover. They desire to be ravished by the Divine. I imagine myself being overcome, infused by the light of God. I see my orgasmic fountain shooting toward the sky, glistening in the sun, fertilizing the clouds.

I glance at Naziha. She has turned on her stomach and is once more asleep. Perhaps, in the morning, this interlude of passion will seem like a dream to her. Sleep refuses to overtake me. I gently kiss Naziha's shoulder, carefully slip out of bed, and pull the covers over her body. I once more get dressed.

In the courtyard, I take a lit torch and leave the quiet darkness of the house to return to the river, hoping to once more gaze at the moon playing with the waves and recapture my earlier feeling of wonder.

The echoes of my footsteps reverberate in the narrow, stone streets. A guard, taking me for a thief, gruffly blocks my path to demand my identity. Satisfied, he lets me continue. Outside the walls, my torch casts an amber glow into the clear distance. I look toward the river and long to touch those ripples of lightness. I walk down the stone steps leading to the grassy bank and extinguish my torch. In the silence of darkness I stroll on the soft, moist grass, carefully listening to the barely audible sound of my steps. I take off my shoes to f eel my bare feet against the wetness of nature. Behind me, in the distance, I hear a movement but do not want to turn, thinking it must be someone like me, walking to forget, to remember, to understand. I continue, ignoring the growing sound of rustling. Suddenly a heavy, sharp object crashes down on my skull and all vanishes.

The coolness of the air sends shivers down my body. The chant of the muezzin reaches me, and I become aware of a splitting pain in my head. I open my eyes to find myself sprawled in the dew of the grass and stripped of everything except my long white underwear. I will have to walk home, nearly naked, while everyone heads for the mosque. I should be grateful the robber at least left me my underwear!

I stay in bed all day, haunted by 'Abdallah's advances and by the nearly violent urgency of my own desire for that light essence I experienced in the hermitage.

Naziha brings in my meals and gently strokes my forehead. Her kindness is truly moving. Late in the afternoon, a servant hands me a letter. It is from 'Abdallah. The scene by the river once more flashes before my mind; an uneasy feeling rises in my stomach. I break open the seal.

"Please forgive my fantasies, which can surely do you no harm. My physical desires do not affect the connection of our minds." I reread and smile.

The leaves of the poplar trees are strewn on the ground. Heavy rains are beating the stone buildings making them shine in the grayness. Autumn has always filled me with soft affection; it is a time when nature gently recedes into sleep to prepare for the renewed blossoming of spring. It is a splendid death filled with hope.

Before prayer, an announcement rings through the mosque: our Caliph, Abd al-Rahman III, has just died at the age of seventy, in the Islamic year 350, 961 for the Christians. Mournful cries rise toward the high ceilings. Wailing fills the large space and rushes out the doors into the wet courtyard. I too am stunned. The caretaker of al-Andalus is no more. Who will lead the empire? Who will ensure our stability? The Caliph's reign of forty-nine years has brought self-confidence and wealth to al-Andalus. Now, who among us does not feel like a lost child, even for a fleeting moment? I cry with the rest, tears of sorrow, tears of hope for a future to equal the past.

The day after the announcement, my father returns from his trip. He finds Cordoba in a somber mood of mourning. On the day of the funeral, the whole city dresses in white and pays homage to their dead Caliph. Great choral processions, accompanied by musical bands, wind through the streets.

It is late afternoon, and the family sits in the main courtyard, near the fig tree, quietly drinking coffee.

"It was Abd al-Rahman III who took on the title of Caliph, freeing us from the Abbasids of Baghdad," my father explains when my brother Husan questions the depth of his grief. "And Abd al-Rahman III has built al-Andalus into an economic and cultural power."

"Abd al-Rahman III has paved a solid road for his son, al-Hakam II," Husan points out. "He has left him a powerful empire to rule."

"I predict al-Hakam II's reign will be even more glorious than his father's," my half-sister Lobua says proudly. Lobua is enthusiastic about the prospect of a new ruler. She does not waste her time in mourning. I know she feels Abd al-Rahman III's son will better serve her ambitions. "At forty-seven, he has already shown his preference for learning," she adds.

"As well as for little boys," chuckles Saida, my father's first wife. Her round bosom merrily bounces under her light blouse.

"Everyone has weaknesses," my father sternly points out.

"Weaknesses in a leader could foreshadow the weakness of an empire," Saida counters, biting into a large date.

"I predict great times to come," my father retorts, clearly annoyed with Saida's pessimism.

"Al-Hakam II will build Cordoba into the center of the world," predicts Lobua.

"And after?" asks Saida.

"Contrasts are the way of the world, the way of God," my brother Ali joins in. "Empires are built and destroyed."

"Why can we not simply progress? Are chaos and destruction necessary?" I ask. Though I am deeply saddened by Abd al-Rahman III's death, more than I would have expected, I agree with Lobua and hold great hope for al-Hakam. II.

"The ways of God are intricate and complex," my father muses.

"Surely man has a say in the direction of the world," I venture. "Surely, we are allowed control over our own development."

The past six months have sped by at surprising speed. I have attended numerous poetic recitals at private homes, and endless arguments with 'Abdallah and Shihab have kept my mind sharpened. Languorous evenings have been spent with Naziha, exploring her body and her past. Not only is she highly exciting and passionate but also loving, humorous, and patient. Her pride has softened, and I believe she is truly content in our home. I feel tremendous gratitude at having found her. Shihab now claims that my constant winning at chess is due to Naziha. Both 'Abdallah and Shihab are very amused by my high spirits. They insist that physical release aids the imagination and gives clarity to the mind.

I have hardly thought of Esther since she left. However, when my father returned from the trip, to my surprise, one of my first questions was about her.

Since Abd al-Rahman III's funeral, I have been eagerly looking for Esther, without success. At last, I see her waiting by the fountain in the courtyard of the mosque. I make an unsuccessful attempt to calm my excitement before breaking into a run. As soon as she sees me, a flush rises to her cheeks, and she bursts into laughter. By the time I arrive beside her, I too find myself reduced to helpless merriment. After such a long separation, we are unable to utter one sensible word to each other. Finally, we gain control of our mirth and leave the mosque, past ragged beggars, colorfully attired singing minstrels. We pass through the city gates to the open road, curving toward the sun-lit hills. In a short time, we arrive at a Muslim cemetery bounded by olive groves and cypress trees. Inside, tanners have placed their hides to dry atop the graves. We stroll past graves of intricate mosaics, grand family mausoleums. The thrill of once more being with Esther adds an extra shine of brilliance to everything I see. My awareness is heightened to a finely sharpened pitch. We sit down on a turquoise tiled grave. The sun is shining in a clear sky, though the air already holds a winter chill. The walk has warmed us and we open our overcoats to feel the freshness of the breeze.

Esther presents me with a package wrapped in yellow silk cloth. I quickly open it to find a magnificent manuscript by Ibn Qutayaba. It is written in careful calligraphy with delicate border designs of gold and royal blue. If death were to take me this instant I would welcome it gladly. My smile caresses Esther and I imagine cradling her weightlessness in my arms. Suddenly, I see Naziha's yielding body before my eyes. The taste of her skin, her wetness is alive on my tongue. I feel my face burning and quickly turn away before Esther notices my embarrassment.

We exchange stories of the past six months, continually interrupting each other in our excitement. The air grows colder, too cold to sit still, and we walk around the cemetery, weaving around the graves, admiring their colors. Esther tells me the Jewish cemetery is not at all gay. It is clothed in uniform grayness. "Only sadness hangs in the air," she tells me. "It holds no joy. Christian cemeteries are not happy places either. I do not know why but Muslim cemeteries have always been a favorite of lovers—they are not only for the dead." Perhaps we feel that love is close to death. The intoxicating, carefree joy of love can only be found again after death, in paradise.

At night, I slowly undress Naziha by the light of the oil lamp and lie beside her glowing naked body. I touch her lips and lightly run my hands down to her thighs, savoring the texture of her skin. I blow out the lamp and explore her body with closed eyes. I feel the heat of her growing desire. Slowly, the image of Esther materializes before me. I look into her dark brown eyes and lightly touch her shimmering white skin. I see her laughing with abandon. Naziha's sighs are transformed into Esther's sparkling breath. No! I quickly open my eyes to obliterate Esther.

Naziha presses against me, arms tightly wound around my waist. As I am carried on the wave of desire, I once more close my eyes. Esther again appears, head thrown back, mouth open in pleasure. My eyes follow the smooth whiteness of her neck. A wave of unexpected anger splashes over me. I don't want to think of Esther while I am with Naziha! My palms press harder and harder against Naziha's body. I bite into her shoulder and hear a soft yelp. My legs push hers apart, and I grab her buttocks, kneading them with full strength, feeling my nails digging into the soft flesh. With my eyes once more wide open, I become thoughtlessly rough in my need to obliterate another's face.

Wasted with exhaustion yet not at all satisfied, I allow Naziha to cradle my head in her arms. Her fingers lightly play with my hair. She tries to soothe me, sensing the battle within. Her touch creates the opposite to the desired effect. Her very touch evokes tight nervousness, and I jump out of bed.

Standing by the fountain of the courtyard, shivering under the darkness of the sky, I hear Esther's voice as the water sprinkles into the bowl below. I am miserable. I cherish Naziha, and she has given me such unimagined, rich pleasure. Yet, I long for Esther.

Time passes in a haze until our next rendezvous. I hurry to the kiosk of the pleasure garden by the river. As I approach, I see her already sitting inside. She looks more beautiful than ever with her straight black hair loosely covered by a light blue scarf. The coolness of the air has brought a flush to her cheeks. I hold the book I had brought for her close to my chest and wonder if I should have written a note inside. Perhaps a poem. I step into the kiosk, and Esther immediately jumps up to ruffle my hair.

"I am glad you are back to your natural auburn color. I much prefer it to the black I saw before I left for the trip." She smiles.

"Don't you think the black made me look more distinguished?"

"The auburn makes you look more mysterious. It gives you an air of difference."

I laugh and hand her the book. Upon seeing the cover, she lets out a cry of joy. It is the interpretation of the Torah by a well-known Jewish scholar.

"I can't wait to show it to my father!"

"Does he know of our meetings?"

Esther hesitates. "No. The book will give me an opportunity to tell him I have seen you."

It is too cold to sit still for long. We return inside the walls to stroll the streets near the Great Mosque. Al-Hakam II has ordered the construction of a new hospital opposite the Mosque. He has commissioned several schools to be built for the poor, as well. Esther tells me she met numerous scholars in Fez who have been invited by al-Hakam II to teach the poor here in Cordoba for a handsome salary. Lobua has been right about al-Hakam II. He has become a ruler with exceptional sensitivity to the lower classes, combined with awareness to intellectual progress. Cordoba is becoming a strong magnet for the seekers of the world.

We enter the covered market and stop at potters' shops to examine their ware. We go into the inner market to admire the luxury goods on display. There are ivory boxes from Alexandria, gold jewellery from Baghdad, delicate porcelain from China. The beauty surrounding us is amazing. The usual cacophony of market sounds transform into a musical score. The aromas are distinctly rich, uniquely redolent. I am infused by a new appreciation of life, of man's ability to produce such sublime creations.

When it is time to part, I find my feet suddenly heavy. We finally say our farewells and reluctantly walk in opposite directions with both of us continually turning back for one last wave, one last look.

The lecturer's words pass through me. The streaming rays of the sun entering the open doorways have captured my attention. Shihab knocks me alert with his elbow. Startled I turn to him; his response is a conspiratorial smile. He probably presumes I was dreaming of Naziha. I make an effort to focus on the words of the lecturer, a distinguished older man who has taught in the great cities of the world. His specialty is Malikite law. He delivers his knowledge with serene confidence, unmitigated certainty. How unlike 'Abdallah, for whom the questions are never far!

After the lecture, just outside the Mosque, Shihab and I are blocked by a newly arrived royal procession. Judging from their banners and clothing, they are from the Christian territories. A richly jeweled hunchback is at the head of a long trail of horsemen. Recently, numerous Christian ambassadors have come to tour Cordoba and pay their respects to al-Hakam. II. At first, I felt tremendous pride that all these foreign infidel rulers came to kiss the hand of our Caliph. Now these processions are commonplace, even a nuisance since they disrupt the normal activity of the city.

"I heard my father say that Ordono IV was expected to pray at Abd al-Rahman III's tomb and proffer his respects to his son," Shihab tells me.

"What could he want?"

"His kingdom, Leon. He needs al-Hakam's help to get it back."

"Why would al-Hakam bother helping an infidel?"

"Sancho, the present ruler of Leon, was to give us ten fortresses but did not. Al-Hakam probably thinks if he helps Ordono IV to power, he will finally get his fortresses," Shihab drops a coin into a beggar's palm, then adds, "I think Sancho and Ordono IV are cousins."

The sound of a horn rips through the air, its sharpness startling the onlookers.

"Is this Sancho the Fat?" I ask as a vague memory glimmers in the background.

"He was fat . . ."

"I remember, Hasdai, the Caliph's Jewish doctor, helped to cure the man of his fatness in exchange for the fortresses." I laugh. "Sancho was enormous. He needed four men to help him get on his horse."

"Sancho has neglected to pay his doctor's bill." Shihab eyes an attractive slave girl nearby.

"Next time he can turn to Christian doctors for help," I say.

"And die. Christian medicine consists of praying over the sick. They're not a very advanced lot in the northern territories."

"The Christians here have at least learned from Muslim science." I remember Sebastian and against my will feel called upon to protect my mother's religion.

"That's probably why a lot converted to Islam."

"They were quick to recognize a superior culture."

"It's not hard to be superior to the Christians," adds Shihab. "I visited Toulouse with my father a couple of years ago. Those people are barbaric!

They have no baths. They hardly ever wash. As well, their cooking was inedible."

The procession finally passes, allowing everyone to return to their activities. A minstrel with a white face, ruby lips, a multicolored peaked cap dangling little bells, and a tambourine in each hand sings of a Holy War in Castile; a war attended by a hundred poets to praise the bravery of the fighting men and a hundred sword sharpeners to hone the blades for the glory of Allah. *At least my mother had the good sense to marry a Muslim,* I tell myself.

The gossip of the day picked up at the market from storytellers, acquaintances, relatives, or friends always finds its way to our family suppers. The evening meal is a time for news: personal, cultural, and political. The volume of our discussions liberally rises and falls, undulating with emotion.

I look at Lobua perched on a cushion, clearly ready to make an important announcement. She waits for the servants to exchange the dishes on the tables before starting.

With a beaming smile on her face, she puts up her hands asking for silence. "I was called to a meeting at the government palace today. I have been appointed to go to Fez in search of manuscripts for al-Hakam II's library."

"That is an honor," Kinza, her mother, cries out and turns to my father. "Don't you think, Ahmed?"

"You will be staying with your brother, Jamal, of course," my father says, naturally concerned about his single daughter.

"Of course," Lobua replies in her haughty manner.

After the usual noises of objections and congratulations, the conversation moves to another topic. Lobua leans over to me and whispers, "I saw you in the garden near the fountain with a beautiful black-haired girl."

"That was Isaac's daughter. We have become friends."

Lobua winks at me.

That is encouragement enough to take her into my confidence. "I think I am falling in love." I sigh deeply.

She laughs with understanding. "Passionate love! That sweet agony!"

"How long does it take to fall in love?" I ask.

"It could take a year, a month, or it can happen in a flash. But the suffering can last forever."

Suffering? I am astonished by her last remark. Why should there be suffering, I wonder?

'Abdallah has been offered a teaching post in Baghdad and is about to leave soon. My father has invited him to the house for a farewell festivity. I am thinking of ways to avoid being present since I feel certain 'Abdallah will make one last declaration of his love for me.

He has been quite persistent since that night by the river, after the Sufi meeting. He thinks words are enough to seduce a person. To this end, he has been regularly sending me poems he himself has composed. They have had no effect. Though I am often mesmerized by his words, my body feels no desire. Being a very attractive and highly intelligent man, he should have no trouble finding a more responsive student in Baghdad. He deserves adoration and love. Perhaps, if I did not have Esther, I too would be tempted.

At the end of the lecture 'Abdallah walks out with me, his arm around my neck, his fingers caressing my cheek. In the courtyard, Esther is waiting by the ablution fountain. I quickly leave 'Abdallah and hurry in her direction. Of course, he follows me.

"You have sat in on some of my classes?" 'Abdallah says to Esther, sitting down by the fountain and sending a group of white pigeons flying into the air.

"I am flattered you remember. I have never said a word in your lectures." Esther smiles shyly.

"How could I forget such a hauntingly beautiful face?"

Esther blushes, but quickly tries to cover her embarrassment. "I enjoy your lectures. I like the way you encourage students to find their own answers."

"We must all strive to find our own answers. At the same time, we must be aware of the answers others have found before us. How else is knowledge to progress?"

"Sometimes we Muslims spend too much time writing commentaries on old answers. Too few make an effort to find new answers," I add a little too eagerly, trying to enter the conversation.

"It is important to have a healthy respect for the past," Esther points out.

"But with a view to the future," I say quickly.

"He's one of my best students," 'Abdallah flirtatiously smiles at Esther.

I am furious at him for playing with her. I protectively turn to Esther, "Why don't we go to the covered market?" I begin to move away.

Esther follows me. I turn and find 'Abdallah close behind. "You don't expect me to leave you alone with such a beautiful young woman," he says with a wink.

I flash him a look of sharp anger, but he simply laughs and fully turns his charms on Esther. As Esther responds to his words, I find myself growing more and more annoyed. Nothing I say can induce 'Abdallah to leave us. My effort to be rid of him inspires him to be even more flirtatious with Esther. She gaily giggles at his recitation of love poems. She is so enjoying herself that she is clearly reluctant to leave when the time comes.

I clench my fists as I look toward the sun. "It's getting late," I say more urgently than I had expected. I now want Esther to leave 'Abdallah's company and hope this statement will send her on her way.

"Yes. You are right," she replies reluctantly.

I take a strong aim at a loose stone underfoot. I miss and painfully stub my toe on a step.

Esther and 'Abdallah exchange a long farewell. 'Abdallah conveys his deep desire to see her again at his lectures. This is the first time I have actually been happy to see Esther go.

Once alone with 'Abdallah I become despondent. I have lost my chance to be alone with Esther. I should not have been so afraid of being rude in front of her. 'Abdallah and I walk in silence through the street of the spice vendors. The pungent odors I normally enjoy now make me nauseous. I walk from darkness to light, through the pools of sunshine flooding down from the square skylights of the cement roof. I am hardly aware of 'Abdallah. I reprimand myself for my cowardice.

"So, can I presume you to be in love?"

"I don't think that matter concerns you. Logic is more suited to your line," I snap.

"On the contrary, I know quite a lot about love."

I remain stubbornly silent.

"This is a very interesting situation, don't you think?" 'Abdallah smiles, enjoying himself.

"I don't think I quite see it from that perspective."

"Try. You love Esther . . ."

I turn to him with a barely controllable feeling of violence.

"Yes"—he laughs—"whether you know it or not, you love the girl . . ." he pauses, " . . . and I love you."

I check my desire to physically lash out at him.

"Yes, I am afraid I do love you," 'Abdallah continues sadly. "The question is where does Esther stand?"

Judging by what just happened, she clearly preferred 'Abdallah's company to mine. She hardly spoke to me or even noticed me. Before she left, she gave 'Abdallah a warm smile while I received no more than a limp wave.

"I envy you," he says quietly.

My throat is tight. I turn away to stare at the spices in copper bowls.

"I envy you because I think Esther loves you as well."

Did I hear correctly?

"Yes, she does, I can tell by her eyes. Even though I tried to tempt her by sweet words . . ." He laughs. "No need to look so surprised. You are a beautiful boy and she is a beautiful girl. You have a naturally elegant and graceful carriage, with eyes that burn to know. That is very seductive."

"You really think she loves me?" I ask, afraid to give sound to the words.

"I can only wish that you would love me half as much as she loves you."

Suddenly I am filled with warm affection for 'Abdallah and resolve to attend his farewell party.

Our main courtyard is decorated in brilliant colors of brocade and silk draped over the branches of trees. The brass tables of the reception room are laden with the finest delicacies Cordoba can offer. A flute, tambourine, and pandora play in one corner of the room. My father has decided to serve date, fig, and grape wine, which are clearly making a number of guests more exuberant. Visiting scholars from all over the world have been invited to wish 'Abdallah a good trip. His friends recite farewell poems in his honor. I too have composed a poem which I recite with great flourish. Everyone is curious to know why he is leaving Cordoba just at a time when everyone is coming here. Some claim Cordoba has surpassed Baghdad in glory and learning. Our city no longer needs to look to the east for inspiration; at last, it has become the inspiration of the world. 'Abdallah assures them he is not planning to stay in Baghdad forever; he simply wants to personally verify the political situation.

Late in the evening, in search of fresh air, I stroll out into the courtyard with several scholars. Soon 'Abdallah joins us. He takes me aside and leads me behind a brocade hanging.

"I want to personally say good-bye to you because who knows when we will see each other again." His voice is filled with emotion.

I lean over and hug 'Abdallah. I will miss this man who has been my best teacher. 'Abdallah gently kisses my cheek and then moves his lips to find mine. I kiss him back and then put a firm hand on his shoulder. 'Abdallah forcefully pulls me closer, his hands traveling down my back. I push him away.

"Don't you know by now? I am not interested."

"I thought you might take pity . . ."

"You do not need pity, 'Abdallah," I say gently. "Remember the logic you are so proud of."

He takes a step back, his head bent toward the ground. "Sometimes logic proves weaker than emotion."

"Soon you will have a fresh group of students, a fresh group of people around you. You will fall in love with someone who will return your affections."

'Abdallah forces himself to smile. "There are not many like you."

At night I hold Naziha's body in my arms but derive no more than superficial pleasure from the contact. During the day, in the courtyard of the mosque, I search the faces coming through the gates. A whole week passes without sight of Esther.

Finally, my patience runs out. Caution becomes insignificant. I decide to send Esther a note asking her to meet me on a specific day. I must be certain she alone will get the note: no one else. I will send a female slave to deliver it to her in person.

After great deliberation, I choose a female slave who has been with us for several years. I impress upon her the importance of this mission and watch her leave.

When the servant returns, she tells me apologetically that Esther was not at home. She had left the note with the house's female slave who promised to give it to Esther personally.

The days are gray with winter showers. Thick downpours send water rushing along the pebbled drainage of the streets. Nature perfectly understands my mood. The day I had indicated in my note to meet Esther brings only a light drizzle, interspersed with clear sun. I look upon this change as a hopeful sign.

I walk into the pleasure garden and immediately notice her sitting in the kiosk. I break into a run and arrive before her breathless as well as speechless. I reach out to caress her hair.

Its softness surprises me. I run my fingers through it, and then lightly touch the smoothness of her cheeks. She turns her head away, and I let my hand drop.

"Someone might see us," she says. After a short period of silence, she turns to me in helpless frustration, "What are we going to do?"

"Get married," the words roll from my lips before I have time to think.

Esther bursts into tears. "I can't get married till I'm twenty-four. That's two years away."

"We'll wait. There is no need to rush."

"But I don't know if my father would ever let me marry you. A Jew cannot marry outside the faith."

"That's ridiculous. I will persuade him. I'll talk to him till he cannot say no," I reply with confidence.

"My father won't even talk to anyone about marriage till I'm twenty-four."

"On your twenty-fourth birthday, my father and I will talk to him. How can he refuse? He and my father have been partners for years. He has seen me grow up."

Esther's tears are still rolling down her cheeks. "Religion does something to people."

"Trust me."

"I do trust you, but I also know my father."

Esther's tear-filled eyes stare into the distant paleness of the sky. She pulls at the scarf around her shoulders.

"Your father adores you." I try to comfort her. "He thinks the world of you. How can he possibly refuse you what you want?" I reach for her hand.

Her eyes drop to the ground. Fear rises to my throat. Perhaps I am not the one she would want to marry. Perhaps my passion is only one-sided.

"That is, of course, if you do want me," I say quietly.

I hear Esther take a deep breath. "Yes." She exhales. "Yes," she repeats firmly and turns to me.

"Then we can make it work." I smile; the smile turns into a chuckle and the chuckle bursts into full laughter. Esther too is laughing. Is love not stronger than religion?

Sheep have been slaughtered for Aishah and Mustafa's wedding. In the open space surrounding our country house, large tents, decorated with silk and hung with oil lanterns, have been set up. Bouquets of red and white roses are everywhere. Orchestras and dancers entertain the innumerable guests. Singers sing and poets recite in celebration of the couple's happiness. My father is proud to give one of his daughters to a freedman, and he has been extravagant in planning the festivities. Esther, here with her family, is magnificently dressed in a silk azure shift, her long black hair providing a brilliant contrast. A magical quality envelops her. Her white skin gives off a silky glow reminding me of a bubbling brook in bright sunlight. We exchange looks of complicity but are careful not to be alone together.

When Naziha comes over to put her arms around my waist, I stiffen. I have never told Esther about Naziha. Perhaps her father mentioned something about a concubine to her. I do not know, but this is not the time I want her to find out. I tell Naziha to stay close to my mother in case she might need help with something.

I tease Aishah about her life after marriage. Her bond with Lobua will no longer be as tight as before. She tells me she already told Mustafa she intends to continue working with Lobua, helping her search for manuscripts.

A man stands up on a podium erected before one of the tents. Everyone falls silent. The crowd slowly gathers around him as the air fills with curious expectation. Suddenly the man begins to sing. A powerfully deep voice soars above our heads. His vocal chords reach toward the highest peak of the mountains, toward the eternity of the sky and the luminosity of the stars. He moves into a series of repetitions, which demand everyone present to join in. Voices rise attempting to achieve unison. Then the crowd falls silent again allowing the man to sing alone, expressing the joys and sorrows of the world and praising love that conquers all.

The melody rises and falls. The singer's voice fades to barely audible. People lean closer, straining to hear. The voice suddenly bursts forth again in clear longing, to just as suddenly die, leaving absolute silence.

The crowd explodes with enthusiastic cheers.

The orchestras once more begin to play. Dancing girls appear among the crowd. I see my Uncle Sadr enjoying the music and gazing appreciatively at the beautiful girls gyrating nearby. Uncle Sadr is a judge and the person responsible for helping me choose law. He leads a pure and exemplary life that will surely be rewarded in the hereafter.

Though I talk to everyone and dance until I can hardly stand, my heart is with Esther. I am always aware of where she is.

Whenever I look at her, her eyes find me. Or my eyes involuntarily move over the crowd until they find her watching me. Invisible threads of awareness bind us.

Food is served throughout the night. The singing and dancing are endless. The spontaneous recitation of poetry, to the happiness of Aishah and Mustafa, is constant.

The call of the muezzin at the break of dawn signals Uncle Sadr to lead the prayers in the open air. Jews and Christians politely move to the background while Muslims begin their ablutions.

IV. Forbidden Love

One afternoon, I take a short cut through the Jewish quarter on my way to Shihab's house. I pass through a small park in the middle of a square and spot two people strolling around the central fountain. Something catches my eye; the movement of the woman is familiar. I look again more carefully. Her back is turned toward me, yet I feel I know her. They stop. The man faces her. He has a full black beard and is earnestly presenting his point. She is nodding in response. With a sudden movement of her head, she flings back her long hair. Slender, delicate fingers reach back to pat the hair in place.

I know! Those gestures are Esther's. I search for a hiding place and dart behind the thick trunk of a date palm. From this position, I continue to observe, my heart wildly pounding. They start to move around the fountain again. Their shadow plays upon the falling water. White pigeons scatter into the air before their feet. When they come into full frontal view, I clearly see Esther. The man with her is about ten to fifteen years her senior. He is continually smiling and glancing at her. She keeps looking at the ground or ahead of her. They turn. Again, their back is to me. The ridiculousness of the situation dawns on me. Why am I hiding? Why do I simply not go out and greet Esther? Must I spy on her? I try to suppress my feelings of jealousy. I see the man reach for her elbow. I jump into the open and walk straight toward them. As soon as Esther notices me, she bursts into a smile. The man follows her eyes. His smile immediately fades.

"Sulayman, this is Simeon, a good friend of my brother, Ibrahim."

Simeon gives me a slight bow.

"Sulayman is my father's partner's son," Esther explains.

"Then you, too, are a merchant," Simeon observes.

"I'm studying to be a judge," I correct him.

"A Muslim judge?"

"Of course."

"Of course," Simeon repeats, nodding his head in satisfaction.

"Simeon is a doctor but often counsels people in legal matters." Esther is clearly uncomfortable.

"You'll excuse us, won't you?" Simeon takes Esther's elbow with a tight smile. "I was just about to escort the young lady back to her house."

"Of course." I hesitate, confused. Simeon coaxes Esther after him. She turns around to flash me an apologetic smile before they disappear down a narrow street.

Heavy of spirit, I walk out of the Jewish quarter and along the outside walls till I come to the next gate. I turn back into the city, past donkeys, carpenters, and masons fixing up an old Roman house. I walk down a side street and knock at a finely polished cedar door. A servant opens. I walk through the sun-drenched courtyard past citrus trees planted around the central fountain. Off the portico, inside a cool room, Shihab is reading cross-legged on a cushion with a little table of sweets beside him. He looks up from his book as I enter.

"Why such a sad face?"

"I'm in love." I sink into a nearby cushion.

"Who is it this time?" Shihab laughs.

"What do you mean, this time?"

"The last time it was Esther."

"It's still Esther," I answer, annoyed.

"Why so sad then?"

"I just saw her with another man."

"You're jealous." He laughs.

"Why should I be jealous," I say unhappily. "I know she loves me."

"Are you absolutely certain?"

"How absolutely certain can one be of anything?"

"Yes, true. Then certainty is very subjective. It's a philosophical dilemma." He glances at the book in his hand and pushes it toward me. "Look, the king of philosophy, Aristotle."

I look at the book without interest. "I hate feeling like this. I've never felt jealous before."

"Lucky you. It is a nasty feeling. Very nasty."

"Have you had it?" I ask.

"Sort of," Shihab says evasively.

"How can you be jealous only sort of?"

"Well . . ." he hesitates. "I guess I can tell you. It's been well over a year now." Shihab's fingers trace the pattern on the rug. "Remember 'Abdallah?"

I nod.

"I wanted 'Abdallah to love me, and I was jealous that he loved you."

"You loved 'Abdallah?" I ask in disbelief. It had never occurred to me that Shihab harbored such feelings for 'Abdallah.

"I respected him tremendously. I thought he was brilliant, and I wanted him to want me."

"You wanted to be his lover?"

"Yes."

"Why did you not say something to me about this before?"

"What could you have done? I could see you were not interested in him. And when I flirted with him and made suggestions, he laughed, humored me, and simply patted my cheeks."

"Yet you bear me no grudge?" I reach for a sweet.

"I was jealous of you, but you were still my best friend."

"And now?"

"Now I'm having a wonderfully illicit affair with a poet fifteen years my senior. She is mad about me."

"Do you love her?"

"I don't think so, I just thoroughly enjoy her loving me." He laughs.

I think of Naziha. How simple it would be if I loved her!

"I don't think you need worry." Shihab puts a comforting hand on my shoulder. "Esther loves you."

I turn to him in surprise. "What makes you say that?"

"The way she looks at you. The way she listens to you. The way the two of you laugh together."

I nod without conviction. I should make an effort to love Naziha. But for Naziha, I feel only affection.

Two days later I find Esther waiting in the courtyard of the Great Mosque. Time has inflamed my feelings of jealousy rather than soothed it. Reluctantly I walk toward her, afraid to face the truth. As I reach her, I see tears flowing down her cheeks.

"My father wants me to marry Simeon," she bursts out and covers her face with her hands.

It takes some time for the words to register.

"But you are not yet twenty-four," I say stupidly.

"My father suggested we marry on my twenty-fourth birthday."

My mind is racing in ten directions at once. "What have you said to your father?"

"I was very vague. I couldn't just say I didn't want to marry Simeon because then he would ask me why and all I could reply was that I loved you. Then he would know I've been seeing you alone and get angry."

"I haven't even said anything about us to my father." This is not how I had imagined life to work. "We're going to have to move fast," I say, trying to be logical. "I'll talk to my father, explain the whole situation, and urge him to invite Isaac to lunch as soon as possible."

Esther quickly nods in agreement, eager to accept whatever plan I present.

"Why does your father want you to marry this man?"

"He thinks it's a good match. Simeon is intelligent, is stable, has money, is respected, all those obvious things."

"How do you feel?"

"Sulayman," Esther says in exasperation. "How can you ask me that? I want to marry you, not him."

I feel tremendous relief, a sudden lightness overwhelms me.

We walk along the outer walls of the Great Mosque, past a construction crew installing lead heating pipes into the walls of al-Hakam II's new charity hall. We continue into the narrow winding streets of the Jewish quarter. When we arrive at the fountain where I had seen her with Simeon, I whisper with a vehemence that threatens to bring tears to my eyes, "I will marry you." I dig my nails deep into my palms until I feel them sink into the flesh, drawing blood.

Esther nods, biting her lips, and disappears down a small street.

"I would like to talk to you alone," I whisper to my father after supper.

"Let's go to the library. We'll be served tea there," he answers.

He leads me along the dimly lit portico. The cascading fountain thunders through the silence. At the other side of the courtyard, he pushes open the intricately carved wooden door.

Inside, he lights the lantern hanging from the ceiling and motions me to sit down.

"Can we close the door?" I ask, aware of my nervousness.

"Ah, this is a serious matter indeed."

My father lightly closes the door as I take a cushion by the wooden table. He sits opposite me on a leather puff. The oil lamp casts a golden hue of warmth and comfort over the library.

I pull up a knee to rest my arm on it. I notice my hand shaking and quickly drop it down beside me. My father waits. I had spent a long time preparing an intelligent presentation for this moment but now find my mind annoyingly blank.

"I want to get married," I blurt out.

My father's good-natured laugh eases my anxiety.

"Shouldn't you wait till you finish your studies?"

"There is no time."

"Time?" my father asks, not understanding.

A soft knock on the door silences me.

"Come in," my father calls out.

The slave girl brings in the mint tea on a tray and places it on the table between us. She takes the silver kettle and, holding it high above the glass, pours the translucent, steaming green liquid into each cup. The aroma of mint fills the room.

My father nods, and she quickly leaves, closing the door behind her.

The steam from the two cups of tea curls high into the air.

My father picks up his glass and gently blows on the surface of the liquid before taking a sip.

"Am I to understand that you are in a hurry to get married?"

I explain the situation to my father, going into greater and greater detail. I tell him about my love for Esther, how we have been seeing each other regularly. I tell him about Simeon. Every joy, fear, and hope is translated into words. After what seems like a very long time, after my father has already drunk three glasses of tea, I finally come to the end of my story. My father leans forward, elbow on knee, hand stroking the empty glass on the table.

I pick up my untouched glass of tea. It is already cold. I quickly drink it down, suddenly aware of my dry throat.

"My dear Sulayman." My father sadly looks up at me. "Of all the girls in Cordoba, does it have to be Esther?"

I can hardly believe his words. "But she's beautiful, intelligent, funny. She is everything I want."

"And she's Jewish."

"Mother is Christian. Besides Jews don't eat pork, like Muslims."

"Yes." My father's gaze lowers. "This is going to be very difficult."

"All we have to do is invite Isaac and have a talk with him."

"All? . . . And what do you think Isaac will say?"

"He's your partner. He's known me since I was little. He knows the family. I think he would be honored."

"My son," my father strokes his beard. "You're so young, so idealistic."

His words are incomprehensible to me. My heart is throbbing in my chest, shaking my insides. My throat is painfully tight.

"Your grandfather, may God rest his soul, had no objections to having his Christian daughter marry a Muslim. Your grandfather probably would not have cared if she had married a pagan as long as he had money. Also, it is very common to have the Christian natives of al-Andalus marry Muslims. However, most of the Jewish population is not native to al-Andalus. They came to settle here about the same time as we Muslims. They came because they wanted to continue living as Jews. We Muslims gave them that liberty, unlike the Christians."

"Are you saying Isaac will object to me being a Muslim?"

"Yes. Also, we would be putting him in an extremely uncomfortable position. He and I have been partners for years. He would be most embarrassed to refuse this request. And I can assure you, he will refuse it."

My father's words do not penetrate. "I'm not asking Esther to convert. Mother is still Christian."

"You would be taking Esther away from her community."

"She can visit any time."

"Visiting and being a part of a community are two different things."

"It has made no difference to mother."

"A lot of Christians have converted to Islam. They are still converting. They have a more, shall we say, open view of Islam. After all, they were the second monotheistic group. The Jews were the first. The Jews feel perhaps a heavier responsibility to maintain their original beliefs. I know of very few Jews who have converted to Islam."

"I'm not asking Esther to convert." Why does my father refuse to understand?

"For Isaac, Esther would have to turn her back on Judaism if she were to marry you."

"Esther loves me," I loudly declare.

"I can see you do not accept my word that Isaac will refuse to allow Esther to marry you."

Hesitantly I shake my head, no longer certain of anything.

"I will speak to Isaac." My father lets out a troubled sigh.

"No. Ask him to lunch, just the three of us. Then you can talk to him."

"All right." He sighs in resignation.

The morning before Isaac is to come for lunch, I meet Esther in the park by the river. A frosty wind shakes the branches of the trees. The fountain we have always loved is spraying cold water in our direction. We retreat toward drier land. Esther is visibly trembling under her leather jacket, while my nervousness brings on continuous waves of nausea.

"I am terrified your father is right," she says, staring at the fountain of water chaotically dancing in the wind.

"Would you feel any less Jewish marrying me?"

"Yes."

Surely, I could not have heard right.

"But I would still marry you," Esther adds quickly.

"What's more important—religion or love?" I ask in exasperation.

"Would you convert to become a Jew in order to marry me?"

My mouth opens but no sound emerges.

Isaac arrives in exceptionally good spirits. My father and I lead him into the reception room where the tables for lunch have been laid. Isaac is enthusiastically telling my father that Yusuf, his son, has found a new tribe of carpet makers, a sophisticated tribe with a long knowledge of carpet weaving. My father listens, his mind clearly not on business. As we begin to eat, Isaac notices his news is not meeting the expected response.

"Ahmed, are you feeling well?" He looks at my father in concern.

"Yes, yes, of course," my father clears his throat. "You see, I have invited you to lunch today to discuss something other than business."

Isaac laughs. "You have my ears."

My father examines his hands, turning them over for a careful inspection. In the ensuing silence, I grow increasingly apprehensive. I must act.

"This is . . . shall we say . . . social business."

"Ahem!" My father loudly clears his throat and puts a hand on my arm to silence me. He repositions himself and straightens his back. "Isaac, please forgive me, but I have a request I must put before you on behalf of my son."

"Yes, by all means." Isaac smiles patiently.

My father takes a deep breath and audibly exhales. "Sulayman would like to marry your daughter, Esther."

Stunned, Isaac turns to me, mouth open, partially chewed food clearly visible.

"He loves her deeply," my father adds, as an apology.

Slowly, deliberately, Isaac wipes his fingers with the napkin and leans back into the cushion.

"Is that right?" Isaac examines me with veiled suspicion. "May I ask how it happened that you fell in love with my daughter?"

"I met her a couple of years ago at your house when we were all there for lunch," I explain. "Then I met her several times at the Great Mosque when she attended some of the same lectures as myself. After the lectures, we sometimes went for walks together."

"I see." Isaac steals a quick glance at my father who is the only one eating. "And now you want to marry her?"

"It's natural, Isaac, is it not?" my father offers.

"Yes, it is natural, unfortunately," answers Isaac.

"Why unfortunately?" I stutter, my throat tight.

"How exactly do you envision this marriage?" Isaac looks squarely at me.

"We get married. It could be in your house, I'm sure my father would allow that. Then Esther comes to live with me here."

"And?"

"And we have children . . ."

"And?"

I silently shrug my shoulders not knowing what to answer.

"And these children, my grandchildren, what religion will they follow?" asks Isaac in a reasonable manner.

Confused, I look at my father. My father nods for me to answer.

"Well, of course, they will follow Islam."

"Yes"—Isaac smiles—"of course." He pauses. "I think your father can understand that I want my grandchildren to be brought up according to the Jewish faith."

"That's impossible," I quickly reply.

"Yes, I know." Isaac smiles slightly. "That is exactly how I would feel if one of my sons married a Muslim girl who wanted to bring up her children in the Islamic faith."

"But Muhammad was the last prophet on earth and Judaism is one of the roots of Islam," I protest.

"Yes, but Islam is not a root of Judaism." Isaac turns to my father. "If you will forgive me for saying that, Ahmed."

"Please, go on, I fully understand. We all have our beliefs."

Desperation has replaced my confusion. "Esther and I love each other, and we would like to get married," I say, trying to simplify the situation.

"If you are willing to convert to Judaism, I would be more than pleased to have you as my son-in-law."

"Surely, you don't expect me to ..." I am deeply insulted that Isaac would think of suggesting conversion. The Arab Muslims have been the ruling class; for nearly three hundred years, we have worked to create al-Andalus into a major political and cultural force. Isaac should show only gratitude.

"No," he answers quietly. "I don't. That is why I cannot allow Esther to marry you."

I appeal to my father whose elbow is on the table, palms pressed against his forehead. "I tried to warn you," he says to me gently.

A sickening sensation rises in my stomach. I am on the edge of an abyss. Overcome by dizziness, I jump up and run into the courtyard. Bracing myself against the trunk of a citrus tree, my stomach heaves, ejecting rice, lamb, vine leaves, raisins. This luncheon has been useless, worse than useless.

The following day, I meet Esther in the courtyard of the Great Mosque. She is nervously playing with a strand of her hair. As soon as she sees the expression on my face, her hand flies to her mouth and a look of horror clouds her eyes.

"Oh, no," she cries grabbing both my arms. "Tell me what happened! My father has said nothing to me."

"It's not possible," I whisper. "I can hardly believe it. Your father will not allow it."

A sob escapes her lips. She looks wildly around at the people, the pigeons, searching for something to arrest her attention. A growing mass in my throat threatens to choke me.

Since the lunch with Isaac, I have sunk to the bottom of a deep, narrow well, unable to see the light.

I grab her arms. "Let's go by the river."

We quickly walk through the courtyard, through the walled city gate toward the Roman bridge. Just before the bridge, we take the stairs leading down toward the river, past the high brick wall with its intermittent watchtowers. Beyond the wall, on higher ground, are the raised pleasure gardens where we have often met before. We have never dared to come down the stairs alone, so close to the river. We were afraid someone might see us. Now neither of us is thinking about reputations.

There are not many people here at this time, in the late morning. Cows graze on the opposite bank. We lean against the brick wall, and Esther bursts into sobs, gasping for breath, her shoulders shaking. The cruelty of the situation has paralyzed me. Now, holding Esther's shaking body in my arms, I look up from the depth of my well to be struck by the blinding light of the situation. An inner dam bursts and a torrent of tears rises to my eyes. My throat yields to an agonized moan. I tighten my hold on Esther and bury my face in her hair. Her hands, which had been trying to dry the uncontrollable tears, suddenly move around my back to grasp me. I do not know how long we stand clasped to each other, shaking with sobs. Finally, we break away. Esther's eyes are a puffy red. Mine must look the same. We have just stepped over an invisible line, into a new and harsher reality.

"No matter who I marry, I will always continue to see you," she says, caressing my cheeks with a wet palm.

"Nothing will come in the way of our friendship." My voice is hoarse.

"Nothing."

I look toward the river. "But I love you," I say almost petulantly, not knowing what I will do with this enormous love in my heart. Who will I give it to?

"I will never stop loving you, no matter who I must marry," she says with determination.

We slowly walk to the edge of the river and wash our faces in the water.

"I don't think we should see each other for a few weeks," I say. "It would be too painful. I think we should each face the reality of the situation alone."

"No . . ." Esther begins to protest.

"I will miss you terribly, but I don't know if I can bear seeing you, knowing that I will never be able to have you."

She finally gives a reluctant nod and bends down to splash cold water to her face.

At home, I spend most of my time in the library trying to lose myself in books. I read the words but cannot understand their meaning. I must reread sentences three or four times. A dull pain throbs in my head. The odd tear drops on a page, and I blow on the wet spot to help it dry, to stop the ink from running.

Naziha comes to my bed at night. I cannot abide to have her beside me. Her very flesh is a cruel reminder of another body I will never hold in my arms. I send her away, knowing I have deeply hurt her.

My father and mother complain that I am not eating enough. They must be right because my clothes feel bigger, my cheeks look more sallow.

One night, as I am lingering in the courtyard, Aishah comes to me and takes my hand.

"I am sad that I cannot give you some of my happiness."

"Time will heal," I say.

"Yes, Allah alone knows why Esther was not given to you. There must be another woman out there, waiting for you."

"What if I don't want another woman?"

Aishah strokes my hand. "None of us can know what Allah has planned for us."

If only I could take solace in the knowledge that this has been ordained for a Divine Reason. I cannot. I must fight somehow. I must find a way.

My concentration during lectures wanders in such an obvious manner that two of my professors talk with my father to urge him to discipline me with a stronger hand.

Shihab wins the fifth game of chess in a row. He is furious with me, yelling that I am allowing my mind to become a wet sea sponge. I usually win, but recently the appeal of the game has vanished. I make careless moves that give Shihab an easy advantage. He hurls verbal abuse at me, hoping his anger will shake this lethargy from my system. I cannot rise to meet the challenge. Head bowed, eyes to the floor, I allow him to freely vent his displeasure. After yelling and throwing cushions at me for a length of time, he finally stops, exhausted. His eyes turn to the ceiling, entreating Allah. I bury my face in my arms, unable to call up the will for either action or reaction. Shihab, sliding down beside me, encompasses me in his arms and rocks me gently back and forth like a baby.

"Al-Hakam II has asked for volunteers to join his Sacred War against the frontiers of the Duero River," I mutter weakly. "Perhaps I should go and fight."

"You do not need to die just because you have been unsuccessful in love," Shihab scolds.

"Risking my life will bring me closer to God and help to distance Esther from my thoughts."

"Maybe you will die."

I quickly raise my head. "Then I will go to paradise having fought in a Sacred War," I announce ceremoniously.

"Are you ready for paradise so soon?" Shihab smiles.

I sink back to lay my head on Shihab's shoulder. "Having Esther is the only true paradise."

Shihab holds me at arm's length, a look of shock on his face. "Sulayman, you, a devout Muslim! How can you utter such a heretical statement?"

I cover my face with my palms. "To know what you want and never be able to have it is one of the cruelest tricks of life."

"You cannot know what life has in store for you. Allah has refused you Esther because there is another path you must follow."

Belief can sound so logical. Allah has other plans for me that do not include Esther. What if I do not agree with Allah's plans? How dare I be so blasphemous? How painful it is to bend to God's will!

My nights are restless. Naziha cautiously keeps her distance. I cannot find it within me to reach out to her. I am standing at the edge of an abyss, paralyzed by the vast emptiness before me. Can Isaac really refuse our happiness? Do not Jews and Muslims pray to the same creator?

As I stare at the sky through the wooden lattice window of my room, I tell myself, Isaac must have come to his senses. He must have realized his grave error. He knows me well; he knows the prestige of my family. How could he hope to find a better match for Esther? Soon, he will tell my father that his daughter can be mine after all. My spirits rise. For days I maintain a buoyancy of new hope.

Days turn into weeks. My father mentions nothing about Isaac having changed his mind. Hope turns to anger.

I go to the warehouse where Isaac and my father are in the midst of preparing for the next trip. They look up in surprise when they see me.

"We were just talking about you," Isaac says.

I smile, my heart pounding wildly.

"How would you like to come on the next trip with us?" My father asks.

I stare at them, uncomprehending.

"Esther?" the word escapes my throat.

Isaac looks down at the books before him. "No, Esther is not going on the trip this time and neither am I. I will stay behind to help prepare for her wedding."

"Her wedding?"

"Soon after our return, Esther will be getting married," my father explains.

"Of course, your whole family is invited," adds Isaac with a proud smile.

I silently turn around and walk out, unaware of my physical environment. I am falling down a gaping crevice of infinite depth. I pray to Allah. I pray that he allow me to die soon. My legs carry me toward the nearest mosque. I take off my shoes and enter the courtyard paved with cool mosaics. As I perform the ritual ablutions, the touch of the water against my skin reminds me when Esther and I washed our tear-stained faces in the river. A sob escapes my lips. I begin to pray, silently repeating the Qur'anic verses. I focus on every word. At first, it takes tremendous effort. Memories of Esther keep intruding. Anger and despair well up to obliterate all meaning. Gradually, the words gain more and more clarity; they contain and rock my boundless agony. Very slowly, the verses open a door to release the painful tightness. My mind moves onto a wider field and glimpses a distant horizon. I bend forward to touch the cool marble floor of the mosque with my forehead.

V. Fez

The boat glides away from the port of Algeciras, from the rock of Gibraltar, rigidly rising toward the sky like an obstinate, double-humped camel. I watch al-Andalus recede, become one with the body of water. Distance will help, my father advised. On deck, I gaze toward the clear blue sky, cloudless, limitless.

Aishah and Mustafa stand beside me. They joke in an attempt to make me laugh. I smile weakly.

"In a few days, you'll feel better. You'll see." Aishah strokes my hair.

"Instead of coming south, I should have gone north to fight. Perhaps I should have opposed father," I say.

A few days before leaving, I had announced during supper that I was going to volunteer for the Holy War in the Christian territories. My father became so angry that he had a coughing fit.

"There are paid soldiers to fight Holy Wars," he had said upon catching his breath.

"There is also a flank of volunteers," I reminded him. "Mustafa was once one of them."

"I joined at a time of great confusion in my life. The war served to clear my head, to remind me of my real purpose in this world," Mustafa explained.

"If the Holy War can do the same for me, I would be grateful," I replied.

"Sulayman," my father said firmly, "you are not a fighter but a thinker. Remember that! You would be throwing away Allah's gift if you used your muscles instead of your brain."

My father refused to allow me to join the Holy War. I did not have the energy to oppose him; it seemed easier to succumb and follow him to Fez.

"The Holy War is not for people like you. I myself would not join the volunteer group again," Mustafa had added.

Yes, I should be studying. I am one of the privileged ones, the bright ones. But these days my mind is incapable of accepting new thoughts, new ideas. Everything I hear washes over this amorphous mass in my head, nothing sticks. I stare down into the opaque greenness of the water. A desire to quietly lower myself into it and disappear overwhelms me. Aishah and Mustafa move farther down the deck. I lean over to a nearby donkey tied to the railing and stroke his nose. I gaze into his inquisitive large eyes and feel an irrational wave of affection. *Specifics, I should focus on specifics*, I tell myself and continue stroking the donkey. Logical specifics, as 'Abdallah might say.

In Tangier, while the slaves unload the rolls of silk and brocade from the boat, I accompany my father to hire camels and a guide for our continuing trip to Fez. Near the camel market, caravans arrive and depart for various corners of Africa.

Merchants exchange goods, stories, and information amid noisy bargaining. In the background, the sculpted minarets of the mosques rise high above the town which begins on flat land near the sea and moves back over the hills protecting the harbor.

The long rhythmic ride to Fez atop a camel has a surprisingly calming effect on me. The rocky terrain of Morocco is a sobering change from the gentle hills of al-Andalus. Our nightly stopovers at the caravansaries bring us together with other travelers converging from various parts of the world. News of Baghdad, Egypt, and Europe are exchanged over skewered lamb and fried eggplant.

Aishah is given the name of a new bookseller in Fez. One of the merchants has just delivered a fresh cargo of manuscripts from Basrah to his shop. She is urged to visit him soon and is assured of finding rare and beautiful books for the Caliph's library.

When my father proudly tells the group I am studying law, a traveling scholar recounts the story of an Egyptian judge run out of town because of his drunkenness. My shock evokes an explosion of laughter.

"Your son needs to live a little," chortles a man with a scraggly gray beard, sitting next to my father.

"He must travel the world to acquire the robes of experience," hollers another.

I dig my heels into the rocky terrain and tightly gripping a pomegranate, stick my thumb through its brittle flesh, forcing the red juice to squirt upward and over the ground. One day I will know much more than all these men put together. One day they will look up to me.

"Cairo is famous for its corrupt judges," continues the amused scholar. "A woman can bribe a judge by offering herself to him for a night or two."

"That's unheard-of in Cordoba," I announce proudly.

The man scoffs. "There are men everywhere who live without fear of Allah."

By the time we near Fez, I realize the trip has cleared my head and forced my eyes to open, to look outward. The change in landscape and people has fluffed up my spirits.

The city's magnificently jeweled blue and gold mosaic gate lead us into a complex structure of narrow winding streets looping into the main market road that leads downhill into the center of the city. We head for the family warehouse where my brother, Jamal, is handling the business in Fez, and is in the process of receiving a new shipment of carpets. With a last burst of energy, we unload our merchandise of silk, brocade, and tapestries. Our guide and servants are sent to sleep in the merchants' Inn, while Aishah, Mustafa, my father, and I go to Jamal's home.

Jamal's wife, children, and my half-sister Lobua rush into the courtyard upon hearing our voices. At dinner, the latest family news is exchanged, including my own attempt to marry Esther.

Aishah leans over to whisper something to Lobua who then treats me with extreme kindness and sympathy. However, hearing Esther's name once more plunges me into the depths.

Later, in bed, the fatigue of the journey releases me into deep sleep where my dreams take me to distant lands. I am standing on an island in the middle of the sea. Slowly, the island begins to separate beneath my feet. The two parts of land are drifting farther and farther apart, stretching my legs in opposite directions. In a panic, I cannot decide on which side of the island to place both feet. Suddenly a terrific storm rises with gusting winds and slashing rain. The islands are thrust back together again by the force of the rising waves. Once more, I stand on solid ground, but the furious winds threaten to sweep me off the island into the surging sea.

Terrified, I scream as I grab onto the trunk of a nearby tree. The tree is wildly shaking in my arms. The raging winds loosen its roots and wrench it from the earth. The tree carries me with it and flies over the angry waves, its roots loudly beating in the air while I still struggle to hang on to the trunk.

We move above the turbulent sea, through clouds, through the raging storm. I can barely hold on; my muscles ache; my feet are helplessly dangling in midair. I despair; will we ever find solid ground? My arms grow excruciatingly tired. I cannot hold on much longer. I glance down. Below, the waves rise up in a white fury; watery fingers stretch upward in an effort to reach me.

Suddenly I wake up in a sweat, my heart pounding.

"Please, Allah, do not let me drown," I silently pray.

The next day in the warehouse, the retail merchants inspect the goods we have brought from Cordoba. My father spends a surprisingly long time with a woman fingering the silk. He is playfully flirting with her. I watch him, amused. In the past, when I had asked him why he had only three wives instead of the permissible four, he told me it was important to know the possibility was always open for a fourth. Possibilities are very seductive for my father.

The woman, while certainly enjoying the attention, is carefully inspecting the various materials, expertly sliding them between her thumb and forefinger. Finally, she makes her decision.

"Sulayman," my father calls out to me, "would you accompany Kerima to her store with the goods and pick up payment at her house?"

"Of course."

The donkey is loaded up, and I follow her through the main street of the Medina. As she walks in front of me, I note the very delicate, light weave material of her clothes that easily sways with the rhythm of her movements. The thick bronze belt emphasizes her slim, almost girlish hips, though she must be at least thirty-five or forty. She slows down, waiting until I catch up to her. Her kohled eyes smile above the violet veil. Her forehead hints at a velvety olive skin.

"We are almost there," she says with a twinkle.

I glance at her round generous breasts, almost too generous for such slim hips. She stops before a store exhibiting rolls of material. An older man, introduced as her brother-in-law, stands behind the counter.

Finished with the unloading, we continue to her house. She leads me down the main street and then turns into a dark, narrow side street. We make a few sharp turns and finally stop before a wooden door. A servant opens and takes the donkey's rope to tie it to a metal ring just inside the entrance.

Kerima orders tea before leading me through the courtyard and upstairs along the gallery into a comfortable room with cushions on a ledge built into the wall and puffs surrounding a large round bronze table. She invites me to sit down, and soon the servant brings the tea in a beautifully worked silver pot. After pouring the steaming liquid into two glasses, the servant leaves.

"Does your husband also work in the store?" I ask.

"My husband died four years ago," she says, casting down her eyes.

"You must be lonely."

"Yes, sometimes, I miss male company. My husband was very good company."

"Perhaps you will marry again."

A sadness clouds her eyes.

"You are a very attractive woman. It should be easy for you to find a husband."

"I do not want to get married," she says firmly. "It's only that I miss male company."

"Yes," I say staring into my glass, also feeling sad.

"Are you married?" she asks.

I shake my head.

She laughs. "I'm sure the day is not far off."

That day might never come, I think to myself as I sip the hot tea.

"Did you love your husband?" I ask suddenly.

"Yes, very much. He was truly an exceptional man."

"That must make his death harder to bear."

"The first year I was in despair, only thinking of death, only thinking of joining him. Then my brother-in-law asked me to be part of the business, the way my husband had been. I gratefully accepted, and the activity of buying and selling keeps me occupied, keeps my mind away from brooding."

"I suppose activity has a way of obliterating pain."

"Very much so."

I look up and smile at her. I am surprised to see she has taken off her veil. Her face is smaller and more delicate than I had expected, judging from those large kohled eyes.

"I don't like to wear the veil, and I know that a lot of women in Cordoba do not wear it," she says as a way of explanation.

I feel slightly uneasy knowing that a veiled woman never reveals herself to a stranger. A veiled woman expresses the beliefs of the men in her family. If those men want to see their women veiled in the street, it means they want to see them veiled before a stranger.

"What if someone should come in?" I ask uncomfortably.

She stands up and closes the latticed wooden door. The sun shining through casts the door's geometric design onto the carpet.

"There is no one in the house right now, only three maids working in the kitchen. Today is one of those rare days when everyone is out on errands."

I watch her slowly move back to her cushion. Delicately, she sits down crossing her legs under her. We sip our tea in silence.

The air feels soft, and I notice tiny particles floating in the beams of sunlight. Our breathing has become audible. I grow warmer and warmer and become aware of my perspiration. An irrational desire burgeons beneath my clothes. Self-conscious, I quickly stand up to examine some manuscripts on the bookshelf by the wall. I force my mind to concentrate as my eyes move over the titles. I notice a book on the four legal schools of Islam.

There is also a book on Mu'tazila philosophy. I have never seen these books before. I am surprised to find them here. She explains that they were her husband's books. With a surge of excitement, I eagerly leaf through them.

"I can lend them to you for a few days if you like." She offers, standing up and coming close to me.

Her deeply rich musk surrounds me. "I would be very interested to read them," I force out a hoarse answer. As I turn around, my arm brushes her breast. I can feel myself blush in embarrassment and curse my light complexion.

"Do take them." She lifts up her arm and runs her fingers through my hair. "Red hair," she says with amusement.

"My mother has blonde hair," I quickly explain.

Her fingers lingeringly move to my cheeks. "And freckles." She smiles, her eyes moist.

She steps closer to me. Her breasts press against my chest.

I hold my breath. An acute yearning burns my insides. The books in my hand drop to the floor. Suddenly my fingers are buried in her thick, lush hair; I am eagerly kissing her lips, drinking in her fragrance. Her body, confident yet yielding, sways in my arms. My nose, lips, and tongue are keenly alive, aware of the slightest nuance. My hands rush down her body searching for bare flesh.

Oblivious of time and space, we roll on the soft carpet, the patterns of light and shade play upon our naked bodies. Her perfumed skin, eager thighs, and malleable round breasts bring to mind the sensuous hills of al-Andalus. The obliterating pleasure of passion caresses my heart, my mind, and my body, leaving only a brilliant, sparkling present.

Out on the street, I look around in both directions. I am in a daze, not knowing which way to turn. I move in a soft, opaque cloud. In my mind is the image of Kerima's undulating body, a body of tantalizing contrasts: the mountainous swaying breasts with their small nipples, the flat stomach, slim angular hips moving to surprisingly soft round thighs—so different from the taut, balanced proportions of Naziha's body. How marvelous of Allah to have endowed women with such varieties of attributes! I turn to my right and follow the curve of the street. I have to ask three people for directions before I find my way back to Jamal's house.

I do not accompany my father into the desert to look for new carpets among the tribes. Nor do I visit the carpet factories with him. Days go by as I read Kerima's books and wander the labyrinth of the Medina, taking comfort in the activity of strangers around me. I lose myself in the sounds and smells of the market.

Suddenly, the scent of nutmeg hits me. I look around. A woman in a nearby stall is grating nutmeg onto unbaked dough. My heart sinks. Esther and I often shared nutmeg buns filled with raisins and apricots. This is all it takes for my sadness to return! I try to fight it off, to strangle it before it can repossess me. I rail against Esther. She should have had the strength to turn against the wishes of her father. If she loved me enough, she would have disobeyed him. The anger gives me strength to once more see a future without Esther. My mind turns to Kerima; her pendulous breasts dance before me. I take the book on law, which had not proved to be as interesting as it first appeared, and head for the shop. Her brother-in-law greets me in recognition. Kerima is not to be seen.

"Can I help you with something?" he asks.

In embarrassment, I look at the book in my hand. He follows my gaze.

"Did you want to return the book to my sister-in-law?"

I look up in surprise.

"She told me you had borrowed two of my brother's books," he explains with a smile. "Though my brother was a merchant, he had a wide range of interests."

"I only have one of the two books I had borrowed."

"Return the other one when you're finished," he says kindly, reaching out his hand for the book.

I reluctantly hand it to him. "Please thank Kerima for me, and I will return the other one in a few days."

Once I leave the store, an irrational fury takes hold of me.

I spot a donkey tethered to the side of a shop, walk over to it, and smack it on its firm behind with my fist. The donkey immediately jumps away, tugging at its rope, loudly braying in protest. Its owner runs out of the shop, yelling at me. I quickly walk away. Suddenly I stop to look around. Perhaps I can find my way to Kerima's house. Numerous narrow winding streets intersect the main shopping artery. How can I hope to find the right one? When I first followed her, I was more absorbed in the movement of her body than in the direction she was taking. I curse myself. I always get lost. I have never met anyone with a worse sense of direction. Jamal will certainly have her home address, and I can ask him for directions.

I stroll over to the Karouin Mosque and absently sit in on one of the lectures. Surprisingly, the lecturer turns out to be excellent. His dramatic presentation stimulates my curiosity.

"How did the Greeks approach logical, scientific observation?" he asks. "How did they arrive at their conclusions?" The lecturer's steady gaze moves from student to student. "First they looked at the universal to develop their thesis, then applied this to the particular. However, it is possible to approach scientific observation from the opposite perspective. One can first examine specifics to arrive at a thesis, and then apply it to the universal. Two very different ways of approaching reason. Sometimes, both approaches lead to the same conclusion. Other times, each approach gives a very different answer to the same question."

Reviewing his comments, it seems to me that reason is not always logical. One can approach both questions and answers from numerous perspectives, thus arriving at numerous different conclusions. For two people to find the same answer to the same question must be an incredible chance. I am amazed that man has managed to progress to this stage of development. I can well imagine two Greeks arguing back and forth about the same point forever, never moving beyond the first plane. There must be an elliptical form of logic built into any thesis whereby, after considerable pulling back and forth, the logic nevertheless evolves through the wear and tear of argument.

At the end of the lecture, I sit on a blue tile bench in the courtyard, contemplating the gently falling fountain. If one can approach a question, an answer, an issue, a situation from a myriad different angles, is it not possible that the companions of the Prophet also saw and heard Muhammad from varying points of view? Then the Hadith, the actions and sayings of the Prophet as recorded by those who knew His companions, must contain a variety of different perspectives. No wonder it is possible for opposing philosophical schools to support their arguments by using the same texts: the Qur'an and the Hadith. Even the Qur'an contains numerous perspectives. A chill of unease takes a hold of me. If the Qur'an contains different perspectives, God Himself must view the world in more than one way. Then what is the final, absolute Truth?

"Sulayman, is it really you?" A booming voice jolts me back to physical reality. I look up to see 'Abdallah. I jump to my feet and swing my arms around him.

"I thought you were in Baghdad," I say.

"I was there for a year and then decided to come teach here for a year."

We hold each other at arm's length and laugh.

"Does Jamal know you're here?" I ask.

"Of course. He told me your father was due to arrive soon. But he never mentioned you would be here as well."

I let my hand drop from his shoulders. "My coming was a last minute decision." I stop. 'Abdallah waits for me to continue. "Isaac didn't come this time," I say as a way of explanation.

'Abdallah takes my face in his hands. "You know you should not have come. You should have continued with your studies."

"I have books with me, and I am studying here," I lie.

"While here, you're going to attend my lectures."

"Of course." I laugh. "You can even give me private lessons."

"Only in exchange for something," 'Abdallah teases.

"Perhaps, perhaps," I say coyly and hate myself as soon as I have uttered the words.

'Abdallah looks at me quizzically but says nothing.

"Tonight you're coming for supper," I announce, "after the evening prayer."

"Even if you had not invited me, I would have come," 'Abdallah counters.

At dinner, I remember Kerima and call out to my brother, Jamal, trying to make myself heard above the commotion.

"Jamal, can you tell me the way to Kerima's house?"

"Who is Kerima?" he yells back from the other side of the room.

"You know that woman merchant I helped the other day. I borrowed a book from her."

"You forgot to bring the money back that she owed us," my father says to me, shaking his head in disbelief. "What's happening to your memory?"

I slap my forehead. Of course, the money. I had totally forgotten. This could be the perfect excuse to return to her house.

"Tomorrow I will collect the money," I quickly offer.

"No need," my father waves his hand in the air. "The brother-in-law brought it in the next day."

"I still have to return her book," I point out. "Jamal, how do I find her house?"

"Give me time to remember."

I hear Esther's name spoken in a whisper to my right. My attention shifts to catch the conversation. Aishah and Lobua are explaining to 'Abdallah what had happened with Isaac.

"I forbid you to talk about that," I shout, stopping all conversation. "That's my own private affair, and it's finished now."

I fall silent as an all too familiar melancholy rises to the surface. My throat refuses to swallow the chewed food in my mouth. I soon leave the table.

A few days later, I attend 'Abdallah's lecture. I am amused to see he still has his provocative style of teaching: questioning his pupils, forcing them to think.

After the lecture, he invites me to his room for the afternoon meal. He lives near the university mosque in a dormitory set up for guest lecturers and scholars. As we enter the courtyard, he instructs one of the cooks to have his meal brought up to his room. We climb two flights of wooden stairs and walk to the end of the gallery. His room is large and comfortable with a cedar writing desk, bookshelves, leather puffs around a low brass table, and a bed in one corner strewn with brocade cushions.

"Everything I need," 'Abdallah spreads out his arms indicating the room.

This is the first time I have been in 'Abdallah's quarters. In Cordoba, I saw him at the Great Mosque or at my own house. There was no need for me to visit him. Now, I carefully look around. The room is very attractive. Everything is compact, within easy reach. A musk of erudition floats in the air.

"I like it," I say as my eyes roam the carpets hanging on the wall.

"Good. Sit down then."

I take a puff; 'Abdallah sits down facing me. In a short time, a knock summons him to open the door. Two women bring in trays laden with various covered dishes, lay them on the table, and then quickly leave.

As we begin to eat, 'Abdallah says, "I am sorry to hear you cannot marry Esther."

A heavy weight descends. I did not want to talk about Esther.

"Love is elusive," 'Abdallah continues. "It depends on another person, therefore, you cannot count on it. You can only count on yourself, what you are as an individual. The development of your inner self should be the most important task. Your first responsibility is to yourself, to Allah, then to the community."

"Law . . ." I begin.

"That's right. And ideas, thoughts . . ."

"I would have become a judge with or without Esther."

"Develop your mind, only your mind will save you in times of distress."

We eat in silence. It takes great effort to swallow the laboriously chewed food. I desperately try to hold back the tears threatening to flood my eyes.

"'Abdallah," I say dropping my hands to my lap, "it hurts too much. I do not seem to feel anything but the pain. I've grown numb to the outside."

"Try to use your logic, your rationale. Don't allow your emotions to guide you at a time like this because they'll pull you down," he says softly.

"What logic?" I cry. "There is nothing logical about this situation!"

"Look to the future. Look forward, not behind you," he stresses.

"God, it's so overpowering, all encompassing. I can hardly see outside of it."

"Now you're close to it. Each day you must consciously think about other things, such as your books or studies. Force yourself to look outside. Time will ease the pain."

I cover my face with my hands and hang my head between my knees. I want to sink into a black hole, curl up, and simply forget about life. I want to sink into the darkness of my sorrow. I hear 'Abdallah move close to me. His hands take my shoulders and gently pull me to him. I lift up my head and bury my face in his neck. He rocks me back and forth, small movements from side to side. His hand caresses my hair. I lift up my head a little and let out a deep sigh. His lips touch my forehead. I turn my face up to his, offering my lips. His face comes close; his lips lightly touch mine. A warm comforting wave brushes my soul. I keep my face turned toward him, waiting for another, stronger kiss. But he simply looks at me.

"No, Sulayman, not now, not when you're feeling like this," he says gently.

"You might never have me again." An impetuous cruelty stirs within and I push away from him.

"I prefer not to have you at all than to take advantage of your present weakness."

In spite of myself, I greatly respect him for his integrity. I silently thank Allah for the warm gratitude that washes over me. "Have you ever felt like this?" I whisper.

"Oh, yes. I know the feeling only too well. It's incapacitating. It is emotional diarrhea. Nevertheless, you must fight. Don't allow it to beat you down, to drain all your energy."

"Logic . . .," I say helplessly.

"Yes. The mind is a wonderful tool, if you use it. You must sharpen it by use. Through thinking and logic, you can grow to understand. And understanding heals."

"Not allowing me to marry Esther is pure bigotry, prejudice. I don't know how my father can be partners with a man like Isaac."

"Try to see it from Isaac's perspective. Try to put yourself in his place. It will deepen your understanding."

"Esther should have run away to live with me."

"You must also try to see it from Esther's perspective. Looking at a situation from several points of view can be surprisingly calming." 'Abdallah smiles.

The lecturer's comments about the various ways of arriving at a thesis flash through my mind. Can I view an emotional crisis from numerous angles? It takes such immense effort. My head is so heavy; to lift it, turn it from side to side, requires considerable strength.

Jamal finally gives me directions to Kerima's house, and I head out to return the second book. On the way, I fantasize about another passionate encounter. However, she is not home. From the height of sensual imagination I crumple back into the physical world; a loosely woven cloth helplessly fluttering on a branch.

When I pass the store, her brother-in-law stands by the counter, and I quickly walk on before he sees me.

I force my mind to focus on abstract thoughts, to seek pleasure in ideas. The lectures at the mosque help me reach toward a higher plane.

I spend a good deal of time accompanying Aishah and Lobua to the market. I sit beside the manuscript copiers, watching them form letters with precision. I look at the peaceful face of one copier. Has he ever known pain? I try to imagine myself in his body. I try to imagine his peace within me.

In time, I grow calmer. My anxiety recedes. The rough, jagged edges become smoother. When depression threatens, I seek out 'Abdallah; he knows how to restore my calm. 'Abdallah has become a surprisingly good friend whose wisdom I have grown to appreciate increasingly. In Cordoba, he had been a friend of my father's and he was my professor. Here in Fez, our relationship has grown more intimate. 'Abdallah has become an anchor for me, a stabilizing element.

At first, our talks revolved around Esther. Gradually they turned to law, philosophy, and ideas. We visit bookstalls together to search for books banned in Baghdad.

One afternoon I go to his room after lunch and find that I have disturbed his nap. It is a very hot day, and he answers the door wearing only a light smock, sleep still evident in his eyes.

I apologize and offer to come back later, but he assures me, rubbing his eyes, that he would have had to get up shortly in any case. I see two books lying on his bed. He has obviously fallen asleep reading. I sit down by the pillows and pick up one of the books, a translation of Plato about Aristotle's last days. I look through it with interest. He comes to sit down beside me and picks up the other book.

"A student of mine gave them to me as a gift. Just this morning . . ." He loses himself in silent thought. "Actually," he continues, "it's a sad story. The father was accused of heresy, was jailed, and then sentenced to death. But he died in jail before the date of execution. These books were his. The son wanted me to have them."

"Probably thinking you too can be a candidate for heresy," I joke.

'Abdallah hits me over the head with the book in his hand.

"Since you're my private student now, you'll be automatically accused as my disciple."

"Never. I will protest the judgment." I laugh.

"They will not believe you. You'll be forced into the role of disciple. Then you'll have to collect all my writings and publish a lengthy commentary."

"You're dreaming!" I wave my arm in the air for emphasis. "I have my own ideas to explore. I'm not going to waste my time commenting on your works."

"How dare you talk to your respected professor that way!" He makes a lunge at me pinning me to the bed.

Laughing, I struggle to get up, but he sits on top of my stomach, his hands holding my wrists down.

"After my death, you will publish a commentary on all my works and thoughts," he commands.

"I wouldn't waste my time." I laugh.

"A waste of time you call it?" he yells in mock horror.

I try to struggle free, now hysterical with laughter. I manage to throw him off and jump on top of him, this time pinning him to the bed, face down.

"I don't know why I bother with such an ungrateful student," he groans into the bed sheet.

"Because I don't accept your cynicism."

He makes a sudden movement that throws me off balance, and we end up in a wrestling match, entangled in the crisp sheets, convulsing with laughter. As we grow breathless and tired, our struggle turns to caresses. ‘Abdallah undresses me, his lips and hands moving down my body. I willingly yield to his desire and lose myself to being loved. It is such soft pleasure to simply surrender to another's hands. As he kneads my body, I think only a man can so expertly know the locales of sensuality. Only a man aware of his own body can play another man's body with such certainty.

I am awakened by the call of the muezzin to find myself lying beside ‘Abdallah. He too has just opened his eyes. We look at each other and smile. I feel so relaxed, so confident in his love and respect for me, that I cannot remember ever feeling so safe before.

“Blondish red hair everywhere.” ‘Abdallah's eyes leisurely travel over my naked body. He chuckles. “Sulayman, you're like a sun god, vital and fiery.”

I look down at my pubic area; blond red hair curling toward my resting genitals. A beam of sunlight entering the closed shutters cuts my body lengthwise; I lie half in light and half in darkness.

“I must go to the mosque,” I say getting up.

“Must?”

“I want to go to the mosque. I have grown to need it. Prayer gives me a sense of precision.” I stop to look at him. “It also allows me a glimpse of greater possibilities.”

“You are lucky, Sulayman.”

Yes, I think to myself, *I am lucky.* I must try to remember that.

I have made several unsuccessful attempts to see Kerima. She has become a dream, impossible to revisit. During the rest of my stay, ‘Abdallah and I regularly see each other, sharing not only physical pleasure but also mutual interest in the latest legal and philosophical ideas. Before I leave Fez, I tell him about Kerima and our one warm afternoon together. He jokingly assures me he will keep an eye out for her and continue where I left off.

VI. Cordoba

Brilliant sunshine hugs the land. Returning home once more fills me with joyous pride. Fez has revived me. My mind is alert. My eyes are keen. Now I see that Cordoba is like an intricately woven tapestry, floral patterns feeding floral patterns. The rich scents of its flowers, fruits, spices, and colors of the subtlest variation are a magnificence to lift the spirit.

The markets bustle with more people than ever before. The population of Cordoba has expanded to enfold an infinite variety of hues: mixtures of blacks, Indians, Chinese, Arabs, and Europeans. People are dressed in the costumes of their land: long-flowing robes of vital colors, large pleated pants gathered at the ankles, the designs of the materials accentuated with gold or silver threads. There are new hospitals, baths, and mosques. More Roman houses have been restored. The expansion of the Great Mosque is still in progress. There are more scholars, come from distant lands, attracted to the freedom and richness of Cordoba. And there are more classes at the mosque.

I once more take Naziha into my arms, as I could not before leaving Cordoba. She again performs the dances of her tribe for me and tells me she has tried to teach them to the women of the household. I am convulsed with laughter as I picture Saida, my father's first wife, doing the fertility dance, her ample breasts bouncing around energetically.

I sink into relaxed, familiar comfort mingled with languorous passion.

During dinner, a few days after our arrival, my father announces that our whole family has been invited to Esther's wedding. An old familiar wave of depression washes over me. I vehemently refuse to go to Esther's wedding. I do not want to see the only woman I have ever loved marry another man, removed from my reach forever.

Concerned eyes glance in my direction.

The next day I find Esther waiting for me in the courtyard of the mosque. She is breathless from running. I am shocked to see her. My deep love struggles with sharp resentment.

"I need to talk to you," she says. "Please come and walk with me by the river."

"How would that look, you about to be married walking with another man?" It is hard to keep the edge of sarcasm from my voice.

"Please," she pleads.

We walk down the stairs leading to the river's edge. By the shore, the enormous water wheel, al-Hakam II has recently built, rotates slowly. Its jugs pick up water from the river and pour it onto higher ground, into the lead pipes reaching to all areas of the city. In an endless journey, the jugs empty at the top then move down again to be refilled. The river leisurely flows in the sun; the waves playfully ripple on the surface without attention to the drama of men. As I longingly look at nature's easy existence, I grow determined not to be alone on the day of Esther's wedding. I decide to hold a large party by the river on her wedding day. I dream of hiring the best dancing girls, the best musicians. Everyone I know will be invited.

"I will marry two weeks from now," she says quietly.

"My father mentioned it."

"On my twenty-fourth birthday, exactly on the day of my birthday."

I am silent, trying to keep an emotional distance.

"Will you come?"

"No," I snap, then force a more civilized tone. "I can't. How can you possibly even want me there?"

"You know I don't want to go through with this," she says to me angrily, almost accusingly.

"But you're not doing anything to stop it."

She looks out onto the river. "No. I am not. I have spent many a sleepless night going over all possibilities. I have asked myself if I was a coward. I've asked myself if you truly loved me . . ."

We stop, and I turn to her in surprise. "How could you doubt my love?"

She continues looking toward the river. "No, I no longer doubt your love. However, your belief in your religion is much older than your love for me. It has deeper roots. It has served you well . . ." She stops. As I watch her, I see her struggling with an invisible, internal force. She bites her lower lip and finally says, "I wish I would not love you as much as I do." She abruptly turns to me and grips my arm. "You know that after the wedding the husband has the right to do what he likes with his wife's body."

I hear myself inhale. My lungs are heavy.

She continues, "I'm afraid. I do not know what to expect. My mother has told me things. It is supposed to hurt. But it's all so vague."

"Have you come to ask me to tell you . . ." I begin in disbelief and anger.

Her grip on my arm tightens, and she moves closer to me. "I love you, Sulayman. If I cannot marry you, at least I want you to be the first one to touch my body."

When the full meanings of her words have sunk in, I stare at her in amazement. "But that could bring you to disgrace. He can have the marriage annulled."

"No. He would not do such a thing. He loves me. Also, I will arrange certain things so that he will never guess."

"Do you know what you're asking of me?"

"Yes. I have gone over this innumerable time. If I cannot have you as a husband, at least I can experience physical love with you."

I throw my hand toward the sky, silently pleading with Allah for strength. "Esther, I went to Fez to try and forget about my love for you. What you are asking me to do will not only bring everything back, but it will make it so much harder to forget afterward."

"How do you think I will feel when someone else must touch my body?"

I put my arms around her, tightly holding onto her. "There is a condition," I whisper into her hair, my heart breaking with the agony and joy of what is to come. "Once is not enough. I must then have you as often as possible, as often as you can get away, up to the day of your wedding."

I feel Esther's head nod in agreement. I take her shoulders and look into her face.

"I know a monastery just to the north of Medina al-Zahra. We can go behind its walls and no one will ever see us."

Esther takes a step backward. "A monastery?" she asks with distaste. "A Muslim and a Jew making love by a monastery?"

"Appropriate, don't you think?" I comment sadly.

"A monastery would be a constant reminder of our differences. It would be too painful . . ."

"Is it not more painful to marry someone you don't love?"

"What choice do I have?"

"You could go against your father's wishes and simply run away," I say with more bitterness than I had intended.

"Yes, I suppose that would have been my only other choice."

I detect a well-controlled streak of anger in her reply. "I could not have reasonably expected you to give up Islam."

I look at her in confusion. "What do you mean?"

"You think I should have walked away from my community, from Judaism. But could I not have equally expected you to become a Jew in order to marry me?"

"I was not expecting you to convert. You would have been free to practice your religion."

"Don't you understand, if I leave the community, I leave the religion."

"No, I don't understand. You know my mother is a Christian, and she remains true to her religion though married to my father."

"Christianity is different. There is no prejudice against Christians. They have political power, not here in al-Andalus but in the rest of Europe, in Constantinople, in Byzantium. However, the Jews have lost all political power to ensure the survival of their religion. All they have are communities scattered around the world in societies dominated by a religion other than their own. If I step out of the community, I step out of Judaism."

Her words have hardly penetrated my consciousness. "You actually thought I should convert to marry you."

"It had occurred to me."

"That would have meant renouncing Muhammad, the last Prophet. How could I do that? It would be equivalent to going against the Word of God."

"According to your religion, yes. According to mine, no. And historically Judaism has much deeper roots than Islam. Without Judaism, there would have been no Jesus and Christianity, no Muhammad and Islam. How could you dare to suppose, you with a young religion like Islam, that I would give up Judaism, the oldest monotheistic religion in the world?"

"Islam is an improvement and refinement on both Judaism and Christianity. It is a continuation . . ."

"What if I say it is a perversion of our beliefs?"

I feel my face flush with anger. I clench my fists. If Esther would be a man, I would certainly hit her. We have killed people for saying less. Sensing my mood, she quickly backs down.

"Try to see it from my perspective. If I leave my people and in a few years the political system changes where the Muslims turn against the Jews, I will grow to hate you as well as myself."

"It is the Muslims who allow the Jews to live in peace. We give you liberty to practice your religion, a liberty that no Christian state would give you. How dare you criticize Islam? How dare you criticize the power that has allowed you to be Jewish?"

Esther lets out a long, deep sigh. "God is stronger than the love of two human beings. I don't think it is good for us, Sulayman, to discuss questions of religion."

"No. Perhaps your upcoming marriage is for the better. Perhaps your father was right."

Esther stares down at the ground.

"Should I accompany you to the gate of the Jewish Quarter?" I ask coolly.

"No, it's not necessary," she replies weakly.

"Then please excuse me, I am going for a walk by the river."

I turn away from her. After a few steps, I glance back and call out, "Enjoy your wedding." Esther does not acknowledge my words.

I continue by the shore. When I reach the next watchtower, I turn back again, but Esther is already out of sight. I walk over to the wall, lean against it, and beat the stone with my fists. When I can no longer stand the pain, I stop and flex my fingers, silently praying to Allah to obliterate my pain.

The steaming summer day with its scorching sun turns into a heavy night of dark heat. My party by the river is in full force on the day of Esther's wedding. People wear as little as possible. The fresh air coming off the river is a welcome relief. Tents with lanterns have been set up on the grassy slope of the bank.

Carpets and cushions are luxuriously spread out for the hundreds of guests. Grape, fig, and date wine flow freely. Hired slave girls proffer trays filled with an assortment of delicacies. Singing, music, recitation, and laughter fill the warm air. As the night progresses, the party becomes increasingly more boisterous. Dancing girls slowly shed their clothes; their nearly nude bodies undulate in the moonlight. Couples tease each other. Music entwines with desire. Songs blaze with longing.

The first light of dawn reveals bodies curled in embrace among cushions, on carpets, in the dewy grass. I lie in the arms of a slave girl, immobile with wine. Servants carry me home and put me to bed.

It is dark again by the time I awake. My head is throbbing.

Every movement creates pain. I remain flat on my back and stare at the cedar ceiling. It moves in dizzying circles. I shut my eyes. Tears well up and flow down the side of my face, into my hair. Uncontrollable sobs wash my sorrow. Can one ever wipe away a memory?

A week later, as I am sitting in the library reading a book, my father comes in sporting a grave expression. I immediately think he has made a bad business deal. He brushes aside my suspicions.

"Well, it is quite clear that something is wrong," I say, putting the manuscript on my lap.

"How serious are you about becoming a judge?" he asks sitting down on a cushion.

"How could you doubt my sincerity?"

"I am simply questioning the depth of that sincerity. You see, I want you to know you do have other choices open to you. My business, which is certainly thriving, can use someone with your skills."

"The material and carpet business interests me but law excites me."

"Then you are determined to follow your intended course?"

"Of course. Why need ask?"

"Your recent actions have put a shadow upon your ambition. The nudity and drunkenness at your party have become local gossip. There is a chance that you might not be allowed to continue with your legal studies."

"I don't understand."

"Sadr was here yesterday."

I look down at my hands in shame. I feel my father's scrutinizing eyes upon me, and a rising blush burns my cheeks.

"If you sincerely want to be a judge, surely you know that the life of a judge must be above reproach."

I remain silent, not daring to look up.

"Remember what happened to el-Hadrami just a few months ago?"

Still staring down at my hands I nod, seeing the scene of el-Hadrami shaved bald, paraded through town atop a donkey. A large procession chanting, "Adulterer!" followed behind.

El-Hadrami had been accused of sleeping with one of his clients, a married woman. After the humiliating parade, he was expelled from Cordoba. Perhaps in Egypt nothing would have happened. Here, in Cordoba, with its devout judges not even deigning to go near political power, staying away from all that might soil their conscience and reputation, here, in Cordoba, his punishment was considered light.

"I advise you to have a word with Sadr. Go and see him at his house right after the second prayer."

I nod, still not being able to look up. If I can convince Uncle Sadr of my sincerity, if I could get him on my side, then surely I would be allowed to continue. Uncle Sadr is a very gentle and honorable man who strictly follows the written word. As a judge, he is beyond reproach. Over the years his quiet dignity has earned him a respected reputation in the city and beyond. I must plead my case. What would I do without law? Losing law and Esther would be certain death. I would have nothing; no purpose or place in life. An agonizing pain grips my chest.

My sleep is haunted by nightmares. I wake with a start then lie in darkness, in fear of my future. Do I really want to be a judge? Yes, my soul cries out with overwhelming force. Then why did you give such a debauched party? Did it drown your grief? Of course not. I curse myself for lack of foresight. I should have the strength to rise above my agony. Strength, where does it come from? I feel like a crumpled rag, trampled by the armies of the caliphate. Can I stand up again? I must have reason to stand up. To be a judge; to learn the Justice of God; to know a higher, more sublime order. To understand a world that stretches beyond emotions.

After the second prayer of the day, I head for Uncle Sadr's house. It was my admiration for the man that had first put the idea of becoming a judge into my head. When I was young, I often watched him dispense justice at the mosque. He always provided the right answers and passed judgment to the satisfaction of all parties. He was such an impressive figure sitting beside his scribes, all eyes turned toward him. I wanted to be like him, to be able to provide the right answers, to be the mediator between God and men.

A servant takes me through the courtyard into the library where I sit down to wait. It is a house of quiet beauty to soothe the mind. Peace surrounds me, and the atmosphere of solemnity is not unlike what I often find in the mosque. Sadr shortly appears at the door. He rushes over to embrace me.

"I haven't seen you since you came back from Fez," he says warmly.

"I've been very busy," I explain.

"Of course, of course," he nods.

He explores my face in the ensuing silence, which lasts uncomfortably long. Finally he asks, "Why would someone who wants to be a judge throw a party like the one you did last week, with wine, drunkenness, naked girls, fornication? I hear a number of young boys were also seen dancing in the nude."

Slowly and reluctantly, I explain that I had little control over the direction of the party because I myself was overwhelmed by the desire to forget. I tell him about Esther. I tell him of my grief and how that grief had interfered with good judgment.

"Everyone grieves," says Sadr kindly. "But you cannot allow yourself to be pulled down by your grief. With the help of Allah, the Merciful, the Compassionate, all things pass, including grief."

Sadr studies my reaction before continuing. "As a judge, you carry the Word of God. To do so effectively, you yourself must be clean. If not, you are soiling the judgment of God. Do you understand?"

"Yes, I do. What happened last week will never happen again. I will not allow my emotions to debase me again."

"You must now go to the chief cadi and explain your situation, otherwise you might finish your studies but find yourself unable to practice."

I make a humiliating appearance before the chief cadi of Cordoba. After I confess my lack of moral turpitude and vow not to fall into such error again, the cadi sits me down to outline the grave duties of a judge. A judge must be a moral example. A judge cannot allow himself to stray precisely because he has been appointed to bring Divine Justice to the people.

After the evening prayer, I stay at the Mosque to meditate. I breathe in the Peace of Allah. Each breath is medicine for my tortured soul. Next to the Divine, my grief is so unimportant. I must rise. My spirit must rise to reach the all-embracing Divinity. There is so much to learn, to understand. Will I ever be worthy?

I must search everywhere to discover Divine Truth. I must read everything. I must know what other men have discovered and go one step further, one step closer to the Truth.

I absorb myself in the controversies of the day. Shihab and I spend weeks trying to determine the exact meaning of Sacred knowledge. If the Qur'an is the source of all Sacred knowledge, then where does scientific knowledge fit in? We finally decide that human knowledge must exist beside Sacred knowledge. However, what is the source of human knowledge? How do doctors and scientists discover new knowledge pertaining to their fields? Can they obtain it from a Divine source other than the Qur'an? Ultimately, is all knowledge sacred, whether it originates from the Qur'an or not? Both Shihab and I agree that to ask questions is so much easier than to find answers. We reason that if there are Divine answers, and then surely there must be Divine questions. At one point, we are reduced to laughter as we contemplate the difference between a Sacred and a human question.

At night, I read until fatigue overtakes me. I question everything. I engage in long discussions with visiting scholars my father invites to the house. I press them for the latest theological and philosophical issues. They tell me that though Divine knowledge is perfect, man must use his intellect to interpret and apply this knowledge. I fondly remember 'Abdallah; he would certainly agree with them. I wonder, when will I be ready to interpret Divine revelation?

A new force grows within me. Nevertheless, underneath this force is still the grief, the desire for the unattainable. I try to bury the grief under my rapidly accumulating knowledge. During the day, I am unaware of it. At night, when I am with Naziha or alone, it floats to the surface.

After the midday prayer, I walk to the pleasure garden by the river and sit on a tiled bench by the fountain. I listen to the music of the water falling from the higher bowls into the lower ones. I glance at the shimmering ripples on the river's surface.

The sun plays with the water, swathing it in silver and gold. As a calm infuses my body, I remember the Sufi hermitage I had once visited with 'Abdallah.

I get up and walk across the Roman bridge to the other side of the river. My feet carry me to the house, impelled by an incomprehensible force.

Inside the hermitage, I have difficulty explaining to a disciple why I have come. I stutter in confusion. He smiles, gently takes my arm, and leads me into one of the rooms of the main courtyard. I recognize the Sheykh sitting on a cushion before a small, carved wooden table on which is a long roll of parchment paper flowing to the floor. He holds a rosewood rosary in one hand and a pen in the other.

"He just arrived, perhaps you should talk to him," says the disciple and leaves us.

The Sheykh motions for me to sit down on a light blue and yellow brocade cushion near him. "This is not your first time here. I remember you," he says.

"Yes, I have been here before."

"Our meetings are usually at night or Friday afternoons," he says. "You cannot join the hermitage as a disciple unless you have first attended at least some of the meetings."

I nod but remain silent. An overpowering shyness has taken hold of me.

"Why have you come?" the Sheykh asks gently.

"I am not certain."

Long silence passes between us. I cannot move. I am suspended in time, in space.

"Why don't you sit in the courtyard for a while? Then, if you desire, you are welcome to return in the evenings or Friday afternoons."

I nod several times, smiling gratefully. I get up and go into the courtyard. Cross-legged, I sit on the marble floor before the round pool of water and lose myself in the delicacy of the water lilies basking in the rays of the sun. The fountain in the center has stopped flowing. The water is calm. I breathe in the peace. A disciple is meditating in one corner of the courtyard. I close my eyes and time passes without awareness.

I return to the hermitage repeatedly until I become a regular at the nightly meetings.

I am introduced to Sufi poetry filled with verses declaring passionate love for God. The poems vividly reveal a desire to be united with the loved one. Had I come across these poems outside the hermitage, I would have mistaken them for simple love poems; poems of high passion. Their explicit language shocks me. I am shocked because some of the feelings expressed are all too familiar. Had I not felt this way about Esther? Did I not desire her with such thirsty passion?

"No," the Sheykh tells me. "In the desire for God, one loses the sense of self. There is no you and the other—the soul must identify with its own Divine source and realize that the soul and God are one. The culmination of Divine love is absolute unity."

"But why do my own feelings for Esther resurface when I read these poems? Why do they not point in the direction of God?"

"Your identification with the poems are solely on a physical plane," the Sheykh explains. "It is only through love that one can see God. However, this love is of a spiritual nature. Your definition of love remains on the material plane. Still, the material plane is a start, the only start we have as people. You can take the love you feel for another and rechannel it toward God. You need not negate the physical love. Use it as a starting point. Build upon it. That love can be used as a stepping-stone to God. You must expand your love and go higher, much higher, toward the Divine."

Unexpected joy rushes through my being. I can learn to love God, to reach for Divine Truth, by having loved Esther! I no longer have to suppress my grief. I no longer have to obliterate my love, to do battle with it. I can maintain it without sorrow.

I can expand upon it. As one piece of knowledge leads to another, one love can lead to another. My heart opens, and I am suffused by such aching tenderness.

I arrive at a small open square near the street of the wood carvers. Three Qur'an chanters, accompanied by a guitarist, sing out the Word of God. They stand beside a mosaic fountain, the glazed colors glistening in the sun, rejoicing in the rhythm of the song. Their clear, unified voices rise toward the blue sky, high above the falling water. A nearby Judas tree is in full spring bloom; lovingly, its rich pink flowers hug the bare branches. Donkeys, tethered to its trunk, lazily bask in the sun. Listeners, enchanted by the sweet rhythm of the singing, lose themselves in another world.

I too allow the chords to carry me away. The Sufis would probably say we all gain nourishment from the same source, yet look at the diversity produced. The voices reach toward the high notes and then suddenly plummet to the shadowy depths. Their tonality reproduces the diversity of which they sing.

A tap on my shoulder breaks the magic. With a start, I reemerge into the physical world to see Esther flushed and smiling shyly beside me. We have not seen each other in over a year. Though I clearly recognize the Esther I had once known, I just as clearly see that she has changed; she has acquired another layer of experience.

A sudden stab of fear contracts my heart. I want to turn away. I do not want to be reminded. Do I still love her? I say a silent prayer to calm myself.

"It has been such an effort not to come and see you at the mosque," she says.

I lead her away from the rhythmic chant. The voices of the Qur'an readers follow us a little way down the street of the wood carvers. The aroma of fresh cedar permeates the atmosphere. Men and women carve and polish different colors and grains of wood. The sound of their tools mingles with exchange of information. We turn the corner to the covered street of the brass workers. The ceilings are rounded and dotted with star-shaped skylights. We pass through the beams of sunlight; bright, piercing tunnels through the dark, cool atmosphere.

"How are you?" I ask, feeling calmer.

"Probably as well as you."

I pause, debating whether to tell her. I decide that spoken out aloud, especially to Esther, will make it seem more real. "I have taken my love for you and have tried to elevate it to a spiritual plane."

"My love for you has been transferred to my son."

I am surprised. "You are already a mother!"

"What else is marriage about? Though Simeon is a wonderful man, I would find our life unbearable without children."

Her presence beside me brings on familiar warmth. But I am surprised to discover I no longer have that intense longing. Nearness no longer translates into desire for possession. Our talk becomes easy as if we had been seeing each other every day. We exchange small events of our lives. We laugh, even tease each other. However, when it is time to separate, we are both struck by sudden anxiety. We fidget with our clothes and do not dare to look the other in the eye.

"I would like to think of you as a friend," Esther finally says, still looking down at her sleeve. "If something happens I would like to be able to call on you. If I need to talk, I would like to know you would be there. Is that a lot to ask?" Her head, as if lifting a heavy weight, tilts up to face me.

"No. Our friendship cannot be touched by anyone."

"It is precious," she says very quietly.

"I will let you know my whereabouts. Wherever I am, you will be able to reach me."

As I am about to leave the mosque, a tremendous uproar draws me toward the gate leading to the Roman bridge. The area is thick with people. Fear and anticipation hang in the air as everyone faces the bridge, toward an event beyond the gate. I ask someone what is going on.

"An insurrection," cries the man.

"The farmers are rising up against al-Hakam II," adds another.

"They don't stand a chance," offers a third.

I rise to my toes in an attempt to glimpse events over the sea of heads. On the far side of the Roman bridge is a large crowd menacingly waving a variety of metal and wooden farm instruments high above their heads. They are marching across the bridge, toward us, toward the city. Their thunderous shouts are incomprehensible, but their fury is unmistakable. Sounds of hooves suddenly hit the stone pavement of the bridge, and cavalrymen, swords drawn, ride at great speed toward the farmers. The opposing sides meet at the center of the bridge; gleaming swords and rusty farm implements clash. Bodies crumple to the ground. Blood spurts over the bridge into the water. After a horrifyingly long time, the fighting slows. The farmers recede to the other side of the river leaving behind many of their numbers, dead and mangled in a pool of glistening red. The horsemen maintain their position in the middle of the bridge, forming an impenetrable wall with their blood-splattered horses.

Can a leader, no matter how good, be popular with everyone? Al-Hakam II, despite the innumerable problems with the various Christian states, with rulers backing out of treaties, has managed to hold onto a relative truce of peace. His efforts at negotiation rather than immediate battle have improved people's lives. The city of Cordoba is rich in scholarship and innovative architecture. There are schools and hospitals for the poor where brilliant scholars lecture and the most renowned doctors practice. All financed by the Caliph. Still there are those who find al-Hakam IV's policies objectionable. The people are restless. Their needs never end. Is there always room for improvement?

My brother Ali's marriage to Noeima is a joyful celebration. However, the birth of their first child brings chaos to the house. The two women who have come to help with the delivery rush out into the courtyard to confer with Kinza in the corner. Kinza, suddenly panic-stricken, rushes to find a servant and then sends him off. In a short time al-Ghifari, the doctor, comes in accompanied by Labbanah, his daughter. They march through the first courtyard, into the second courtyard and disappear into Noeima's room.

Having watched these proceedings from the library, I now become curious and ask Kinza what is going on. Kinza can only cry, her shoulders shaking, and the scarf around her neck trembling.

I cautiously go to Noeima's room. Labbanah stands guard at the door and does not allow me to look in. I inquire about the state of affairs. She quickly glances into the room and then leads me away into the first courtyard.

"Noeima's baby was born terribly deformed. My father was called to administer the necessary medication to hasten the baby's death," she explains in a professional manner.

"Poor Noeima." I hold my head in distress.

"Death is never easy," Labbanah replies.

"Are you helping your father?"

"Yes. I am apprenticing to be a doctor."

"Have you witnessed a lot of deaths?"

"A number, yes."

I look at her calm manner and am surprised. She is probably no more than twenty-five; a glowing woman with smooth burnished skin, bursting with health.

"Death does not bother you?"

"Death is the will of Allah. Why quarrel with destiny?"

"How simple!" I am amazed.

"It is simple. People complicate it with misguided desires."

She returns to Noeima's room. I put my hands under the fountain, feeling the cool water upon my palms. In the first courtyard, Kinza's grief-stricken voice cries out for Ali. It seems life has decreed suffering for everyone. Tears come to my eyes as I see Noeima's gentle smile before me. She is still young, I tell myself, and she will have many more children.

Several times, I meet Labbanah at the market, shopping for herbs with her father. He proudly tells me how many people she has already cured in her young life. In spite of the innumerable illnesses she must have witnessed, her laughter is gay and carefree. I find myself slowly drawn toward her. I begin to seek her out.

When I mention her to my father, he immediately thinks she would make a perfect wife for me. He suggests my mother speak with Labbanah's mother. I protest. I do not desire marriage.

The Sufi meetings infuse me with an inner calm. I have become a permanent member of the hermitage, joining doctors, secretaries, judges, musicians, and artisans. All of us contribute financially to the support of the Sheykh and his disciples.

I have grown close to one particular disciple, Jahm al-Din, a young man of my own age. His boundless enthusiasm for the mystical immediately attracted me. He is a terrifically curious and optimistic person willing to take whatever path necessary to commune with the Divine. I look upon his courage to face all obstacles as a soothing example.

"Divine Justice can only be defined in terms of love and beauty," says Jahm as we sit in the courtyard after the nightly meeting.

"I don't think I would define Divine Justice in those terms," I reply.

"You would not, but a true Sufi would. A Sufi would also say that justice can only be meted out through forgiveness and mercy."

"If you talk of justice on a personal level, I would agree. But justice is required on several levels."

"There is internal justice and external justice. As a cadi, you would be dealing only with external justice."

"Before I can deal with any form of justice, I must know the Qur'an by heart, be familiar with the Hadith and Sunna of the Prophet, not to mention the consensus of the community. These are all Divine sources. They will bring me closer to God and His intention for man."

Jahm only smiles quietly, indicating that there is no need for a discussion since I have a fixed point of view. I believe he himself has an equally fixed, though different, point of view. It is hard for us to meet since neither is willing to leave his position. His stubbornness can greatly infuriate me.

I walk toward the Roman bridge in the darkness of the night. Stars sprinkle the sky as skylights sprinkle the dome of the market. Is there knowledge higher than the written word? I tell myself that first I must be familiar with the written word before contemplating a higher order. Surely the written word will lead me to discover the Divine order.

Also, I must learn the application of the written word. For the moment, I am simply a student. Only in application can writing live; application will help me gain a deeper understanding of Divine Justice. The practice of Justice will help me to understand men, God's creation; it will also bring me closer to the Truth. Did not the Mu'tazila philosophers say that for man to realize Divine Justice on earth, he must use his reason?

VII. Law

When I am thirty years old, in the Muslim year of 358, to the Christians 969, I am finally appointed a judge, a cadi. I begin to practice in the portico of the Great Mosque where I have often listened to other judges pass their verdict. The authority of my position has naturally elevated me in my own eyes. Whereas before, I would look toward my professors for answers; now, people look toward me for answers. I shoulder this serious responsibility with great pride. At last, I am beginning to look upon myself as a man. Once I grow comfortable with this new phase of my life, I turn my attention to Naziha's future.

One summer afternoon, we are sitting in the women's courtyard, sipping coffee under the shade of a citrus tree.

"The time has come for me to give you your freedom," I announce ceremoniously. "Of course, I will help you with whatever you require to start a new life."

Naziha looks at the fountain in silence. Then turns to me. "What would you like me to do?"

"Naziha, you have been with us for more than seven years. By the grace of Allah, you have earned your freedom. It is no longer for me to decide what you should do."

"Would you like me to go or to stay?"

I laugh uncertainly. It had never occurred to me what I would like. I simply thought the time had come to grant Naziha her freedom; it is a just act on my part, born of logic not emotion. My father always gives a slave his freedom after seven years, sometimes even sooner. "Of course, I would like you to stay. You are most welcome to stay. I adore you, you know that."

"I ask you one thing. I want to go and visit my country and family. Then I would like to return to you. I am happy here."

I look into her eyes. The pride I spotted in them that first day at the slave market is still evident. The face is open, smiling. A wave of gratitude cleanses me, allowing me to see her true worth. I had not realized how much I would have missed her had I never seen her again. She has certainly provided me with a great deal of comfort over the years. My gratitude at having Naziha almost touches feelings of love; though, sadly, there is no tingling, no heightened awareness, only comfortable affection.

In the mornings, the brilliant clarity cast by the summer sun is still vernal. By midday, the rays have burnt through all the freshness replacing it with heavy, palpable dry heat. I find it takes physical effort to walk through the sunny patches of the city. The atmosphere presses down on the shoulders forcing the limbs to move slower. Every step I take brings an awareness of my body's ponderous weight. All seek the relief of shade. In the summer months, I practice in the mornings and return again between the fourth and fifth prayer to handle a few more cases. Sitting at a rectangular table, I hold court in the shade of the portico assisted by my four counselors. Wasil, my court clerk, records the testimony of the plaintiffs, defendants, and their corresponding witnesses. I usually have two professional witnesses on hand to vouch for the character of the witnesses brought to us by the plaintiff and defendant. The reliable testimony of just witnesses is of key importance in Muslim law. I have great respect for this process.

Wasil is extraordinarily efficient; he keeps the registers and files in immaculate order. A jilwaz is also on hand with his whip to keep discipline at all hearings. When necessary I call upon the police to mete out punishment or take the culpable party to prison. I have everything I need to help me carry out justice.

Cases of divorce, inheritance, family murders, and innumerable other crises pass before my eyes. I eagerly immerse myself in every case. My enthusiasm infuses my counselors and Wasil with greater pride in their work. Before me, all are treated with gentle humility. I am honored to serve the people of Cordoba, to set them on the just path.

To date, in my experience, working with law is similar to mathematics—it requires strenuous mental exercise, mental acrobatics. I find the practice of law is tempering my powers of reasoning. The knowledge I have accumulated over the years is at last focused toward a specific goal. As the cutting edge of a blade becomes finer and finer through sharpening, so does the mind.

Everyone in the house notices my enthusiasm. Aishah and Mustafa say I exude satisfaction when I return from a morning session of holding court. My father and brothers are proud at the evident respect people show me in the mosque and the market. In the evening, I never fail to tell Naziha about some aspect of a case. She laughs at my exuberant energy, pleased to see me in high spirits and full of optimism.

There is no other place I would rather live than in Cordoba. My life is flowering to fulfill its Divine goal as Cordoba is gaining wider and wider fame. Under al-Hakam II, my city has become the highest center of learning, attracting students from distant lands. The population swells with young people eager for the latest knowledge the world has to offer. The bookstores are filled with the writings of modern scholars as well as numerous translations and commentaries on the Greek masters. Any manuscript one desires can be obtained here.

I often stroll through the market to bask in the culture igniting the air. Debates take place anywhere and everywhere; in the squares, the pleasure gardens, the marketplace, or the courtyards of mosques. The exchange of knowledge and ideas fills Cordoba with a heightened energy that even peaks the curiosity of the common man. The city also attracts builders, minstrels, musicians, and singers eager to learn the newest techniques of their trade.

This vibrant excitement seeps into my soul. Sitting in court, listening and judging cases, is no longer enough. I desire a direct participation in the exchange of knowledge. After considerable thought, I decide to teach Islamic law in the afternoons. The curiosity of the students forces me to rethink old beliefs and explore recently discovered concepts.

"Could knowledge and understanding be carried to an extreme?" asks Harith, a student from Baghdad who is always surrounded by the girls.

"No," I reply. "There are no limits to knowledge. It is not within the possibility of man to know everything. Only Allah has infinite knowledge."

"Well, then, could seeking knowledge reach perverse levels?"

"Knowledge can be twisted or manipulated to serve a particular purpose. But then it can no longer be called true knowledge," I reply.

Giggling erupts from the students.

"Tell him," a fat student urges Harith.

"Yes, you must tell him what you told us," coax the girls.

"Do you have something to tell me?" I ask Harith.

The giggling fades to expectant silence. Harith allows for a dramatic pause, clearly enjoying the attention.

"I have been spending the last year studying in Fez where a number of cadis are working on a treatise based on hypothetical cases. They are attempting to determine exactly at what point succession to an estate opens up when the owner of the estate has been turned into stone by the devil." There is another dramatic pause to allow a few suppressed giggles to surface. "Also, they have ruled that if a mouse falls into melted butter and drowns, the butter cannot be used as oil for lamps since the air would be polluted by the impurity of the dead animal's flesh."

A wild round of laughter threatens to explode. I myself have a hard time keeping a straight face.

Harith calmly continues, enjoying the rapt audience attention. "The theologians have also decreed that it is not permissible to ride a camel, donkey, or a horse which has drunk wine because of possible contact with the forbidden substance through the sweat of the animal."

The class finally gives vent to a riotous outbreak. I myself start to cough ferociously trying to hide my laughter for it would be most disrespectful to openly laugh at the activities of my colleagues in another land.

At night, I eagerly relate Harith's story to the family. Before I can finish, I am rolling with laughter along with everyone else.

"Did you keep a straight face during the lecture?" my brother Husan asks.

"With difficulty," I blurt out between fits of tearful laughter.

"Allah is gracious," my father says, wiping the tears from his eyes. "That is good entertainment."

Deep within, a faint question begins to take shape. How is it possible that theologians and cadis dare use Divine Law in such absurdly shameful ways?

Emerging from the steam baths near the Jewish quarter, my Sufi friend Jahm and I hear exquisite singing accompanied by an orchestra. We look around but can see nothing. The music grows louder as it approaches the baths.

"It's the funeral," says Jahm.

He is right. The funeral procession rounds the corner and moves past us. The lamenting Jewish community is carrying the body of Hasdai ibn Shaprut to the cemetery. Following the coffin is a contingent from al-Hakam II's court, a great number of Muslims, as well as numerous Christians. Will the Caliph ever find a replacement for him? For decades, Hasdai had been the court physician for Abd al-Rahman III and al-Hakam II. He was also an excellent diplomat and a famous patron of Jewish poetry and writing. I have often heard about him and had great respect for his activities. Esther had lavishly praised his integrity. The thought of Esther brings a warm glow to my heart. I search the faces of the mourners, hoping to find her among them.

"Allah has called him," says Jahm simply. "Now he will truly know the meaning of life."

The procession continues through the city gates moving with rhythmic grace, bodies swaying in unison to the chords of the music.

"This physical world is the lowest form of reality," continues Jahm. "Your actions may be admired by other men, but the real question is whether they will also be admired by Allah."

"Man must try his best to fulfill his potential here on earth. I think Hasdai did that."

"Best according to whose definition?" Smiles Jahm.

"Muhammad defined that for the Muslims, Moses for the Jews, and Jesus for the Christians," I point out.

"Each of us acts according to his own interpretation," Jahm says calmly.

"How can it be otherwise?" I ask in exasperation.

"We must try to seek direct communion with God."

"We cannot all negate physical reality in an effort to commune with Allah." The severity in my voice surprises him.

"Why not? Then there would be no more killing." His answer rings with the annoying purity of hopeless idealism.

I shake my head. Though there is an element of truth to Jahm's words, sometimes his comments bring to mind an innocent child.

One day I enter the Great Mosque for the first prayer of the day and suddenly stop, along with everyone else. After nine years of construction, the mosque is finally completed. Heaven has clearly inspired its beauty and grandeur. The marble columns linked by the horseshoe arches line up toward eternity. The brilliant sunshine flooding through the skylight above the mihrab accentuates the predominantly gold mosaics and the intricately engraved white marble panels. This mosque is truly a reflection of paradise. The speaker mounts his elegant wooden minbar for his Friday talk before prayer. I reluctantly lower my gaze from the sparkling mosaics to focus on his words. The low voice rings through the mosque as he announces that al-Hakam II has nominated his eight-year-old son, Hisham, to be his heir apparent. Everyone is ordered to take an oath of allegiance and to mention his name, after that of the Caliph, during Friday prayers.

Despite the glorious beauty surrounding the announcement, I am deeply shocked. I am not alone. Al-Hakam II has numerous relatives of mature age who would make a more suitable successor. How could a young boy be expected to rule?

The Saturday after the announcement, misgivings stir in the marketplace. The movement of the crowd expresses unease. People wonder if al-Hakam could be persuaded to name another successor. Just because Hisham is the son of Subh, his favorite concubine, it is no reason to make him a ruler. People's anger turn on Subh. She must have pressured al-Hakam to make such an announcement, everyone says. I sadly wonder why rulers confuse affairs of the heart with politics. I considered al-Hakam II to be a wise man.

He is known throughout the world for his intelligence. It seems intelligence cannot always save one from error.

The city falls into turmoil. Furious arguments break out in the baths. Something must be done, people urge. Others say we must patiently wait for the future to unroll. They insist there is no need to take action; the situation is not urgent.

"That's right," someone yells through the steam of the bath. "Wait till it becomes impossible to act!"

"It is written," comes a dismembered reply.

"If God wills it, everything will be fine," a chorus answers.

Within days, the fear and misgivings dissipate. The city regains its normal pace. I too grow confident and optimistic that al-Hakam II has made the right decision. By the time he dies, Hisham will be a grown man. Till then, he can educate his son to be worthy of his future role as Caliph.

After several years of holding court and referring to the various texts containing Divine decrees, I am thoroughly familiar with the word of the law. I become adept at reciting needed passages and previous cases with their accompanying judgments. I quote at will passages of the Qur'an, the Hadith, or the Sunna. My mind is alert and keen when dealing with the word of Allah and the meaning of the words gain a deeper significance. Each time I pass a judgment, and support it with a relevant quotation, I take time to reflect upon my words. I have never passed a judgment mechanically, as some people in the field of law are known to do. I believe my role, as a judge demands conscious diligence; not only am I responsible to the people, but also to Allah. I feel myself move closer and closer to the Truth. *Soon,* I tell myself, *soon all will become clear. Soon, I will know.*

One day a case comes before me concerning a business transaction. A plot of land was exchanged for services rendered by a farmer. Now, the owner of the land claims the farmer has not fulfilled his required work and does not deserve the land. I carefully listen to the testimony. A feeling of unease comes over me as the plaintiff outlines why he is claiming back his land.

There is an overconfident and superior manner to the man's gestures. His delivery and his words seem at odds. Slowly it dawns on me that the man is lying. The story of the defendant, the farmer, is much more plausible. Both men have the required two witnesses to give supportive evidence as to the characters of the accuser and accused.

After everything has been heard, Wasil, my counselors, and I discuss the case. I point out that the plaintiff was obviously not telling the truth. The counselors say that the witnesses for the side of the plaintiff were more respectable than for the side of the defendant; therefore, it makes no difference how I judge the performance of the plaintiff. I try to argue, without the least success. They claim the case is clear and the verdict obvious since it perfectly parallels a case mentioned in the Muwatta.

Later Wasil takes me aside. "I am surprised this is the first time you have noticed someone lying."

I do not understand his meaning.

"Forgive me for being so blunt," he continues gently. "You have been paying such close attention to the word of the law that you have not noticed the people who have come before you."

"You yourself have told me my judgments have been impeccable." I naturally feel I must defend myself.

"Yes, they have been impeccable, viewed from the perspective of the law."

Is there more than one way to look at Truth? More than one perspective? Why has he not said this to me before? Have I missed something all these years? For the first time since I have become a judge, I make an effort to listen more closely to the people. A number of cases go by where my judgment disagrees with that of the counselors and Wasil. They repeatedly point to the letter of the law to support their stand. I am forced to bow my head and agree with them.

I am frustrated and confused to suddenly find myself so distant from accepted opinion. What I now perceive to be just is legally unjust. This development creates a painful inner tension for me. I cannot use observation in my judgments, nor can I use logic. Wasil was right, if I follow the letter of the law, my judgments are impeccable. But there is no room for me to move beyond the written word.

I make an effort to follow accepted tradition and use my power of reason to fit cases to precedent. Yet, an invisible rope, once taut, is loosening. I try hard to tighten it once more. *The written word of the law is of primary importance*, I tell myself. Divine Justice is perfect. For a short time, I regain my sure footing of an earlier period.

A little later, another case comes before me where a woman is seeking divorce from her husband on the grounds of cruelty. The husband denies her accusations. The woman presents three witnesses, one male and two female, who attest to her good character. Though the woman is certainly beautiful, I doubt her word. Something about her manner sparks my suspicion. When I bring up my objections with the counselors, they say that according to evidence we must grant the divorce.

Several months later, I accidentally discover that the woman is about to marry her male witness. Obviously, he was lying on her behalf when giving testimony.

During a game of chess with Shihab, I broach the subject of my frustration. I ask him if he too has experienced similar situations in his role as judge. Shihab deals with cases of inheritance and his specialty is the administration of charitable endowments. He tells me that in cases of inheritance, he has certainly come across situations where the parties involved were lying for their own benefit, yet he was powerless to contradict them.

"After all, I cannot say I don't believe them when they have presented the required evidence." He shrugs. "I simply follow the letter of the law."

"How do you personally deal with that?"

"I accept that this is part of justice." He contemplates the board before making his move. "The presumption of shari'a is that whoever swears will tell the truth because they are terrified of the consequences of a lie. However, that is not the case. People are often more concerned about a material gain than about spiritual retribution. It is not my place to teach them their religious obligations. When the time comes, they will pay for their misdeeds."

"As judges, are we not supposed to show them the correct way, point them toward the right path?" I remove his queen.

Shihab shakes his head. "Within limits. Our role is very clearly prescribed. There is no room for us to step outside that."

"What about Truth?"

Shihab starts to laugh. "Sulayman, you must have realized that we are not always allowed the luxury to act according to the Truth."

"Do you not find a discrepancy between being a judge and wanting to follow the Truth?"

"What you believe to be the Truth is not necessarily what someone else believes to be the Truth. That is why the laws have been written down for us—to make it very clear what the Truth is."

"At times I find myself applying the Truth, as written down, but witness an untruth upon which I cannot act. I find that debilitating—I find right action, at times, has been taken away from me."

"Sulayman, you amaze me. You have not lost your idealism. Not in the least."

Having won the game, I leave Shihab. I am restless. An inner tension drives me to the book market in the hope of finding an exciting new manuscript to divert my attention. I pass through the pools of sun cast by the star-shaped skylight of the domed roof. The smell of parchment paper hangs in the air. I peruse the stalls, casually looking at the displays. A brilliant cover design catches my attention. I open the book to find a collection of Sufi poetry. Just as I begin to read the verses, shouts assail my ears. I turn in the direction of the commotion and see the inspector of the market, whip in hand, pulling a man onto the street from a nearby shop. He holds the man's neck down with one hand and brutally flogs his back with the other. The inspector is a big, muscular man wearing a small leather vest over a green cotton shirt and loose matching pants gathered at the ankles. The man he is holding is of slight build, his fear making him appear even smaller. The whip leaves dark lines on his long white robe.

"This man is cheating good Muslims. Take heed!" The inspector cries and gives the man another hard lash.

I put the book down and quickly leave. I hurry to the pleasure garden near the zoo and sit by a rectangular pool with a fountain of thin jets reaching toward a cloudy, fragmented sky. I pull my overcoat tighter to keep out the cold. Is it possible to administer Divine Justice in a practical form? Could I reasonably hope to get a deeper insight into the Justice of Allah by administering his words to others?

I seek solace in my teaching. My doubts about the practice of justice are reflected in my lectures. I urge my students to think for themselves, to analyze. The Divine revelations of Muhammad occurred over three hundred years ago, I point out. Is it not possible that the laws presented to our prophet were simply meant as a starting point? And that starting point is the Qur'an. Does not the Qur'an itself admonish against blind following? Does it not encourage people to study, question, and think?

The more familiarity I gain with the law, the more aware I become of its rigidity. The door to independent thought and interpretation of Qur'anic verses closed at the beginning of this century, after all the Hadith of the Prophet had been collected. Now there is no more room for creative judgments. So, what is my place in the legal system? Am I simply required to follow precedent? Is this Divine Justice?

Why is it that the farther away we get from the time of the Prophet, the more rigid we become? The less we trust ourselves, the more we expect conformity of our fellow men.

After a Sufi meeting, I complain to Jahm. I am getting no closer to the Truth. At one point, I thought I was heading toward that glimmer of light. Now a veil has dropped, shielding my view.

"There are several levels to Divine Justice," Jahm explains. "You are dealing on its lowest level. To learn you must seek on a higher plane. Everyone must. The people who come to you as a cadi learn from you because you are higher than they. For you to learn, you must seek a higher teacher."

"That is partly why I come to the hermitage."

I return to the hermitage increasingly. I find myself seeking out Jahm's company with greater regularity. With him I am able to vent my frustration. If I can logically understand the turmoil inside, surely I will be able to find the cure. But questions only cause greater aggravation. Jahm listens with patience. The more patience he demonstrates, the more anxious I become.

My father does not understand my distress. The family tells me I should be proud of my role as cadi. They say people speak of me with such respect. They look at me with concern and announce I must be tired. Husan suggests I go to a camel race with him. Ali thinks a horse race would be better. "Al-Hakam II has just received some magnificent horses from Majorca," he tells me. Aishah suggests I accompany Mustafa and herself to the next archery competition. She says I might find it calmer than a horse or camel race. In addition, Naziha climbs into my bed at night, stroking and kissing my body. Getting no response, she leaves sadly.

Jahm is the only one who seems to understand, who does not make me feel ungrateful at questioning my good fortune.

"How, how can you ever find the meaning of Truth in letters?" asks Jahm. "How can you ever express the Eternal Spirit of the Law which man, a temporal being, has fixed in writing?"

"That is exactly what I have said to my students. I am not listening to my own words."

Jahm smiles, a smile of inward peace. "How can the written word convey Eternal Truth? How can it ever hope to express the Law of God? The only way to reach the Eternal is by reaching upward, not by bringing it down to the physical level."

"Philosophers have grappled with the spirit of the Law. There have been works written . . ." My voice sounds hallow.

"Those are just words and if they do not change, as everything in the physical world must, then those words will become meaningless."

"What are you saying?" I cry in exasperation.

"Sulayman, law in practice will never give you the Truth since it is only a symbol of a much higher reality. You must look at that reality."

"What must I do to see?"

"You must find the Truth for yourself." Jahm presses on. "You must have the courage to go forward and discover your own path toward God."

"How?" I tightly clench my fists, hoping to hold back an overwhelming sense of desperation.

"There is no one answer. Our Sheykh will give you one possible route. Another Sheykh will point you in a different direction. Ultimately, you must find the right road yourself. No one can give it to you," says Jahm.

I witness the swelling of Cordoba. The book market has more and more magnificent manuscripts from distant lands. My own family blossoms to produce more and more children running through our three courtyards. Aishah and Mustafa have two sons and one daughter. Husan and Niama have added another two sons. Ali and Noeima have two sons and two daughters. And Naziha, unable to carry the full length of her term, lost two. My brothers and sisters were touchingly sympathetic. My mother cried, holding me close to her. I felt strangely removed from their sorrow. Though I mourned with Naziha, I felt a great distance between my inner self and the reality of the situation.

Harith ibn Adham, an ambitious student with an agile mind, comes to watch me at court in the mornings and stays after lectures to walk with me in the market. His inquisitiveness is the only thing to give me pleasure these days. Thinking he must be missing his family, I have invited him home several times for supper.

One afternoon after the lecture, in the middle of the summer heat, he suggests a ride into the hills where the air will be cooler.

We tie our donkey to a low hanging branch and settle on top of a northern hillside, under the shade of a large oak tree. The heat is less oppressive here; the atmosphere is lighter. Still, the leaves with their serrated edges hang limp from the lower branches. There is no evidence of even the slightest breeze.

Harith immediately strips down and lies naked upon the undergrowth, his eyes blissfully closed.

"You too should undress," he suggests. "It's easier this way."

I admire his youthful body; transparent beads of perspiration glisten on the olive skin of his chest where the black hairs are beginning to grow. He is already eighteen or nineteen yet his legs are free of hair; there is only a rich cluster of black around his genitals. I smile, thinking of 'Abdallah. I glance into the distance, at the gently rolling hills surrounding us. Their curves are soothing to the eye. Amazing how nature can caress the soul! Lightness infuses my tense muscles. My eyes return to Harith's outstretched body. He has put his hands behind his head, exposing the silky cluster of black hairs at his armpits. My eyes move down. Harith has a wonderfully proportioned body with slim, long legs. My gaze leisurely travels over the taut limbs. I can understand why the Greeks sculpted marble figures of your boys. There is a fresh eroticism to tight, smooth lines. Harith slowly turns over on his stomach. The dark olive skin of his back glistens in the sun. Naziha's skin has a similar sheen though a deep brown shade.

I pull my shirt over my head and quietly lie down on the ground, grateful I still have a capacity to enjoy the body. I have not totally died within.

In the month of Safar, when the autumn breeze should already be chasing away the heat of summer, I visit my Uncle Sadr to pay my respects on his birthday. To my surprise, I find him without visitors. He tells me that nearly a dozen people have just left a short while before my arrival. He leads me into the coolness of his library off the portico. His daughter soon brings in a steaming silver kettle of mint tea and places it on a low brass table. Sadr pours the tea into the two pale green porcelain cups and sits down on a cushion. His neatly trimmed beard is now filled with gray hairs. A distinguished tranquility surrounds him.

"Sulayman, you look rather tired," he says observing me carefully.

"I am happy to say that you look in full health." I laugh.

"Yes, I thank Allah, may He treat you as well as He has treated me."

"It pleases me to find you in good humor on your birthday."

"It pleases me less to see you with such a distressed appearance. Tell me. How is everything with you?"

I take a deep breath. Should I approach the subject uppermost on my mind? This is not a topic of conversation on my uncle's birthday. I decide against it and simply smile.

"Tell me," he urges. "We're alone and I hardly ever see you alone these days. I would feel honored if you opened your heart to me."

I take another deep breath and sip the hot tea. I stare at the blue and white tiled floor. The carpet has not yet been laid down for the winter. "You have been a judge for many years," I finally say quietly.

Sadr nods, waiting for me to continue.

"Have you ever had any negative feelings about your work as a cadi?"

"Negative? What do you mean? Specifically."

"Have you ever felt that the people coming to you were not very intelligent? I don't mean uneducated, simply not intelligent."

"The duty of a cadi is to point these people in the right direction."

"Yes, of course. But do you ever feel frustrated by the repetition of the cases?"

"No," he says slowly. "I never tire of helping people to follow the correct path."

I look out into the courtyard. My eyes rest on the falling water of the fountain. I shake my head and turn back to him. "Does that give you enough of a challenge?"

"I do not look to Justice for a challenge. The Law is Divine. It is there to be accepted. My duty as a cadi is to pass it on."

"Do you feel you understand Justice?"

"I don't think there is anything to understand about Justice. What is there to understand about the Absolute? It simply is." Sadr tilts his head to one side and kindly smiles.

"Yes, I agree with you on one level. But I cannot help feeling there are other layers I have not yet grasped."

He quietly ponders my comment before replying. "Have you thought of becoming a mufti? Producing fatwa might provide you with more of a challenge."

"A mufti is not required to come up with original thoughts. He simply reworks existing laws."

"The mufti develops new ways of looking at existing laws."

I nod in frustrated silence.

"Think about it," urges Sadr. "You are a good cadi. You have a good reputation."

I look up at him in surprise.

"Yes, I hear about how you are doing. You are my nephew. I make a point of knowing."

I am touched by his kindness. He is a good man, and he has taught me a great deal.

The only place to give me peace is the Sufi hermitage.

"The Kingdom of God is within you," says the Sheykh. "To know the meaning of Divine Justice, you must feel the light, beauty, and love of God. You must seek within, not without. Within is the Absolute. This physical world is but a shadow."

"Then why is it here in the first place? What is the purpose of this world?" asks a follower.

"It is but one landscape of the journey. Your soul must seek the Absolute, no matter where you are. You must seek that higher spiritual world where we are all One. Because that is reality," says the Sheykh.

Why is it so difficult? What is holding me back?

"You will have to make a decision at some point," says Jahm as we stroll by the river under the moonlight.

"What do you mean?" I ask.

"You will know when the time comes."

Jahm stops in the light of a lantern coming from a nearby cottage. He looks at me in silence for a long while. I grow uncomfortable.

"Before you can proffer justice, you yourself must lead a just life," Jahm says at last.

"I am leading as just a life as I know how," I protest.

"Have you found the Truth?"

"No . . ."

"Do you want to find the Truth?"

"Of course," I snap.

"You are not leading a just life till you do everything within your power to discover the Truth. You must be just with yourself before you can be just with others."

I silently beg Allah to tell me what to do.

"Look within," Jahm says softly.

VIII. Truth?

Thunderclouds stir in the sky. I feel raindrops on the palm of my hand. I hurry, pressing close to the wall, watching the raindrops grow larger and larger as they hit the stones of the wide road girdling the city. The thunder grows louder, more menacing. I draw my waterproof coat tighter around my body and glance up to see a few dozen Berber equestrians galloping toward me. The vision of their colorful military attire is a startling contrast to the wet atmosphere. I slow down to watch them pass. Backs straight, heads held high. Berbers are zealous Muslims, recently converted to the faith. Abd al-Rahman III had refused to allow Berbers into the army. Al-Hakam II, his son, has taken a great liking to Berber horsemen and has brought over several thousand from the hills of Northern Africa. My father once said Abd al-Rahman III considered them a treacherous people. Al-Hakam II, a great lover of horses, has grown to admire their skill with these animals and has chosen not to see their treacherous side.

The stones under my feet are now totally wet. I hope to arrive at the gate before the beating rain drenches me. People are running, knowing how the winter weather can suddenly change from bright sunshine to a hurtling waterfall. I peer into the aqueous atmosphere and see a sheet of water moving toward me. I too break into a run. By the time I reach the gate, I am fully soaked. Rushing through the narrow streets, I try to avoid the water gushing down the center drain.

At last, I reach Shihab's house. He forces me to quickly strip and gives me dry clothing. I stand in the library, my back pressed against the warm walls. My palms search the tiles trying to locate the pipes carrying the boiling water.

"Ah," I breathe out in rapturous relief as I press the sole of one foot against the wall.

A girl brings in a pot of coffee and cardamom honey cakes.

"These cakes will put the energy back into you," says Shihab.

I sink into the cushions against the warm wall and luxuriate in the heat behind my back. "Sometimes it takes so little to make one feel fully alive," I say in amazement while taking a bite from the cake.

"Have you been feeling dull lately?" Shihab laughs with such force that crumbs of cake come flying from his mouth. "Your mind is always churning with such intense questions. I am surprised you can sleep at night."

"The problem with you, Shihab, is that you've grown too comfortable to suffer spiritually."

"My dear Sulayman." He laughs heartily. "Tell me, is suffering a necessity?"

"I haven't decided yet. When I find the answer, I will let you know." I joke.

"No. When you find out, hold onto the secret. Don't spread it around."

I slowly take a sip of coffee, savoring its bitter taste. "I envy your tranquility."

"You should. I am to marry soon," Shihab loudly announces.

This is a complete surprise. "Do you have someone?"

"Arrangements are going on right now. She is a true beauty, like a deep red rose with its lusty petals just opening to maturity. When you see her, you will really envy me." He bursts into another round of laughter.

"You certainly are in a good mood."

Shihab stops laughing and looks at me curiously. "I wish I could say the same about you, Sulayman."

Feeling suddenly uncomfortable, I adjust my position on the cushion. I reach for my coffee cup and pause to stare into the deep brown liquid. Shihab watches me in silence.

"I feel I'm missing something," I finally say still looking into the coffee cup. "I can hardly explain." I stop, trying to collect my thoughts. "Being a cadi is no longer giving me enough satisfaction."

"I never looked for satisfaction." Shihab carelessly shrugs his shoulders. "To me being a cadi means prestige, as well as power."

"Yes. That's true. There is power. Is that enough for you?"

"Do you remember, when we began, we always talked of law in such ideal terms? We had high expectations of working with the Word of God." He pauses. "Since then I have learned that being a cadi is a mechanical function requiring little thought."

"Mostly, it requires blind faith."

"Do you enjoy the prestige, the power?"

Gazing into his empty coffee cup, Shihab lets out a deep sigh. "I know that in meting out law, I am meting out the word of Allah."

"Are you sure you are meting out the word of Allah? Are you sure all your judgments are correct?"

"It is a question of belief, isn't it?" An edge of sarcasm laces his voice.

"Do you believe all your judgments are correct?" I press.

"I don't ask myself such questions. I don't go to such extremes."

"How can you do otherwise?"

"I fulfill a function, a necessary function. And "—he shakes his forefinger at me—"I do good work."

Am I so different? Why is it so difficult for me to feel satisfaction? People show me respect; my students hold me in high esteem. Yet, I do not feel deserving of their praise.

In the hermitage, gazing at the water lilies in the pool of the courtyard brings me peace. The ripples created by the fountain move outward to the perimeter, gently rocking the large green pads. Gradually, more and more people arrive and settle down in the courtyard, ready for the evening lecture.

The Sheykh, surrounded by his followers, smiles. His eyes sparkle as the ripples of water shine in the sun. "Seventy thousand veils separate Allah from this physical world. In the process of birth, from the highest point to the lowest, every soul passes through these seventy thousand veils. During the first half of the journey, the soul passes through light and sheds its Divine quality. During the second half of the journey, the soul passes through darkness and puts on the physical form. Here, on earth, the soul must teach the body that it is a child of a much higher plane. The soul must make the mind aware of the veils through which it has passed and encourage it to lift those veils one by one to see reality. And the mind must help the soul to rediscover the trip back to the One."

"How can this be done?" asks an astrologer.

"It is a slow and difficult journey. The stages may be mastered through discipline, but man has no control over the spiritual states these stages will bring. Man can do a certain amount of work, after that we must simply trust in God."

"The spiritual states descend from God," offers one of the disciples. "But they might only descend for a very short time, as glimpses of the Absolute. Man has no way of holding onto these states."

"On that highest level," offers a female disciple, "the passionate desire to be one with God, that union of the lover and the loved one, is finally achieved."

A number of the followers, including myself, have difficulty grasping these words. We exchange looks of bewilderment.

"Did God not say in the Qur'an that believers should close their eyes?" asks the Sheykh. "That means your physical eyes should be closed to better see with your spiritual eyes."

Do I have to close my eyes to see?

I pay careful attention to the people who appear before me in court. I not only listen to the words but have also begun listening to the spaces. At first, the spaces reveal very little. Gradually, as my perception grows more refined, I can sense an essence: a need, a trickery, and, most shocking of all, I can sense an evil—pure bad intentioned evil. And some of these people who come before me have a judgment passed in their favor simply because they know how to present themselves. Though Malik writes that the intention of a person is to be given great consideration, the evil intention never comes across in an obviously clear way. Yet, the evil is unmistakable.

During a walk by the river, I bring up the question of evil with Jahm.

"A great Sufi once said that things are known through their opposites," says Jahm twirling a wild rose between his fingers.

"Then," I reason. "Allah must have also created evil."

"Allah has created all. He has created all to help us move toward the Light."

"You mean Allah has created both good and evil?" I ask in disbelief.

"Yes, He has emanated them into the world."

"That's heresy! You're saying that Allah contains evil within Himself."

"No. Allah is eternal, absolute, and pure. He has the power to create whatever we need in this physical world to help us reach the light. The recognition of evil allows us to define the good."

Jahm continues to twirl the rose between his fingers. "You can say that heaven is Absolute unity, whereas hell is diversity. The good and evil of earth become the positive and negative of Absolute oneness. But within the Absolute, the positive and negative are united."

"Are we to unite good and evil here on earth?" I ask hesitantly.

"We must find a balance till evil no longer means a negation of the soul. All criminal acts are an absorption in the physical at the expense of the spiritual. If we can find a balance, we can begin to strive toward unity."

We walk in silence. I grab at the branches of a willow tree.

Jahm tosses his rose into the river. "True alchemy is about the transmutation of human nature," he says with a beatific smile.

One Friday morning, I find Jahm at the steam bath. He is sitting on the marble ledge, his back against the ocher clay walls. A beam of sunlight from one of the star-shaped skylights falls on his face. His body is surrounded by thick steam, his eyes are closed. Three other people are sitting on the ledge engaged in animated discussion. Jahm seems oblivious. I sit down beside him and touch his shoulder. Slowly, very slowly, his eyes open and, equally slowly, he turns his head toward me and a quick smile brightens his eyes.

"You are exactly the person I should have drawn to me," he says.

I laugh. "Why?"

"I was meditating on Truth. Reason can only take you so far toward knowing the Truth, after that you must appeal to Allah to guide you the rest of the way."

I nod, wondering where he is leading.

"How can you know Divine Justice?" he asks cheerfully.

"Through the study of the Qur'an and the Hadith," I answer, though I already suspect this to be not totally correct.

"Where does reason come in?"

"In understanding," I reply.

"Has understanding helped you to get any closer to Divine Justice?" His eyes sparkle beneath the wet lashes.

I shake my head. "Law has brought me close to a segment of society I never knew existed."

"That's very good. You must know all segments of God's creation." He closes his eyes and pauses to think. "There are three pathways to the Truth—Revelation, Reason, and Mysticism. I think you have traveled two of the pathways, Revelation and Reason. You have yet to travel the third, Mysticism."

I look toward the dome, at the star-shaped skylights allowing a shock of sun to filter down through the steam. Patches of round brightness sit upon the wet clay floor. I fold my arms across my chest. A strong attraction draws me toward the world of the spirit. Yet, I am terrified to approach.

I am not ready to follow the path of Mysticism. Something is holding me back. I try to rationally define my reasons for reticence. My mind refuses to provide logical answers. Simply, I am not ready. I know the rigid formality of the law will never give me what I seek. Yet, there are certain things I must still do before I turn my back on law. I cannot understand my inability to make the necessary change. What more can the life of a cadi possibly give me?

Jahm has had the courage to commit himself to a mystical path. Perhaps by watching him more closely, by seeking out his company more often, I too will acquire the needed strength to leave my position. Through his influence, perhaps I will be able to give up the material world.

I go to the hermitage more often. To my surprise, I rarely find Jahm there. Before he was always there. Now, he seems to have disappeared. The Sheykh tells me Jahm has gone into the mountains to be alone and meditate. Months go by and I fail to see him. The Sheykh spends time with me alone, giving me guidance. However, I grow impatient, something draws me to Jahm. My desire to talk with him grows to absurd proportions. I need him.

Perhaps because he is close to my age, I reason. I keep returning to the hermitage to sit by the pool of water lilies. Waiting.

One morning as I am about to enter the Great Mosque, I pass a beggar in rags. I reach into the purse hanging on my belt and drop a few coins into his hand.

"No, Sulayman, not from you." He returns the coins. I look up in shock and recognize Jahm's face. He is considerably thinner, and there are dark circles around his eyes. However, the eyes themselves hold a deep pool of luminosity.

"I have been going to the hermitage almost every day looking for you." I am startled by the anger in my voice.

"So the Sheykh tells me."

I unfasten the purse from my belt and try to hand it to Jahm, "Here, take all of this."

"No, Sulayman, you are a friend."

I look at him, wanting to help in some way yet knowing he does not need my help. On the contrary, I need him.

"When will you be at the hermitage?" I ask.

"Soon you will find me there."

As I have been seeking out Jahm, Harith has been seeking out my company. He has drawn closer and closer to me and has begun to confide in me. His father, a doctor, wants him to return to Baghdad to apprentice by his side. Harith is not ready to return.

He has begged his father to allow him to remain one more year. He is waiting anxiously for a reply.

"Why do you not want to return?" I ask as we sip coffee in the market.

"There is still so much knowledge to absorb here."

"Medicine would not put an end to your learning. On the contrary, it could open up new doors of discovery."

"There is knowledge I cannot obtain from medicine and, once I commit myself to it, I cannot turn back."

"Apprenticeship with your father does not mean commitment to medicine for the rest of your life. If you find it does not suit you, you are free to try something else. I have not followed my father's business."

Harith stubbornly shakes his head. "I can't explain it. I know it is not reasonable, but I am not yet ready to apprentice with my father. I want to continue studying with you."

"I too am seeking knowledge." I drink down the last bit of coffee. "I am sure your father could provide you with much more than I."

"Only I can know where to seek the knowledge I need."

I look at Harith in admiration and put my arms around his shoulder, saying quietly, "Knowledge demands courage."

I am sadly thinking of myself.

When I arrive home after midday prayer, I enter a house filled with grief. All the women are crying. Aishah comes running to greet me and whispers, "Mother has died."

The news of her death is not a surprise, we had all anticipated it. Mother has been sick for several months. Still, a flood of emotions rises to the surface. I leave the women's courtyard and go upstairs to the gallery overlooking the fountain.

Everyone has congregated downstairs. Here, I am alone to walk the gallery and give myself to my grief in private.

I struggle with a vibrating mass of sorrow in my chest. My mother, who has given birth to me, has died. Now, at the age of thirty-five, I must look after my own evolution. Was it not always I who was responsible for that? Yet, I feel as if the umbilical cord has been cut a second time. I must step out into the world without fear. What is there to fear? Allah, tell me! By Your all-knowing grace, grant me the answer!

A cool wind caresses my tear-streaked cheeks. I look down into the courtyard and see my father standing still before the fountain. I can feel his grief. He must be particularly saddened by my mother's death since Saida, his first wife, has also died just a few months ago. Now Kinza is left alone to look after his needs.

The next day Sebastian, my mother's brother, arrives at our house; Sebastian who I have not seen since my grandfather's funeral. My father respects Sebastian's wishes to give my mother a Christian burial. My father well knows that is what my mother herself would have wished.

Once more, I find myself in the Christian cemetery. The air is filled with the ululation of the women of our household. This time, when the call of the muezzin rings through the high-pitched cries, I remain staring at the grave through my tears. I feel Sebastian glance at me. I do not have the energy to lift my head to meet his gaze.

As we walk back to the house, he puts his arms around my shoulders. "I will be staying at the monastery in the mountains for the rest of the week. Please, come and see me whenever you like."

A few days after the funeral, I take the donkey and head toward the mountains. The monastery has changed little since the last time I was here. I even recognize some of the same people.

Sebastian leads me into the dining room. It is empty now, well after the noonday meal. The stonewalls contain silence. We sit down at one of the long wooden tables near the wall. I smile at Sebastian. His hair is still the same color as mine with only a few white hairs around the edges. He looks slightly rounder than before and now delicate red lines etch his cheeks.

"You have become a man," Sebastian tells me. "The last time you were still a boy. You wear your maturity well."

I wonder what it takes to make a body into a man. Before I can verbalize my thought, Sebastian asks about my mother. He is suddenly curious about numerous aspects of her life. He asks questions I am unable to answer, and I suggest he have a chat with my father. Sebastian bends his head toward the table.

"I loved Catherine. I have not been able to stop thinking about her since receiving the news of her death. How little I know of her life! How little I know of who she became as a woman! I only remember the little girl of my childhood."

I press my palms together. "I remember her as my mother. I too know little else of her. I cannot say what she was like as a woman."

"How many facets are there to a person?" I wonder "After a lifetime you hardly know yourself, how can a lifetime be enough to know another person?" His fingers travel the smooth wooden surface of the table, back and forth, back and forth, slow, short trips parallel to the edge. He looks up at me. "How are you keeping, Sulayman?"

These days, every time someone asks about my state, I return to the same point. When will it be otherwise?

"Law is not giving me the answers I had once hoped to find."

Sebastian laughs, a sudden spurt that dies as quickly as it started. "I can say the same for my religious calling. I was hoping to feed my soul. Instead, I find myself entangled in the politics of religion. You would never expect politics in religion, would you? Politics in the house of God."

"Is it necessary to engage in those politics?" I ask.

"I am trying to disentangle myself." Sebastian hesitantly shakes his head from side to side. "I entered the political arena of religion thinking the issue was God. Instead, I find the people who claim to represent God want power over the soul. To achieve power, they suppress the soul with fear. How different is that from kings and queens who use fear to gain power over the body?"

"You must break away from the layers of dogma to reach God," I suggest. Will I ever be able to follow my own advice?

"I entered the order because I wanted to help men get closer to God. Recently, I feel as if I myself have lost touch. God seems so distant. Being here in the monastery is helping me to look into myself."

"Religion provides boundaries for the majority of people, boundaries within which to live. Those who seek more than the average need to reach beyond those borders. One must be brave to travel uncharted territory."

"But first one must see the borders in order to cross them."

"Yes, the faculty of sight must be trained," I say quietly.

We sit in silence, warmly smiling at each other. I reach across the table to put my hand over Sebastian's.

"We must never stop asking question, Sulayman."

Unfortunately, we are not always ready to listen to the answers, I think.

I visit Sebastian several times before he returns to Leon.

When he leaves, I feel as if a good friend has departed. Perhaps one day I will make the trip to visit him in Leon.

To my surprise, Jahm appears at one of my lectures. When I finish, Harith and Jahm are waiting for me. I present Jahm to Harith and the boy's face clouds over with jealous suspicion.

Amused, I explain to him that Jahm and I have been friends a long time. As the three of us walk out of the mosque, I notice Harith looks rather dejected. However, I must gently tell him that I would like to walk with Jahm alone, since we have not seen each other for a while. Harith, without another word, marches away from us.

Jahm softly laughs. I feel I must defend Harith but Jahm waves my words away.

"I am certain he is a good student," he says. "I have come to invite you on a trip into the mountains, to Ronda."

Coming from Jahm, this is an unusual invitation. "When?"

"In a few days."

"You know I have court in the mornings and I have my lectures."

"I am sure you can take off a week."

We walk through the main gate in front of the Roman bridge, past two severed heads impaled atop the gate.

"I don't know," I say quietly.

"It might prove a good experience. Nature has a surprising amount to offer if you are willing to spend the time to accept her gifts."

I still hesitate.

"Think about it," Jahm urges.

I do not have to think about it for long. Within days, Jahm and I are riding on donkeys through the mountains of al-Andalus.

The hills are more rugged toward the southwest. Golden stone is often visible through the green shrubbery. After several days of travel, we head into the valley where a wonderful expanse of smooth cultivated land appears before us. In the distance, the clouds sit between the hills adding a dreamlike quality to the landscape. We take the road between the fields and head straight into the clouds, around the hill.

Suddenly I halt the donkey in amazement. Just a short distance ahead of us, standing perpendicular, reaching toward the clear blue sky, is a gigantic reddish golden rock. The rock, engraved with vertical lines terraced to the top, sports a hat of green grass and trees looking absurdly small from our vantage point. A little further, along to the right of the trees, the walls of the city are visible. The walls and its fortifications look to be a continuation of the rock: they have been built from it, giving the whole a homogeneous, organic effect. At the very bottom of the rock is a little creek curling around it. Beside the creek stand several enchanting farmhouses with red-baked tile roofs. Such magnificent country! Such variety of landscape! I thank Allah for giving me the wisdom to accompany Jahm.

"Atop that rock is Ronda," Jahm announces. "The Romans built that city for fortification. You'll see there is a Roman bridge over a deep chasm connecting two rocks. Below the bridge runs the creek. Further down from the Roman bridge, connecting two other rocks, is the Arab bridge. The town is built in layers."

I follow Jahm as he leads his donkey around the rock where the land tapers down to farming lands. We climb a steep road.

Higher and higher. I feel as if I am ascending to heaven, past whitewashed houses, past Persian lilac trees in full bloom, past white and yellow jasmine bushes growing up the side of the rock.

An old fig tree with its large leaves swoops its branches toward the ground. We climb higher. I can now see the top of the minarets rise above the city walls. At last, we pass through the enormous wooden gate with its sharp brass studs.

"We'll leave the donkeys at the caravansary, and I'll take you to the highest point of the rock."

I am enchanted. Ronda is made up of several tall rocks standing close together. Houses, built of golden reddish stone, rise from the deep crevices of the rocks. Further down, on the vertical terraces of the rocks, are shrubs and trees leaning toward the running water below. Looking down into the distant water, into the darkness, I feel terror rising up. I quickly turn to the sky for reassurance. Jahm leads me to a lookout tower and takes me inside. We climb the tight stone circular staircase. At the top, we emerge onto a square landing, into bright sunlight. I gaze out, toward the landscape surrounding this enormous rock. My breath catches in the base of my throat. The rock goes down and down into the creek and rises again on the other side in the form of smaller rocks clothed in trees. Beyond the smaller rocks are the hills, rolling smoothly into the distance, carrying groves of olive trees, almond trees, plum trees, citrus trees. On they roll to eternity.

Jahm sweeps his arms through the air. "God is everywhere. He is the One Universal Spirit manifesting through infinity of forms. God is the spiritual seed planted in the dark womb of earth."

"You think Allah is a tree or a plant growing in the earth." I laugh.

"Sulayman, the earth is a symbol of the material universe."

"As everything material experiences growth, so too should the spirit blossom. The spirit should grow with the knowledge of its own divinity. That knowledge will give us immortality while our physical bodies will decay and die."

The valley flows before us. The beauty of Allah seduces me, tugging at my heart, urging me toward Him. I see the supreme balance of his creation, the supreme unity of the whole. How inadequate I feel! How insignificant in the face of such Divine beauty! I withdraw into myself, into the sad self-pitying darkness, into the deep crevice of the rock. Jahm notices my sudden shift in mood.

"You must look outward, upward. Allow yourself to grow into that Divine Spirit which we all carry within. See it. Know that you are much greater than your physical form."

"Sometimes I despair," I say in a barely audible voice. "Will I ever understand Allah through the practice of Justice?"

"Surely you know the answer to that."

I nod sadly. The law I practice is several layers removed from Divine Justice.

"Remember the end of Surah twenty-eight, 'All things will perish save His magnificence. His is the judgment, and to Him will you be brought back in the end.' That is Truth. You, I, all of us are a part of Him."

I nod. His words oppress me rather than lift me up.

We spend time in the baths, wander through the town, and sit atop rocks in prayer. Jahm ceaselessly talks of the importance of love: self-love, love of nature and humanity, universal love. Slowly, I allow myself to open. I feel myself grow larger. I touch the valley below and the translucent blue sky above. I expand from my center to embrace the One and weep tears of joy.

When the time comes to leave, and we descend into the hills, the expansion diminishes. Once more, I return to the smallness of my earlier life.

I have attended several Muslim funerals, a few Christian funerals, but this is my first Jewish funeral. Isaac, my father's partner and Esther's father, has died. I should hate the man for having withheld happiness from me. Yet, I carry no hate for him in my heart. I have grown to understand him, and my understanding kindles compassion.

The rabbi standing beside the grave chants the prayers in Hebrew. A large circle of friends and acquaintances, swaying in rhythm to the words of the rabbi, mourn among the tombstones. The emotions death evokes are the same no matter what one's beliefs. Do we mourn the person who has died or do we mourn ourselves? Can our difference evaporate in death? Do Christians no longer need idols? Do Jews no longer believe themselves to be the chosen ones? And Muslims? Does the Sunni and Shi'a controversy fall away? Does the jihad cease to be important? In death, do we all become One?

I visit Esther while she is sitting shivah. However, the women are in another part of the house. I manage to make contact with her in the passageway between the two courtyards. Her kohlless eyes are red and swollen. Her face is pale. I long to comfort her, to hold her.

"I must see you alone," she whispers, hoarse with tears.

"Meet me at the western entrance of the market after midday prayer in one week. And bring a donkey."

She leaves to rejoin the other women. The heavy pain she leaves lingering in the air evokes the deep inner well of my own grief. I long to dissolve this burden but events only continue to add to its weight.

Sitting sidesaddle, we make our way up the mountain. Esther is leading, determined. Our journey is made in virtual silence. I wonder why she has taken this chance: a married woman, alone with a man. Perhaps she needs an old friend's comfort at a time of such sorrow. We turn up a hilly road, lined by trees and bushes. Finally, we find a deserted clearing, far from people, from houses. She stops near a large, ancient cedar and ties her donkey to the trunk. She takes a beautiful green and gold brocade blanket from the back of the donkey, unfolds it, and spreads it under the tree. We settle down on the ground and look out through the crisscrossing of innumerable branches at the city below us. Medina al-Zahra, the caliphal residence, is to the north, the city stretches out to the south, toward the river. Hundreds of minarets reach toward the sky. It is a cloudless day of brilliant sunshine. The late morning has not yet reached unbearable heat; the air still holds the fresh coolness of the night. The leaves on the trees are still. The vegetation in the sunlight is scorched a pale yellow. An easy calm surrounds us. I can almost believe that nothing but this instant matters.

I look at Esther. She picks up a dry leaf from the ground and crumbles it to tiny bits in her palm. She carefully places the broken leaf at the thick base of the cedar. What can I say to her? Are there proper words? But proper words are currency between strangers. I reach over to caress her hair.

"The sadness will pass," I say.

"You are right. Sadness has a way of passing," she turns toward me, "as does happiness."

She bursts into sobs, hiding her face in the palms of her hands. I move close to her on the blanket and put my arms around her shoulders. She gently pushes me to lie down. For a long time we are still, her body pressed against mine, her face on my chest, her sobs slowly ebbing away. I remember my passion for her. I remember loving Naziha but seeing Esther in the darkness. Time passes. The searing heat begins to peek through the branches. Here, under the shade of the tree, it is still fresh. Esther raises herself on her elbow and leans close to my face. I make an effort to suppress my growing desire by concentrating on the lifeless body of her father.

"Sulayman, I want to obliterate this aching pain, this all consuming suffering. I want to wipe it away," she whispers.

"It will pass. You must have patience."

She pushes herself away from me. "Stop your logic. Logic is no good," she cries vehemently. "I loved my father. I loved him. He taught me everything I know. We talked long hours together about everything. We talked late into the night when most people in the house were already asleep. Who will I share my thoughts and ideas with now? I cannot talk to Simeon. Next to my father, you are the only other person I can talk to."

"Surely, Simeon is an intelligent man."

"Intelligent and condescending. Also, as I have slowly learned, limited. His intelligence does not soar. It moves at an even, lumbering pace." She remains quiet, staring up at the branches. "With the death of my father, I feel as if a part of me has also died."

I wipe the falling tears from her flushed cheeks.

"I am alive, Sulayman, but my inner self is disappearing."

Fury flames in her deep eyes. "Help me!" she cries. "You must help me. You are the only one."

She falls on top of my outstretched body, kissing my face, my lips. Her hands move inside my shirt, around my neck, shoulders.

I quickly grab her wrists and hold her. "No. Not now. Not like this, out of sorrow. You will regret it."

"Yes, now. I want my father to see us, to see that you are the one I come to, not Simeon, the proper respected doctor. It is your comfort I want, your warmth, not Simeon's."

She jerks her wrists from my hand and buries her face in my neck, her hands roaming my body. "Sulayman, do not refuse me," she whispers into my ear, kissing the lobes. "Do not refuse me. Love me."

I shut my eyes and feel her tears roll down my temples. I melt into Esther's desire, ignoring that what we are about to do would condemn us in the eyes of Muslim law. How often have I myself condemned people to the lash for fornication! How is it possible to refuse such deep desire? What extraordinary effort it would take for me to turn away now? How can the law compete with such forceful inner demands? I feel her curves, her skin. I caress, kiss, and taste the totality of her body. I stroke her suffering and lick her longing. We move through timelessness, space falling away around us, living the present in eternity.

IX. Lost

Foreign ambassadors stream in through all the gates of the city to pay their respects. Ululations are heard throughout the day. Men shed tears in the marketplace. Al-Andalus is paralyzed by shock at the news of al-Hakam II's death. I cancel my cases and lectures to mourn. I had expected al-Hakam to live much longer than his father. Abd al-Rahman III used to say that he had only sixteen days of peace during his long reign; to consolidate his empire, he was always engaged in battles either in the north, with the Christian territories, or in North Africa. Al-Hakam II's rule was much more stable and peaceful. He had every reason to live to a ripe old age.

Of course, my shock at his early death is due more to the realization that Hisham, his ten-year-old son, is now heir to the throne. What will a small boy do with such a powerful empire? The chamberlain, al-Mushafi, and the boy Caliph's steward, Ibn Abi 'Amir, are left in charge of Hisham's affairs. It takes little time before I hear that people within the Caliph's family are engaged in a fierce battle for the leadership of the empire. I can well understand why. Al-Hakam has left behind numerous paternal uncles and virile sons who would be infinitely more appropriate as the leader than Hisham. Every day brings fresh news of court intrigue. Fear and uncertainty quickly ripple through the city. Fortune-tellers predict the end of the Umayyad dynasty. Will al-Andalus become as unanchored as I feel right now? Has the empire also lost its way?

During supper one night, my father says, "The chamberlain and steward will rule in the boy's stead." He is clearly displeased at this idea. "Wait and see. That is everyone's prediction."

"Subh, the boy's mother, might hold the real power," adds Aishah.

"I predict a palace revolution," Husan offers.

He is right. People working within the government begin to split into angry factions. Numerous cadis, myself included, put their support behind al-Mughirah, al-Hakam's twenty-seven-year-old brother. The Caliph's Slav bodyguards are also on our side. I throw myself behind this political cause and forget all other concerns to do with law. My political affiliations and involvement in the future of the empire reveal new wells of energy within.

Suddenly, the news of al-Mughirah's death hits the streets. He has been murdered in the palace. Sources claim the murderers are Abi 'Amir, Hisham's steward, and al-Mushafi, the chamberlain. Some of the government officials who supported al-Mughirah are executed. New officials to accept Hisham woo the theologians, muftis, and cadis. Hisham only needs a few more years to reach an age where he could rule with competence, they say. Patience is part of Muslim tradition, they say. The Prophet himself, may God protect him, preached patience. What choice do I have? How can I hope to sway a whole government with just a few cadis? The political situation helped to take me out of myself for a short time. Now, I am once more confronted by my personal frustration.

Hisham is installed as the new Caliph. His first official action is to name his steward, Ibn 'Amir, the vizier. The theologians, muftis, and cadis all agree that for the moment, this is the best solution for al-Andalus. It means two mature men, Ibn 'Amir and al-Mushafi, will rule until the ten-year-old boy comes of age. People begin to breathe a little easier. Still, rumors continue to circulate. One says that Ibn Abi 'Amir, a ruthlessly ambitious man, is Subh's lover. I wonder if al-Hakam's weakness for Subh will also be shared by Ibn Abi 'Amir.

Some of us, suspicious of government events, keep a close eye on the palace situation. We note, with frustrated impotence, that Hisham is not being given a proper education, as befits a ruler. Instead, he is encouraged to occupy his time in meaningless enjoyments with boys and girls. Ibn Abi 'Amir begins to take more and more power into his own hands. The man quickly becomes commander of the army and declares one Holy War after another. Al-Hakam II favored negotiations and treaties; he avoided unnecessary fighting. Not Ibn Abi 'Amir—he must prove himself on the battlefield. *Naturally*, I think to myself, *the support of the army is an extremely powerful weapon and a virtual guarantee to power.* The man does not have a weakness for Subh; he is using her.

In one way, I envy him for his clarity, for recognizing his hunger and ruthlessly reaching to fulfill it. In another way, his failure to consider the consequences of his actions on a larger scale, his inability to see beyond his own personal, small needs, I find repelling, not to say very irresponsible. In addition, irresponsibility in the hands of a ruler bodes tragedy on a large scale.

There is constant movement of the army around the city walls; soldiers, cavalrymen, archers are either on their way to fight or are returning with an enormous amount of booty.

Inside the city, all opposition is ruthlessly purged and suppressed. Ibn Abi 'Amir rules al-Andalus with an iron hand. Some people, particularly the orthodox faction, agree with him. They say people must be given strict boundaries within which to operate. They now say al-Hakam II had allowed too much freedom to reign in the land. The voices of the orthodox theologians rise. I feel al-Hakam II had a natural confidence in his power. He was at ease in encouraging growth. Ibn Abi 'Amir must prove himself. He was not born to power; now that he has it, not by merit but by force, he must hold on at all cost. Oppression is a favorite weapon of the insecure.

Ibn Abi 'Amir ravages Salamanca. He then goes against Ramiro II of Leon and returns victorious. As the soldiers parade through the city, leading Christian captives who pull cartfuls of valuable plunder, the people welcome them with thunderous cheer. Ibn Abi 'Amir is gaining in popularity: among the people and among the army.

Jahm predicts that the man's rule will be the end of al-Andalus. He says that nothing gained dishonestly could bring fortune. Ibn Abi 'Amir has usurped power. In the short term, the political situation could look positive, but the price of his dishonesty will claim its toll. I agree with him.

In the year 366/977, Ibn Abi 'Amir leads a successful expedition into Galicia. The battle yields great booty. The army loves him because he has rewarded them handsomely. I spend long periods of time observing and analyzing his ruling technique. I am astounded by how the man's every action supports his personal ambition. He is buying the army's loyalty through generosity. He is also seducing the people of Cordoba. He is distracting them from internal politics, by forcing them to admire his external military exploits. To further cement his power, Ibn Abi 'Amir marries General Ghalib's daughter. In time, the news reaches the streets that Ghalib, and Ibn Abi 'Amir have charged al-Mushafi with treason and thrown him in prison.

However, Ibn Abi 'Amir still does not feel secure. He now invites Berber soldiers to join his army. The man has mistrusted the Slav soldiers ever since he learned of their allegiance to al-Hakam's brother. Neither does he trust the Arabs. Only the Berbers will accept his position unconditionally. I am amazed at the man's systematic logic. Systematically, he is building a tight foundation, but it is a foundation for his power, not for the future of al-Andalus.

Increasingly, Berbers are brought over from North Africa. Al-Hakam II had only accepted a few hundred equestrians. Now the face of the army goes through a complete transformation.

The city of Cordoba is also changing. Scholars are leaving. I cannot fault them. I too feel an invisible shroud tighten around my brain. Before law only frustrated me; now my frustration extends to various other areas of my life. I am no longer allowed to express my ideas to my students as freely as before.

Ibn Abi 'Amir grows so powerful that he begins to build al-Zahira, his own palace. However, he is still not secure in his power. The orthodox theologians have only given him their reserved support. After all, he is but a common man. Only the Caliph has the right to represent the faith of Allah.

In an attempt to prove his worthiness, Ibn Abi 'Amir begins to copy out the Qur'an by hand. I laugh at his obviously contrived efforts, but the theologians murmur their approval. They also murmur their disapproval of some of the books in al-Hakam II's 400,000-volume library. To appease their concern, the man gathers all the volumes dealing with philosophy, speculative religion, and astrology. I am aghast; this is nearly half the content of the library!

I watch, with the rest of a large crowd, as books are carted down to the foot of the Roman bridge, wheelbarrows upon wheelbarrows overturn their contents of magnificent parchment. An enormous pile grows and grows. Ibn Abi 'Amir orders his Berber soldiers to throw their torches upon the pile of manuscripts. Dead silence hangs in the air. As soon as the torches touch the parchment, a threatening sizzle burns through the stillness. The books catch fire. The gray smoke rises high into the cloudy sky. The books burn and burn and burn.

I sob, mesmerized by the horror. Shihab, standing beside me, notices a book he has read several times during his student years. It was a particular favorite of 'Abdallah. He too begins to cry. I look at the dense crowd. Everyone's eyes are glazed over with tears, whether from the heat of the fire or from distress is hard to discern. A hush has descended over the city. The power of the flame grows; its crackling dance is powerfully hypnotic. No one moves.

The next day, when I go to the mosque, the ambers are still smoldering.

The cadi and mufti express approval of this act. They have always felt the philosophical books endangered belief. The Divine word cannot be questioned. How could I have expected them to respond differently? I am all too familiar with their bias.

Jahm insists that politics are not to be trusted, nor can the theologians who claim to hold the key to Islam. Disgusted with the current situation, he disappears for several months. Upon his return, he talks about his ecstatic visions while sitting under the stars by the river. He rhapsodizes about the beauty of God. One day, as we are walking through the covered market, Jahm looks around and declares that the people need help.

"Fear is totally contrary to the love of Allah. People cannot honestly love Allah yet fear his creation," he says.

More and more scholars are leaving. There are fewer students from distant lands coming to seek knowledge in Cordoba. Harith has left to join his father. I was sorry to see him go. Now, mostly Berber pupils come to my lectures. When I ask them questions, they remain silent. The Berbers follow the word of the Qur'an literally. Most have recently converted to Islam, and they express a nearly fanatical belief in the religion. I begin to lose interest in my lectures.

In court, I find I must deal with more and more cases of heresy. This is a very new experience for me. During the time of al-Hakam II, I never had a case of heresy come before me. I know the police dealt with the odd case, but no more than a handful over a period of several years. Now I see about one case a week. These cases of heresy drag me to even deeper depths of despair. I watch myself perform a task as if I were watching another. I have become numb to the world. No one can rouse me, not even Naziha. As I lie awake in the blackness of night, a faint inner voice urges, "You must find the door. You must wake up and step out."

I am suffocating in my own inertia.

Jahm has decided to bring his knowledge to the people. He regularly preaches in the marketplace, in the little square at the end of the street of booksellers. I often stop by to listen. He is a surprisingly good orator, passionate conviction rings in his voice. Over a period of several weeks, his reputation blossoms. Witnessing the fire of his delivery kindles a tiny spark of hope within. I am grateful for his friendship.

One day, as I am eating a handful of dates and listening to Jahm, I feel restlessness in the crowd that I had never detected before. Palpable tension sits in the air. I look around in an attempt to find its source. A number of police are standing near one wall. It is the first time I have seen them here.

"Allah is in everyone and everything," Jahm's voice rings out. "He is the Universal Spirit infusing all with the Divine Essence. He is above us, below us, on every side of us, as well as within us."

"Heresy!" cries a young man standing on the sidelines with a group of his friends.

"He manifests in an infinite variety of forms," continues Jahm in the same clear, gentle voice.

"God is One!" chants another group of young men, also standing on the sidelines.

The crowd is getting tenser, noisier. People shout angry exchanges. Restlessness ferments under the sun.

"He is the essence that unites us all with All," continues Jahm looking into the crowd, heedless of the growing rage. "Everyone and everything shares in the Divine Nature of Allah. Within us we all contain that Divine seed. Only by looking within will we discover All."

Groups of young men begin to chant, "God is One!" Two of them, with arms flaying, fingers curled in outraged indignation, shove their way through the crowd toward Jahm. As soon as they reach him, they grab at his clothes, tear into his flesh. Horrified, I immediately force my way through angry and panicked bodies, desperate to reach Jahm. Suddenly, a sharp pain paralyses me. I see a bloody line run down my arm, cutting through my clothes, my flesh. The police, flicking their whips, enter the crowd. I double over in pain, dropping to the ground on my knees. People, in a rush to leave the scene, trip over me. I fall and lose consciousness.

By the time I open my eyes, the square is nearly deserted. The stones on the ground are stained with blood. Immobile bodies are being thrown onto carts. Clutching my arm, I force myself to stand up and move away to sit on a nearby bench. What happened to Jahm? I berate myself for not having been strong enough to help him, to protect him.

A couple of days later, as I am holding court in the mosque, a policeman leads Jahm toward me. Close behind them follow three well-dressed men. Jahm, dirty with scabs all over his face and body, happily smiles at me. A sense of dread takes hold. The police officer, pointing to the men behind him, identifies them as the plaintiff, accusing Jahm of heresy, and two witnesses. I am to judge the case. My throat and stomach tighten. The peaceful look in Jahm's eyes is in total contrast to my inner turmoil. I bid the police officer to come closer.

I stand up by my bench, pull myself to my full height, and glare down at him. "Why are you bringing this case here?" I hiss. "Why are you not handling it in your own courts?"

The anger in my voice surprises him. "Jahm al-Din asked to have his case judged by you specifically."

"By me?" I echo in disbelief. I crumple back down on my bench. "How can you possibly expect me . . . ?" My voice is barely audible. I turn to Jahm, silently pleading. Total trust faces my fear.

"The case is clear," explains the police officer. "It is a clear judgment and the man does not protest it. There is no need for our courts."

Wasil takes down the names of all concerned. The plaintiff is called to present his case. My anguish has blocked out sound. I hear only snippets of the testimony. Jahm is a pantheist . . . splinters the Absoluteness of Allah . . . a danger to the population, to honest Muslims . . .

"You fools, you understand nothing!" I silently shout, outrage pounding in my head. "Jahm is a much truer believer and loves Allah with infinitely greater passion than any one of you."

Next, the witnesses come forward to testify to the uprightness of the plaintiff. Meaningless words drone on. Then it is Jahm's turn. I become alert.

"Everything said has an element of truth," he says calmly.

Desperate to hold back the inevitable, I plead, "Have you no wish to protect yourself? Explain to them . . ."

The counselors put a hand on my arm to quiet me. My talking to a prisoner in this way is very inappropriate to my position. I silently beg him with my eyes. Jahm smiles, calm, confident. Flaring anger and helplessness battle within.

The counselors, Wasil, and I take a short time to confer. They all agree that the case is clear and Jahm is a danger to Islam. He must be stoned to death as a heretic. How can I defend him? I can say nothing to sway the judgment. Jahm has sealed his own fate by refusing to counter the accusation of heresy.

I am sweating. Is this truth? The process of law is heretical, not Jahm. Fools! All of them, fools! I glare at Jahm in anger. "Do you have anything more to say?"

"You're sitting in the seat of tradition." He smiles. "You must follow its dictates."

"The case is clear," yells an angry onlooker. "The man must die."

The crowd stirs, craving an execution. The police crack their whips in the air for silence.

Suddenly numb, my long familiarity with legal proceedings helps me to mechanically continue. "According to Muslim law, you have committed an inadmissible sin for which you will be stoned to death." My voice is dead to my ears. I motion to the police officer who brought him.

The man nods in satisfaction. "I told you it was a clear case. Now he is mine."

No, now he is truly Allah's, I think.

Before leaving, I tell Wasil and the counselors I do not want to hold court the next day. I quickly move to a dark corner of the courtyard, lean against the cool stonewalls, and heave up everything in my stomach. My tears blend with the partially digested food on the ground. My body shakes with a violent desire to vanish, evaporate into oblivion.

After prayer, I stay in the mosque a long time. Through prolonged meditation, I try to ease the aching pain in my chest.

I go to the hermitage and ask to see the Sheykh privately. As I am about to open my mouth to talk, my vocal chords cease to function and an enormous dam bursts open. I drop to my knees, cover my face with my hands, and bend toward the ground, sobbing with a force that promises to obliterate me. The Sheykh sits before my bent and trembling figure in silence. Time passes.

Exhaustion brings calm. At last, I uncurl my body, take the hands from my wet face, and stare at the tiled wall before me. Its blue and yellow design is out of focus. I shut my eyes tightly, squeezing out the tears. I open them again. The design is clearer. I shift my gaze to the Sheykh sitting on the cushion, fingering the rosewood rosary in his lap. His eyes hold depths of eternity.

"Jahm will be stoned for heresy," I rasp.

He nods without emotion.

"I was the judge."

He nods again.

"Jahm is not a heretic," I say, raising my voice in anger. "What kind of law is this that forces cadis to pass such a judgment? Against all logic."

He nods again, tranquility surrounding him.

"Where is justice?" I yell. "I killed Jahm. In my search for Truth, I killed the closest friend I had."

"No, Sulayman, it was written."

"Why did I have to be the one to pass the judgment?" I cry. "He asked to be judged by me. He must have thought I could save him."

"Only Allah can save him. Jahm knows this."

I shake my head violently.

"And who are you to say that Allah has not saved him through your judgment?" he says in an exquisitely gentle voice.

Tears again begin to flow. Sobbing once more shakes my shoulders.

"You delivered him to Allah," I hear the Sheykh say.

I walk the banks of the river, staring at the ripples on the surface of the water. In the distance, I hear church bells ringing. A little later, I hear the call of the muezzin, "God is most great! God is most great! I testify there is no deity but God! . . . Come to prayer! Come to security! . . . There is no deity but God!"

I walk, no longer feeling my legs. They move of their own accord—one foot after the other. The river flows, merrily gurgling. I walk. And walk. The sun is sinking lower and lower. The light fades. I walk past summer cottages along the banks. I walk. Darkness descends. I can no longer see the water. I only hear its sound. I walk slower. And grow weaker. I fall to my knees on the grass and lie down in its moist softness. Through the dark leaves and branches, I see the stars. Consciousness fades, slowly disappearing into the depth of the river, the waves flowing over it, cleansing it.

I have done a terrible injustice. By passing the sentence of death, I have hidden behind the words of the law to support the community's insecurity. To the community, only an official interpretation of Allah is acceptable. Mercy and love, both words used by the Prophet, are hardly mentioned, much less practiced. Mercy and love would threaten the existing power structure. Fear of losing power insists on narrow confines. It is fear that is evil.

I have committed a double injustice; an injustice toward Jahm by passing the death sentence and an injustice toward myself for passing a sentence I do not espouse.

In two days time, I appear before the chief cadi of Cordoba. The first time I saw him I was twenty-four years old and had begged him to excuse my reckless behavior. I assured him of my sincerity in studying to become a judge. Now I am forty, and I hand him my resignation.

X. Hermitage

Soon after I resign as a judge, in the Muslim year of 370, 980 for the Christians, the new palace of Ibn Abi 'Amir, just to the northeast of the river, is completed. Its grandeur equals, though many say surpasses, Medina al-Zahra. Hisham, along with his mother Subh, are left in the caliphal palace in virtual imprisonment. All government activity moves down from the mountains to the river; from high ground to low ground. Foreign ambassadors no longer make their way toward the mountains. Instead, they head toward the river to pay homage to the ruler.

The political situation of the day heralds doom. Though I am helpless in the face of external events, I can no longer remain idle in my personal search for the Truth. I must gather the strength to face myself. Now that I am fully aware that written law will never allow me a glimpse of the answer, now that I have purged all possible hope that law might still contain a glimmer of the real Truth, I must turn in another direction. I must have the courage to follow my search no matter what it takes or where it might lead. My mind gains new clarity.

Looking back, it is clear that all events have aligned themselves to urge me in one direction. I must obey the call. In preparation, I organize my affairs. Once more, I grant Naziha her freedom. I offer her a choice; I can either arrange a marriage for her with an honorable man or give her money to return to her own country and set up a small business of her choice. After a few days of tears and reflection, she tells me she prefers to return to the home of her birth. A dull pain grows in my heart.

Once she sets sail from al-Andalus, I know I will never see her again. She has been a constant companion who has given me considerable comfort and joy. I will miss her greatly, but I know there is no room for her in the next phase of my life. The next phase I must enter alone. Accepting my inevitable grief, I help her pack and give her several servants for the trip. They set off on donkeys toward Almeria. From there, they will sail across the sea and continue with camels on land to their final destination.

"You must follow your heart, my son," my father says in the library, tears filling his eyes.

Logically my father understands what I must do. Emotionally, he is filled with sorrow. I too feel tremendous grief knowing I will leave the house that has provided me with support and love throughout my life. I also know that what I now need can only come from a source quite different from the world I have known to date.

I go to the Great Mosque to pray. After prayer, I remain sitting on the mat. People return for the next prayer, and I still have not moved. Time passes. I lose awareness of my physical reality. I am of my body but no longer feel it. I am in a mosque but no longer see its physical limits. I have entered a world of weightlessness, timelessness . . .

After the fourth prayer of the day, I leave the mosque. My feet carry me across the Roman bridge and along the road beside the river until I reach the hermitage. I present myself to Sheykh Mundhir al-Shirazi and prostrate myself before him.

"Sit down," he tells me. "Do not embarrass me with such a posture."

I sit down on one of the cushions against the wall. Time passes in silence. The wooden rosaries shift in his hand.

Finally I say, "I want to be a Sufi."

"Why?"

"Being a judge has not taught me the Truth."

The Sheykh gently laughs. "Wanting to know the Truth is not enough. Wanting is a need arising from your lower self. You must submit to the Truth. You must let your conscious self go. If God is willing, He will allow you to glimpse His Divine Reality."

"I am ready to do whatever is necessary."

"You must first be willing to die." He smiles.

"To die?"

"Yes, you must die . . . before you die."

I sink into silent incomprehension.

Sheykh Mundhir calmly gazes at me. "A bird cannot fly carrying his nest," he says. "You must be ready for the Mystic Path of the Sufi before embarking upon the journey."

"I will do whatever you say."

"The length of time it takes to be ready varies with the individual," he says softly.

"I will dedicate whatever time is required."

In silence, his fingers slowly pass over three round, shiny rosary beads.

"You must first learn service," he says. "Before you can serve God, you must learn to serve men. If you desire, you may be a servant here at the hermitage."

When his words penetrate my consciousness, the shock of their meaning immediately straightens my back. The Sheykh registers my sudden movement and smiles.

A servant leads me upstairs, along the gallery and into a room with four beds.

"You will share this room with myself and two other seekers," he tells me and leaves.

I sit down on the bed and take the Qur'an I have brought with me from my pocket. I lay it on the floor beside the bed. I lie down and allow exhaustion to wash over me. At last, deep sleep and dreams overtake me.

Wrestling a forceful wind gusting around me, I struggle over rocky terrain. I climb large boulders and scuffle with sharp bushes. The wind loudly screeches in its effort to dislodge everything from the earth. Grabbing onto a tree trunk for a short rest I strain to look through the whirlwind of sand hoping to see into the distance. Far away, I can just make out an island of palm trees around a small, clear lake. I once more fight my way through the wind in an effort to reach this calm distant paradise. Suddenly a large snake rises up before me, blocking my path. It comes closer and closer, forming a circle around my legs. The orange, black, and white rings around its body slowly undulate as it moves. Its head begins to casually slither up my trousers. My instinct is to jump away. However, my body is paralyzed. The snake is now curled around my right leg and making its way higher and higher up my body till finally its large head is level with my own. With dispassionate clarity, it looks me straight in the eye. Its forked tongue flickers in and out of its mouth, trying to convey a message. Its thick body is now firmly curled around my waist and chest. I continue looking into eyes of crystalline depth. My fear subsides. I begin to walk again, carrying the snake with me. I once more turn my gaze outward to the island of palm trees. I climb over rocks until I get to an open space. Now only a stretch of sand lies between the island and myself. I look to either side of me and notice a large caravan of camels heading in the same direction. The men riding the camels turn around and see me. They change their direction and begin to head toward me. The camels, walking through the sand kicking up clouds of dust, pick up speed. I know they are about to attack me. I look down at my body thinking the snake will be my protection. It is no longer there. The camels are getting closer and closer. I cannot move. How can I run away and abandon my island? No, I must face the danger. I must reach the island at whatever cost. The riders have drawn their swords and are about to bear down on me. Suddenly, everything snaps to black.

My eyes fly open. At first, I do not know where I am. I turn my head and see the servant asleep beside me. Then I remember.

I spend my days cleaning house, washing clothes, helping in the kitchen, and serving the members of the hermitage. At first, I grit my teeth with every menial task. Could this subservient position lead me to the Truth? I feel as if I am sinking. I no longer have a clear view of myself. My pride rebels. "I am a judge," I insist to the other servants. They smile in response and continue on their way. "I am a judge," I yell in silence. People respect me! They seek my advice! Doubt racks my being. Why have I come to the hermitage? Can I trust the wisdom of the Sheykh? I allow myself to play with the idea of returning home. I can always join the family business. I need not continue in law.

One day I am in the kitchen minding a big copper pot of bubbling liquid set upon an open fire. A number of vegetables are lying on the wooden table beside the stove. A big purple eggplant with its shiny skin catches my attention. I steal a quick glance around me. I am alone, everyone seems to have left. I pick up the eggplant, feeling its weight in the palm of my hand. I curl stiff fingers around its smooth skin and squeeze its body. My grasp tightens until my nails penetrate its purple cloak, bursting open the pale flesh, revealing the seeds of its insides. I clench my fist around its mutilated body and rub the soft, yellow flesh between my fingers. Waking with a start, as if from a dream, I stare at the bruised and now useless eggplant. I put it close to my face and lick its bitter moisture.

Can servility lead me closer to the Truth? I struggle with my doubts, my longings, and my fears. *Courage*, whispers a small voice within. *Courage.*

"Patience nurtures courage," says the Sheykh.

Weeks become months.

On my hands and knees, I pull the wet, soap-soaked rag along the marble paving of the courtyard. It is the middle of the day, and the summer sun floods over me. I sit up to rest. My eyes are drawn to the fountain. The clear water gushes upward then falls down, creating ripples upon the surface of the water. The ripples move outward, causing the water lilies to sway. Lightness fills my heart. I turn back to the rag, lying on the pink marble ground, and continue to clean. The courtyard begins to sparkle. No corner escapes my attention. Every spec is removed. I want people entering this courtyard to marvel at its beauty.

I serve the Sheykh and his disciples supper. I smile at each one in turn, as I place the vegetables and lentils on the table. Then I stand back and watch them eat the food I had helped to prepare. My humble pleasure brings lightness.

At the end of the meal, I gather up the dishes. Cradling them in my arms, I carry them to the kitchen. I return to the dining room bearing plates of figs and dates. Lovingly I place them on the table. I desire to do more for these people, to serve their every whim. I am ready to jump at any command, ready to make every wish a reality. I will work day and night to give pleasure, to make the members of the hermitage comfortable. Joy rises. I want to serve the world. My heart opens, ready to do the bidding of all.

Darkness has long covered the light. Alone, under the brilliant stars, I sit in the courtyard and pray to Allah. The verses of the Qur'an pass through my mind the way the falling water passes into the pool. The verses recede from my consciousness. In the foreground, I see that Truth is not to be understood by intellect alone. The intellect is but one path, one level, with a limited capacity for comprehension. The Truth is much, so much larger. How could I have hoped words would lead me to the Truth? The Truth is not translatable. Truth is not to be comprehended by sense alone. Truth is Absolute and Eternal. Words are a human form of expression; words could never define Divinity. The essence of God must be experienced.

I continue to sit in the courtyard, the verses of the Qur'an carrying my deeper consciousness higher and higher toward the infinity of the night. When dawn brings the chant of the muezzin, the call penetrates my being with greater significance than ever before.

"God is most great! God is most great! God is most great! God is most great!" The sound reverberates toward the dark sky just beginning to be shot through with the rays of the first light.

While buying provisions at the market for the hermitage, I learn that Ibn Abi 'Amir has invaded Leon, sacked Zamora, and has returned with a rich booty of slaves, church bells, and treasures. Cordoba gave him such an enthusiastic welcome that he grew brave enough to declare himself al-Mansur, the victorious, and has ordered his name mentioned at Friday prayers after that of the Caliph. He has also announced that the new coins to be minted will bear the name of al-Mansur. Now that he has dared to raise himself to the same level as the Caliph, he has also ordered all the courtiers to kiss his hand in greeting, as they would do if they were to meet Hisham.

I marvel at people's struggle for such ephemeral gains. They grasp at material reality not realizing everything physical must decay. Few see a larger picture than their own private concerns. Having spent the past year at the hermitage, I can now remove myself from the affairs of the physical world and see it at a distance.

For years, Ibn Abi 'Amir has persistently courted Cordoba with conquered territories, booty of riches, and feigned piety. Gradually the population was seduced, blinded by false grandeur, and they could not see that the newly proclaimed al-Mansur was putting an end to the Umayyad caliphate and the Umayyad family that originally founded al-Andalus. It has taken nearly three hundred years to build al-Andalus into the center of the world. How long will it take al-Mansur to destroy it?

Already the atmosphere of Cordoba has lost its vibrancy. Its spices are no longer as intoxicating. The conversations I overhear in the market regard commerce. There are no more passionate arguments about philosophical ideas. The street of booksellers has become smaller. Fewer books are being sold. Staidness sits heavy in the air.

Humbly I enter the room, awaiting the Sheykh's words. I silently stand before him, my hands at my side, my head bowed toward the floor, waiting. He sits on the cushions, rosary in hand. I am ready to do his bidding. I am ready to bring his tea, to wash his feet and his clothes, whatever he might ask.

"Sulayman, sit down," he says gently.

Expecting an order, I am surprised by this invitation. Awkwardly I take a cushion opposite him.

"You have been in servitude for a year now. What have you learned?"

"In this physical world, there is no person lower or higher than I. The highest and most absolute is Allah."

"And now, what do you desire?"

"The Truth. I see now that I must experience the Truth, to know it in totality."

"Why do you desire the Truth?"

I hesitate. Never have I asked myself why. I flounder. "I want to sense, to feel, to understand the totality. I want to see a pattern in the whole. I . . . I . . . I can hardly explain. I feel an aching desire . . ."

The Sheykh moves the prayer beads between his fingers and allows the silence to resettle before speaking again.

"You no longer need to serve," come the soft words. "You will spend a month fasting, in silence and meditation. Then you may emerge from the fast and silence but you must continue your meditations. Focus on extinguishing every lower, human desire. Whenever you observe within you jealousy, resentment, anything resembling human emotion, you obliterate it. Allow love for the Absolute to grow and fill your heart. Human emotions are but veils that keep you from God. The veils must be lifted. All earthly characteristics along the journey of total love must fall away. Attachment to this physical world must disappear."

I nod and nod trying to memorize his words. I do not fully understand their meaning, but I want to remember the words because I will repeat them to myself later. I will repeat them repeatedly until their meaning attains clarity.

"You are about to undertake the pilgrimage of your life," he continues, "a pilgrimage toward the Divine."

I move into another room, on the other side of the gallery. I am alone here. "The path is lonely," the Sheykh had explained. "You need to learn solitude."

I sit on my bed day after day battling the gnawing hunger in my stomach. I scratch my legs until they bleed, desperately wanting to distract my attention from the hunger. Extinguish the human desire! I must not focus on the hunger. By focusing on it, I give it more strength. However,

I must not obliterate the hunger with pain because that replaces one sensation with another. I pick up my Qur'an and open it. Its golden letters etched on the parchment form a delicate pattern.

"Everything upon the earth passeth away, save His face." (55;26) *Yes, we will all pass away*, I think. People, animals, plants are born and then die. The one common denominator of the physical world is birth, growth, and death. In this cyclical change is unity. Then there is the Absolute Unity, which exhibits no change. Truth never passes away.

" . . . everything is perishable but He; He is the judgment, and to Him you shall be brought back." (28;88) Through our death, we are reborn. Through our death, we become part of the Absolute Unity. We fall from Unity to diversity. In this diversity, there is a cyclical unity of change. This diversity mimics the eternal Unity. The physical world, in its diversified form, reflects the possible perfection of a higher order, the Absolute order. If we are fallen from above, we contain a little of the Absolute within. It is my Divine Essence, swimming in the murky depths of the sea, hidden by the debris of earth, that I must find, clean, and lift up into the light.

For days on end, my head is bent toward the pages of the Qur'an, my eyes following the letters, the words, and the glistening gold. The pages turn. The letters take shape then float up into the air. My room dances with verses of gold. My breathing deepens and slows. My eyes no longer see the letters, only the patterns they form on the page. I grow enamored by the beauty of the golden pattern, occasionally interspersed with touches of turquoise and ocher. The pattern moves and dances before my eyes. The flowing lines braid, unbraid, and rebraid. The golden braid playfully dances out the door. I follow it to the gallery and watch it undulate toward the sky, toward the sun. The golden braid joins the flaming globe to become one with All.

Tears wet my face. I return to the room and lie on the bed, flat on my back. My soul burns with exquisite pleasure as I float up and up, no longer touching the physical. My body is disintegrating, moving apart to become a part of a much, much larger whole, to encompass a Beauty of Eternal magnitude, to cradle all creation and lift it toward its Creator.

I am swimming in my tears. I will disappear to be reborn in totality. My floating self reacquires its weight and begins to sink downward, downward to earth, to my bed, into the physical world. Now I know why the Greeks called the physical world hades, the lowest form of reality. I can fall no lower than my dense, material form.

I struggle to regain the experience of floating. I fight a desperate fight. I plead with God to allow me once more to join Him. There is no reply. I remain earthbound.

"Tell me how I can return? Please help me," I plead with the Sheykh.

"You must not want it. You must be content with what God gives you. You must be grateful for His gifts and not expect more than He is willing to give. You must have patience. You must trust. Surrender."

Do not fight! Do not struggle! Do not be bitter! How hard it is to trust! I can give up wealth. I can serve my fellow men. I can open my heart to creation and love the dry blades of grass in the summer heat. However, how can I give up the light of God once He has revealed it to me? How can I not want it? Desire it . . . long for it?

I let myself go to the routine of contemplation. I focus on detaching from emotions that present themselves. I cultivate serenity. I open my heart and give myself up to Eternal Wisdom. I, who used to devour books and ideas, now look toward the indefinable.

At times, I fall into despair. How difficult it is to maintain the attitude of absolute surrender! It is so hard for my lower self not to meddle, to creep up when least expected and present its demands. Just when I think I have succeeded in disciplining it, it tiptoes back, teasing, bragging, and insisting on attention—laughing at my efforts.

The Sheykh smiles at my desperate pleas. "You must concentrate your energies. You must learn to focus. When your lower self intrudes, remember to look in your heart. You carry the Divine Essence within."

"There is such a battle . . ." I begin, stopping in frustration.

"Pay no attention to those battles for if you give them your attention, the battles will escalate. Do not look at the battlefield of your mind but focus on your heart."

"The power of concentration required is often so difficult to harness," I reply hopelessly.

"To sharpen your concentration, practice reading only one verse of the Qur'an throughout the day and into the night," he replies. "Repeat it over and over to yourself and watch how many meanings of that one verse will be revealed. Only through focused concentration will the meanings come alive."

His gentleness soothes my fears.

I walk to the nearest hill and sit on top overlooking the landscape to the south and the city to the north. I breathe in the sweet air. I sit down under a tree and focus inward.

Slowly, my consciousness drifts toward oblivion. Change means giving over to progression, to a fuller realization of the essence. Change is needed to reach purity. Change is needed for perfection. See all things as one. Any one could become the other. Any one could transform into the other because each holds the seed of all in the body of one.

The Absolute, Perfection, contains all and all contains the Absolute, Perfection. All contains the potential, the possibility to Become.

All is One. One is All.

I am one in All.

I know it in my head; I comprehend it logically. I do not feel it with the totality of my being. I do not experience it with my heart.

Night has fallen. I descend into the valley and make my way back to the hermitage.

One night a man who plays the flute comes to visit the hermitage. Carpets are laid down on the pink marble floors of the outer courtyard. Everyone sits down, ready to listen. Intricately worked bronze lanterns throw delicate designs of light on the scene. Someone closes the fountain. The falling water trickles to a stop. The swaying water lilies settle down. All ears open to listen.

Suddenly the flute emits a high note, commanding focused attention, calling toward the sky. Then silence. Gradually, a calm, even rhythm is introduced. I grow relaxed. Slowly, almost unnoticeably, the speed builds; the pace quickens growing faster and faster, increasingly urgent. I become alert, rising to a higher plane, rushing forward. I rise and rise on the notes. Rays of light infuse the black night.

The music abruptly stops followed by the purity of silence.

Once more soft, delicate chords enter the night. They reach a valley and maintain an even pace of melodic composition. Sweet rhapsody. Gentle caressing. Fragrant jasmine plays with the breeze. The leaves of the olive trees shimmer in the moonlight. Graceful calla lilies dance in ponds. I rest in one place, absorbed in the choreography of creation. The notes dip lower and lower, deeper and deeper.

A high note is introduced! I rise from my peaceful dance, alert. A cluster of high notes builds to a nimble rhythm, urging movement. Once more, I rise and rise, higher and higher. The intensity increases, promising all, pointing the way to eternity. With fluid lyricism, the rhythm stretches to longing. My rise comes to a soft stop. The longing cries out in agony. It recedes to a moan. The notes talk of desire. The notes talk of bliss and union, of forgetting and knowing. They reach higher and higher.

Once more, they burst into wild energy. Unleashed, there is no stopping the ascent. A dance of joy fills the air. The notes play with the stars. The blackness, infused by light, disappears to leave gold. I float on the rays of warmth and love.

The music comes to an abrupt stop. Silence falls. For a seemingly long time, no one speaks. The Sheykh walks over to the musician. He leans down to say something. The two men burst into soft laughter.

I am unaware of time. On my lips is the name of Allah. I desire only to glimpse His Beauty. His name flows from me without effort. My surroundings grow dimmer and dimmer. I no longer feel the floor beneath me. Food is of no importance. I roam among the stars. I visit the moon and help the rising of the sun. I kiss the clouds and caress the translucent blue sky.

Suddenly, my body begins to shake uncontrollably. Clouds burst. I open my eyes and see one of the disciples clutching my shoulders, his face contorted in an expression of intense effort.

"The Sheykh would like to see you," he says in a voice barely audible.

I head down the stairs into the courtyard. My legs feel weak since I have not used them in what seems like a very long time. My muscles are uncertain whether they can carry the weight of my body and any moment threatens to collapse. Is this what babies feel like when they first begin to use their legs? Downstairs, I wobble into the reception room with great effort. The Sheykh nods toward me with a smile and motions me to sit down near him. I collapse onto the cushion.

"The time has come for me to give you a task," he announces without ceremony. "You must now go in search of a hidden treasure. You must find the Philosopher's Stone."

I am not certain I have heard right. "The Philosopher's Stone?"

"Also known as Philosophical Gold."

"Yes. Of course." Not only is my body weak but my mind seems to have also acquired a softness. I try to remember everything I have heard of the Philosopher's Stone. I can recall very little. "But how is that possible?" Confusion replaces the serenity of a short while ago.

"In order to find this, you must leave the hermitage," he says.

My head feels heavy; my legs ache. "How must I begin?"

"You concentrate. You have learned to concentrate here at the hermitage. Concentration is the first step toward the answer. It will take time. Patience is another ingredient to success."

I bow my head toward the tiled floor. Fear born of bewilderment rises from my stomach. I look up at the Sheykh.

"Must I leave?" I ask in more despair than I had thought possible.

"If a bird dies in a cage, he has died in captivity, and perhaps has never discovered how high he could soar," he replies softly.

"Where will I go? Back to my father's house?"

"You will go wherever your legs take you. You will travel and talk to other people. To find the stone you must search."

"Then I will have to ask my father for money to travel."

"No. You have served the members of this hermitage. Now allow the world to serve you. Remember, a bird is content with whatever crumb he finds on the ground."

"You mean, I must beg?" Horror is evident in my voice.

"If necessary, yes."

XI. The Journey

After the first prayer of the day, I pack my scant belongings, including the gold printed Qur'an. Reluctantly and with a dreadful ache in my body, I turn toward the hills. Daylight is just beginning to break through the darkness. The cool winds of autumn chill my bones as I walk the open road. For the first time, the outlines of the rolling hills fill me with dread. The road curls around. I walk and walk. The light grows in the sky to reveal gray clouds. Occasionally the sun peaks through, casting the clouds' shadow on the green hills. My feet begin to hurt; forlorn, I sit down on the edge of a field. I am grateful my cork-soled shoes are in good condition. I wore these when I first entered the hermitage, and I have needed to walk very little since. The cook has packed a little bag of nourishment for me. I now open it and take out a few almonds. I must be careful how I divide up this food. Who knows how long it will have to last me?

With a heavy heart, I once more stand up. I long to return to the hermitage. Why has Sheykh Mundhir sent me away? Was he displeased with me? How could I possibly progress without his aid? Constricting terror weakens my body and forces me to sit down again upon a jutting rock by the roadside. I cannot continue. I will never find the Philosopher's Stone. I have no idea where to look. Who will help me? Jahm flashes through my mind. If only he were with me. Now, when I need him the most. But it was I who put him to death. Tears flow down my cheeks. Sobs of self-pity shake my shoulders. I pull up my knees and sink my head down in utter despair. I will die here: here on this rock. I will die of exposure and starvation. "You can go to your father's house," says a little voice. I look up at the clouds swiftly moving across the sky. A flash of sunlight appears as the clouds rush onward through space.

No, I cannot return to my father's house. I must move forward. I must trust the Sheykh. Perhaps he did not send me away out of displeasure but for my own benefit. I must give this path a chance before abandoning it. I take a deep breath. A few drops of rain fall on my face. I stand up and once more continue my trip down the road.

I walk and walk, watching the clouds rush across the sky. My eyes roam the round hills. At this time of year, there are few fruits and vegetables growing in the cultivated plots. The vineyards contain naked branches. The flowers have all died. Nature is dormant, resting. A light drizzle is putting a shine on existing vegetation. Walking has warmed me. I lose myself in the repetition of my movements. One foot after the other. My body gently sways back and forth. The light drizzle freshens my skin.

Coming from behind me, in the distance, I hear the sound of slow, rhythmic hoofs hitting the ground. The sound grows louder. Soon a man on a donkey passes me, turns his head around, and slows down.

"Do you need a ride?" he calls out kindly.

I shake my head. After all, he only has one donkey, which is already carrying a load as well as its owner.

"This is a strong animal. He can take both of us," he says.

"Where are you heading?"

"Granada."

"That's several days away."

"That's where I'm heading, God willing."

I spend the next week riding behind Salih to Granada. At nights, we rest in caravansaries and the man generously pays for my accommodations. Salih is a man of about fifty-five, with infinite good humor and an easy laugh which at first sounds surprisingly high-pitched coming from such a heavy-set body. By trade, he is a silversmith. He proudly shows me his hands; thick fingers and large palms engraved with deep lines. These hands could grab you from a storm-infested sea with ease.

"My wives complain that I work too hard," he tells me one night as we sip strong coffee just outside the caravansary, under the stars by the citrus grove. "They cannot understand that shaping a piece of silver gives me exquisite pleasure. When I form jewellery with my hands, the turmoil of the world disappears around me. I could be working in the middle of the busiest marketplace, and I will see nothing but the silver under my fingers."

"Do you only work with silver?" I ask hesitantly.

"Sometimes I also work with ivory. On the other hand, if I find precious stones at a good price, I will buy them and put them on a jewellery box. But it is the silver around the ivory and the stones that I love most of all."

"Do you ever work in gold?"

Salih breaks into laughter and vigorously shakes his head.

The next evening, as we relax after supper on a rock, I can hold my tongue no longer.

"Have you heard of Philosophical Gold?"

This time Salih breaks into even louder shrieks of laughter. He does not answer. I press him again.

"Yes. The Philosopher's Stone." He becomes very pensive and continues after a long pause, "Stone is power. It contains enormous force. It holds immortality."

"You mean gold?"

"Yes, if God wills it."

"How can I obtain it?"

Again, a long roll of laughter rings into the night. "You must be ready. When you are ready, you will not ask such a question."

Anger rises in response to his answer. Why have I even bothered to ask this man? He is only a silversmith. How could he know? However, I cannot let it go.

"Do you know how to make it?" I ask this against my better judgment.

"No one can tell you. If you are simply given the answer, it will be worthless. You must find it yourself."

I go to sleep with a feeling of hopelessness. In the morning, I wake up and force myself to look upon Salih with magnanimity. After all, he has been especially gracious toward me who is no more than a stranger to him. With effort, I recover my warmth toward him.

Throughout the rest of our journey, I make no mention of the Philosopher's Stone. In Granada, he invites me to stay in his house. His generosity is boundless. As the days pass, he makes me feel so welcome that a strong urge to stay on indefinitely takes a hold of me.

A couple of weeks later, as we are walking back from the mosque after the last prayer of the day, Salih tells me he can do no more for me.

"I know it is a comfort to rest. Now you must continue your journey, my friend."

I feel crushed and weak and hate myself for it. It has been several weeks since I have left the hermitage, yet I still cannot seem to walk on my own feet.

"I have a cousin going to Malaga on business. You can have a ride with him if you like," he offers.

Reluctantly, I accept.

I hardly speak to Salih's cousin on the trip though he tries hard to engage me in conversation. I hide behind invocations of the name of God. I shuffle my cedar wood rosary between my fingers the way I remember the Sheykh doing. The poor man grows very respectful toward me, thinking me a pious man. His generosity equals his cousin's. He pays for my food and lodging at the caravansaries. I stay up most of the night praying. This clearly makes a deep impression on him.

However, I am ashamed of myself. I know I am hiding behind piety. I am afraid.

In Malaga, Salih's cousin and I part company. He goes to take care of necessary business while I roam the streets in a state of low-tide depression. I sit down on the steps of a mosque to rest. Not far from me stands a young man with a glowing smile on his face: begging. Soon I too will have to beg. Will I find it within me to smile like this young man, to feel his joy? I take out my rosaries and close my eyes. In the infinite darkness of my mind, I try to recall the flute music I heard at the hermitage. I see myself rising higher and higher through the clouds of doubt until finally I reach a clear blue sky with the globe of the sun beckoning me.

I open my eyes and see the young beggar smiling right at me. I greet him with warmth. He introduces himself as Anas. After a short conversation, I discover that he too is a Sufi. My joy expands filling my heart with gratitude as I take him in my arms.

He invites me back to the house he shares with two other Sufis on the outskirts of the city. It takes several hours of walking before we reach our destination. By the time we arrive, I have developed a debilitating pain in my knees and shoulders. Picking up a pot of tea takes tremendous effort. Anas tells me to rest.

"Yazid will be back soon," he says. "He is a man of great power and a healer. He will take care of you."

"Yes," al-Naqarat agrees. "Yazid is in great demand as a healer. Often it is impossible to sleep at night because people come at all hours asking for his help."

Al-Naqarat is in his forties and makes his living with mosaics.

"Laying down mosaics has helped me to see God's grace. It has helped me to the Light," al-Naqarat explains. "I am doing God's work. I am creating beauty. It comes nowhere near the Beauty of God, but it is still a dim reflection."

"You are seeking God in your physical work?" I am astonished.

"Yes. I have passed more than ten years wandering from place to place, developing from station to station. I have studied with numerous masters. The last one has been Yazid. Staying here with him, I have learned that just as he heals and gives to people, I can return to my craft of laying mosaics and also give to people."

I find the man's gracious humility moving. Will I ever reach such a stage?

When Yazid arrives, he greets me with a kind smile and no surprise. It is as if he had been expecting me. Shortly the muezzin calls for the last prayer of the day. From a distance, his voice floats over to the house. We gather in the small courtyard and begin our ritual prayer. Warmth infuses my body and dissipates the tension in my stomach. After prayer, we sit in position and contemplate. Yazid, sitting on his worn prayer mat, slowly levitates into the air and hovers at a point where the branches of the orange tree begin to spread.

"Forgive me," he turns to me with a chuckle after he has descended again, and we have finished our contemplation. "I normally do not do such things in front of strangers. But you will stay with us for a few days so you will no longer be a stranger."

"Sulayman needs your healing power," Anas says as we sit down for our evening meal.

"Yes, yes," Yazid replies, wiping his long white beard on a cotton napkin. "Tomorrow morning, after a good night's sleep."

After breakfast, Yazid tells me to lie down on the cushions, and he sits beside me. He closes his eyes and puts his hands on my knees. He remains in this position for a surprisingly long time. Anas stands by the door.

My knees begin to feel warm, and they start to tremble. Yazid furrows his brows and maintains his hands in position. My knees jerk up and down helplessly and then come to a standstill. Yazid opens his eyes.

"I can do nothing for you," he announces. "Your trouble with your knees has nothing to do with your journey. On the contrary, you do not want to continue on your journey which is why you have pain in your knees."

"What can I do?"

"Rest, contemplate, and face your fear."

"I am not knowingly afraid of anything," I protest.

"Beyond your knowledge lurks another world. You must enter that world and find the root of your fear."

I spend several days in silent prayer.

"You must surrender," Yazid says to me one night over supper.

Who has said this to me before? Jahm? The Sheykh?

"You must allow God to lead you. Do not resist. Trust Him. Trust yourself."

I fast and meditate in solitude. I know Yazid had been right. A part of me is closed, fearful. Sheykh Mundhir, whom I greatly loved, has sent me away. No, I tell myself. He sent you away to do a task, to search for a treasure. He did not send you away in rejection. In my mind, I see the Sheykh calmly sitting on his cushion.

"Love will lead you to the Divine," he whispers gently. "Do not be afraid to love."

Love! I am afraid to love. I am afraid my love will be taken away from me as Esther had been denied to me. I am afraid if I open up again I will receive pain. I, who had been a judge and practiced the Word of God, am afraid! My tears tumble. I sob. My shoulders, so painfully stiff earlier, now move with a life of their own, suddenly loosened, dancing.

However, I felt love at the hermitage, I tell myself. You were protected at the hermitage that is why you allowed yourself to let go. Now that you are no longer there, you do not have the courage to love! You have closed off to protect yourself.

Moreover, how can I find the Philosopher's Stone if I am closed?

Allow yourself to bend to His Will. Why is it so difficult? I thought I was free of my disappointment with Esther. I thought that was over a long time ago. No, I have yet another veil to pass through.

The next day, my knees are much stronger. There is still some pain when I walk but nothing compared to what it was when I arrived. My shoulders have also loosened up. At breakfast, Anas suggests I go with him to Malaga and beg.

"Yes," says Yazid. "You should go with him."

Just when I feel I have licked my fear, I discover another lurking around the corner. Fighting great resistance, I follow Anas to Malaga. My good mood of this morning has soured. I lag behind.

Finally, we arrive at Malaga, and he leaves me in front of one mosque while he heads toward another.

"I will come for you when it is time to leave," he tells me.

I stand in front of the mosque, staring at the other beggars.

Their clothes are torn and dirty. I look down at my own attire and realize that my shirt is wearing thin. It has not been washed in over a week. My shoes are now worn and ragged. My beard is shaggy and unkempt. A wave of self-disgust washes over me. I sit down on the steps of the mosque unable to put out my hand.

I think how I used to enter the Great Mosque of Cordoba and give to the beggars at the gate. How glad I was to be able to give! It made me feel good to give. Now, here, I am on the other side. Begging! I do not need to beg, I cry in my head. Yes, comes the small reply. Do you know humility?

A dirty palm appears in front of my nose, and I look up to see an old beggar. I shake my head and apologize. He smiles a toothless smile and moves on.

In an effort to gain courage, I silently recite verses of the Qur'an. Slowly I stand up and shyly extend my palm. My eyes are closed, my head bent, and I silently repeat the name of Allah repeatedly. A coin drops into my palm. I open my eyes in surprise and look up. The person has already gone on. I put the coin in my pocket and once more extend my palm. This time with more courage. I close my eyes, lift my head, and thank Allah for giving me strength.

By the time Anas comes for me, I have collected several coins. I proudly show him my treasures as excited as a child.

"Good," nods Anas in approval. "You will come with me tomorrow as well."

My heart sinks.

Later that night, I offer my coins to Yazid.

"You keep them," he tells me. "You will need them."

For the next few days, I follow Anas to the mosque in Malaga. Each day is a little easier. Each day I feel a little lighter. One night I count the coins I have collected and realize I have enough to pay for a boat trip across the Strait of Gibraltar to Tangier. Inexplicably, I am elated.

"I am ready to leave now," I tell Yazid at supper.

"Good." He fixes intense eyes upon me. "What are you searching for?"

"The Philosopher's Stone," I say shyly.

I continue to eat in silence. After the last prayer of the day, I go over to Yazid and ask, "Do you know how I can find the Philosopher's Stone?"

"You must combine sulfur, salt, and mercury," he says and goes off to his library before I can ask anything else.

The next day, I set out on foot, heading toward Algeciras. This is a heavily traveled route. Soldiers and caravans pass me. I walk for a number of days, refusing the several rides offered. I often stop by the seaside to look out at the water's movement and changing color. I sit on the sand or rocks contemplating the beauty of creation. I sleep under the stars wrapped in a surprising sense of safety.

Finally, I accept a ride from the leader of a caravan. A young boy on a camel pulls me up beside him. I travel with the caravan all the way to Algeciras where I board the boat across the Strait.

Memories of my trips with my father resurface. The day is overcast, threatening to break into a storm. The water rages and foams, its color opaque, dark, impenetrable. It crashes against the sides of the boat, hurling it from side to side. The sails, taut against the wind, struggle to maintain balance.

I think back to Yazid's words. Combine sulfur, salt, and mercury. This is alchemy. The Sheykh could not have actually meant a physical process. It could not be as simple as that, if it were, everyone would be transmuting base metals into gold. There must be a deeper meaning to this task.

In Tangier, I head for a mosque near the southwestern part of the city, just beyond the hill. As I do my ablutions in the courtyard of the mosque, I wonder why I have come here. I have never been to this mosque, and on the way, I had passed several other mosques yet was not prompted to stop. I have stopped at this one for no good reason.

After prayer, I sit quietly in the mosque, remembering a Qur'anic verse, "What is to come is better for you than what has gone before." (93;4)

At nightfall, I find myself sitting on the cool sand before the gently rolling sea. The waves reach toward me, almost touching my toes, and then recede. Dots of brilliance are scattered in the sky.

A movement catches my attention. I look to my right, and from around a large rock rising out of the water, I see a man. He is walking toward me, on water. Even as he nears the shore where the water is shallow he walks just on the surface, barely disturbing the movement of the waves. He comes out to the sand and sits down beside me. His feet are not even wet, nor is the bottom of his robe.

I move slightly away from him to get a better look. He smiles at me, at my disbelief. He has deep-set dark eyes and wears white flowing robes. His laughter comes as a low melody.

"I am surprised you have not experienced light travel before."

Yes, I have heard of it. Sheykh Mundhir was known to do it. Sometimes he talked of trips he had taken to Bukhara or Samarra to visit friends. We would see him go to his room at night, and in the morning, he would recount tales of his night trips. He told us that we too would be able to travel lightly when we were initiated.

"I have come to give you a message," says the man beside me. "You are looking for something and a man who can help you lives in Ceuta. In a short time, you will have a desire to go to Ceuta. Follow that desire."

"How do I find this man in Ceuta?" I ask.

"He will find you."

The man smiles at me, gets up, and goes back from where he came, on the water and around the rock.

Time passes. I am hardly aware of it. I either pray at the mosque I went to on the first day or beg in front of it should the need arise for food. I meet a group of Sufis who also congregate around this mosque, and we spend several hours exchanging experiences and learning from each other. Most of them are further along the path than myself and hearing them speak of their difficulties gives me hope and comfort.

They invite me to their house. Here I share a room with an older Sufi I had not met at the mosque. He spends his days and nights in prayer, standing before a small window with wrought iron grating.

One day, as I am in the midst of prayer, the name Ceuta flies into my mind. I feel an urge to leave immediately and make my way to that city.

I bid farewell to my friends and follow the coastal road by the sea toward the east. On one side of me is the enormous body of water with its changing colors and movements. On the other side of me stretches hills dotted with trees and shrubs, a rugged landscape that invokes strength and courage. Though I am offered numerous rides, I accept none. From time to time, I share a meal with other travelers. The voyage gives me great pleasure. I pray on the sand and invoke the names of God as I walk. My solitude is never solitary because I know Allah is with me. Peace and serenity envelop me. Times of distress and difficulty come to test man's faith. Everything is unfolding as it should, and either we read the symbols of events correctly and learn or we choose to remain ignorant.

Jahm returns to my mind as I sit atop a rock with the waves lapping against its side. The light spray washes my face as Jahm's smile appears before me. How could I have thought that I was condemning Jahm to death? How could I have thought he died because of my word? Allah had already prescribed his end, and Jahm knew and accepted it. By decreeing his end through the word of the law, I was merely serving the whole in a temporal present for the sake of the infinite. Jahm's death was a gift to me. It was that gift which has led me onto the path of Sufism.

My heart dissolves and opens. The spray of seawater blends with my tears. "Thank you. Thank you," I whisper.

Night falls, and I am still sitting on the rock, fingering my cedar wood rosary.

At last, I find myself in Ceuta, a coastal town that clusters around the shore. Its core teams with urgent activity. I aimlessly walk through the covered market, through its winding streets. My long trip has made me particularly hungry. I am given some nuts and dried dates by a food vendor. Someone else offers me orange juice.

A tall cylindrical minaret covered with blue, green, and gold tile work captures my attention. I head toward it, making my way through the narrow streets, always keeping the minaret in view. At last I arrive at a magnificent mosque, its ocher walls carved with fluid floral patterns. In the courtyard, the tile work matches the minaret in style and color. After prayer, I see a group of people quietly talking in one corner of the mosque. Something about them catches my attention. I approach them to ask for directions to the nearest Sufi hermitage. Two young men offer to accompany me.

During our walk of several hours to the hermitage, they tell me that Sheykh al-Shakkaz is now the master, the one before died only a year ago and he had appointed al-Shakkaz to take his place. They speak with such great respect for the present master that I am led to think that they must be his disciples.

Toward late afternoon, we arrive at a whitewashed hermitage. Inside the courtyard, a man with gray hair and long beard is playing the flute. As soon as I enter, he stops playing and gives me a big smile. My companions whisper to me that this is al-Shakkaz.

"It has taken you a long time to get here," he calls out, beckoning me closer.

A man with deep dark eyes comes out of a side room of the portico. I know him!

"You already met Jalal," says al-Shakkaz with a good-natured laugh.

Jalal, the man I had seen walking across the water, gives me a warm embrace.

"You are welcome to spend some time with us. Later the two of us will talk," promises al-Shakkaz and then picks up his flute again.

True to his word, after supper, al-Shakkaz asks me to follow him into the library.

"Nothing is what it seems," he tells me. "Of course, you already know that. Still, just when you think you know, you find there is yet more."

I laugh. How well I know what he means. I pause to consider his words. "It is not literally the metal gold that I am to find, is it?"

"Gold is the purest metal. Gold is purity of the soul. Only with a pure soul can one be ready to marry God, can one hope to live in the Light, in the Sun of Allah."

"But first I must overcome the baser elements of my physical self," I offer.

"The key is not to rule over your baser elements but to transmute them."

To what can my fears and doubts be transmuted? I have already come close to suppressing them. However, can suppression fully guarantee that they will never rise up again?

As if reading my thoughts, al-Shakkaz answers, "Every negative element has a positive side. You must transmute everything negative within you, every negative thought or feeling, into its equal and opposite positive."

First, I must discover all my fears and doubts. Is this possible? Will there not always be something to emerge from a deep crevice to surprise me?

"Transmutation occurs through contemplation and concentration," he continues. "When you have found the Light, you have found your treasure."

"How will I know when I have found it?"

"You will know."

"What about the sulfur, salt, and mercury? Do they each have a spiritual significance?"

"Yes. But that you must find elsewhere."

The hope I had felt at the beginning of the meeting now evaporates. It is replaced by fatigue and frustration. Why must I always keep searching elsewhere for the answer? Why can al-Shakkaz simply not tell me?

Once more, I set out on the road. I make my way south to Fez. The solitude of the trip takes me deeper and deeper into myself. Even as I recite the verses of the Qur'an, the Philosopher's Stone is on my mind. Must it be so elusive? My mind sways between a physical and spiritual interpretation. Even the conversations I have about it drift back and forth between the physical and spiritual meaning. Could I be searching for more than one Philosopher's Stone?

When I arrive in Fez, I immediately go to my brother Jamal's house. We warmly hug each other. It gives me such pleasure to see him once again. I had not realized how much I had missed my family. His wide smile is as welcoming as always. I tease him about his rapidly graying hair. He proudly calls out his six children. I am shocked to see that they are almost adults now. One of his wives died a few years ago, and he has taken another young wife who has recently given birth to a daughter. I take the baby in my arms and lovingly kiss her bright, smiling cheeks. The eyes, sparkling with clarity, regard me with amused curiosity. Holding the baby close to my chest reminds me how long it has been since I have held another human being this close to me. I wonder where Naziha is right now. I hope she has found happiness.

Jamal's house is filled with good-natured laughter and vibrant energy. He gives me a room to myself and assures me freedom to pray and contemplate. He promises me solitude. No one will disturb me. Laughingly, he adds that my presence will bring good luck to his family.

During my stay with Jamal, I make my way around Fez to find out about the various hermitages near the city. One day I know I can no longer stay at Jamal's. An inner voice tells me to move on.

I seek out a hermitage reputed for its discipline. I have heard that al-Rundi is the master and he has a very strict way of teaching his followers. I ask several people for directions. Nevertheless, I manage to get lost numerous times before finally finding a very large white stucco house surrounded by palm trees.

Inside dwell a surprisingly large number of disciples. They welcome me into the group, and we are soon sitting in a tight circle by the fountain engaged in an animated discussion. I immediately feel comfortable and take pleasure in the beauty of the house. An intricately carved wooden portico and upper gallery surround us. The walls are geometrically carved cedar wood panels painted in gold and red. I realize how important physical surroundings can be. How I had loved Sheykh Mundhir's hermitage! Its serene beauty often helped to calm my soul.

The disciples ask eager questions, wanting to know where I have come from, who was my master. When I tell them I had been educated by Sheykh Mundhir, they want to know about his technique of teaching. Though I explain the best I can, they quickly fall upon my words with barbed criticism. I try to defend him, thinking I had not explained myself properly. They interrupt even before I can finish my sentences. They are quick to point out how certain techniques have proven to be incorrect. I soon realize that al-Rundi's followers are not interested in listening to a different approach. They simply want me to acknowledge that their master's method is the only correct one. Their reaction causes me concern. I want them to share my respect for Sheykh Mundhir the same way they want me to respect al-Rundi.

Our arguments continue for several days until finally, during one of my periods of contemplation, I realize that I should desist from further discussion regarding the ideal teaching methods of a Sufi master. After all, I am here to accomplish a task, not to argue over teaching methods.

Once they see that I no longer contradict them, their antagonism toward me dissolves, and they do whatever is within their power to help. One of them tells me that an alchemist, who has spent his whole life trying to convert base metals into gold, lives near the hermitage. Another follower laughs and says the man has grown gray and decrepit through his fruitless efforts. My curiosity is aroused. From their words, I gather this alchemist works on a physical plane. Though he might not be able to provide me with spiritual answers, he sounds like someone who at least can give me a rational interpretation of a concrete process. Then I could use my imagination to take it one step further.

I make my way to the alchemist's house, which is even further from Fez than the hermitage. Following the disciples' directions, I finally find an old house built on the rocks, surrounded by shrubs and palm trees. This seems to fit the description I had been given. The door is opened by a small, thin man who looks at least eighty years old. He has a white straggly beard and surprisingly clear eyes. Bent at the waist from age, he peers up at me with suspicion. I take great pains to explain why I have come to see him. At last satisfied, he opens his door wider to allow me in.

I enter a small, unkempt courtyard filled with numerous copper and clay vessels of every size and shape. The surrounding clutter gives off an air of whimsical enchantment. There has been no attempt at creating an aesthetic environment. Every discernible object has been or is utilitarian. Moreover, every object seems to be alive with a distinct personality that reveals a fragment of the old man's character. I feel as if I have entered a sacred and magical place. To one side of the courtyard is a little bronze table with a leather puff. He disappears into a room and with spry steps returns carrying another puff. We sit down.

His hands sweep over the courtyard. "My whole house is a laboratory. I have devoted my life to alchemy." He chuckles, rhythmically caressing his beard. "Had a wife once, but she left me. Claimed I did not need a woman, all I needed were my chemicals. She was right. Alchemy is my only passion."

The man is disarmingly innocent, despite his age, as if he were standing naked before me.

"Have you had any success?" I ask.

"I have been searching for over seventy years, and it has taken me fifty years to discover that mercury is spirit, sulfur is soul, and salt is the body."

Ah! I think, suddenly sitting erect. *Why has no one said this?* The Philosopher's Gold has nothing to do with actual metals.

As darkness falls, we are still in the courtyard engaged in deep conversation. I am mesmerized by the story of his quest and fascinated by the man's obvious devotion.

I sigh with a huge relief and think, *Now I know; the gold is within!*

He laughs with an abandon I have rarely seen. Perhaps Jahm laughed like that once or twice.

"I now know the principle," he tells me, his eyes shining like the stars in the sky. "I now know that it is not simply the right combination of chemicals that are needed." He pauses to stroke his beard.

He chuckles toward the sky as his fingers wind their way through his large mass of curly white hair. "Ah, this involves the very essence of nature—its very core."

His eyes lovingly survey the contents of the courtyard, as if remembering how each object has served him in his search. Then he resumes his story.

"Every material thing contains within its makeup the potential to be every other thing. A rock contains elements of all other rocks and gems within it. The reason we see it as a particular rock is because that particular element is the strongest in its makeup. However, this rock also contains the potential to be gold." He pauses to examine the stars in the sky. "Now the elements of sulfur, salt, and mercury also contain the potential to be gold. It is like a child. One must nurture it to maturity, never forgetting that the potential one is nurturing is gold. If you forget, you lose it and must start over again. Moreover, it takes such awesome power to always contain that gold in your mind. Always without ever wavering." He shakes his head and adds quietly, as if to himself, "That awesome concentration."

When the distant call of the muezzin softly floats through the dark air, we are still sitting in the cluttered courtyard. The old man clears some space for us to pray. Later he apologizes for not having provided me with water for ablution.

"There is a well I share with a neighbor, but it is quite a distance from here. Also, I spend my whole day trying to purify my mind. I am sure God will accept that purification as my ablution."

"Yes, it is the symbol of purification that is important not the actual process," I reply, discovering a new understanding of symbolism. "As long as the symbol remains alive, its physical manifestation grows pale by comparison. A symbol is universal, an act is particular."

He nods and nods, though it is clear he has hardly heard my words, he is so absorbed in his own thoughts.

I spend a long time with this old man. During the day, I go into Fez to beg and buy nourishment for both of us. At night, after supper, we often talk until early morning lightness streaks the skies. Sometimes, I spend my days in prayer and contemplation. Other times, I observe the old man at work. I marvel at his focused attention. Nothing disturbs him. A tree may crash to the ground outside his house, and he will not blink. Such absolute dedication inspires reverence.

One afternoon I sit on the puff, leaning against the wall, watching him. Two copper containers and a rock of salt sit on his workbench. He fixes his gaze on the rock, willing it to life with the intensity of his eyes. In a short time, the rock begins to lift into the air until it reaches the man's eye level. I have seen him spend whole mornings with the salt in midair while he sits before it, totally engrossed, turning it around and around with his mind. Next, he turns his attention to the copper dish. Soon a mass of mercury levitates out of the container to the height of the salt and the smooth liquid wraps itself around the white rock. Satisfied, he turns to the other copper dish. He levitates the liquid sulfur to the level of the mercury and binds it around the silvery mass.

He sits in front of this, without physically touching it, his eyes never leaving the hovering object in midair. I watch closely. The three elements seem to grow less and less dense, taking up more and more space above his workbench. Solely by concentration, the three elements, distinguished only by their individual colors, are gradually combined to form a loose, homogenous whole. When the density is uniform, he mentally compresses it into a solid mass, the consistency of rock.

With his eyes, the old man lowers the hovering rock onto his desk. Picking it up with his hands for a closer examination, he shakes his head and hands it to me.

"It is like silver," I say.

"I have often got this type of rock. It is closer to silver than gold. The quantity of mercury I use is very tricky. But then if I use too much sulfur, I cannot get the density I need to make a rock." He shakes his head again. "But then it should make no difference what quantities I use. The element will always contain that small potential for gold. It simply must be activated."

"One day, God willing, you will succeed." I smile.

"This search has given me such riches already. I feel like a wealthy man."

Having watched him work for these past few weeks with an intensity one usually reserves for prayer, I believe him. He is probably one of the few truly wealthy men of this world. The very process of his work is the Philosophical Gold. Ultimately it makes little difference whether he will find it; his dedication to his goal has already purified his soul.

He has found his path. I must once more set out to search for mine.

XII. Freedom

After I leave the old man, I wander through the desert, toward the mountains of Morocco. I walk across flowing sand dunes, guided by the light of the sun. I share food with caravans and listen to news of the world. I move across the terrain of God and sleep in the arms of the earth. I remember the pure happiness of the old alchemist. Perhaps I too can find pure joy in my very search for Philosophical Gold. Perhaps it is the search that will teach me what I need to learn, not the outcome.

At times, I simply sit on a rock and contemplate the grandeur of nature. It is possible to look at the deserted sand dunes, the rugged mountainside, and feel lost in the abyss of time, feel insignificant in the scheme of creation, feel useless beside a grain of sand. It is also possible to look out and feel at one with the nobility of the physical world, share in its majesty and grow within at the realization that nothing stands alone. Within me, I hold the sand dunes of stillness, the mountains of patience, and the subtlety of the shifting winds.

I meet nomads crossing the wide expanse of golden sand. I join them for a time and then continue on my own. The Atlas Mountains loom before me, their snow-capped peaks reaching toward the sky. In time, I arrive at the foothills and head upward. The very climb toward higher ground uplifts my soul. Solitude in nature makes it easy to feel the proximity of God. Striving is now hardly necessary. The outside world no longer needs to be overcome. Here, one has a clear path to God. I climb higher and surrender myself with ease.

On my way up the mountains, I encounter a tribe of Berbers living in caves and tents along a terraced slope. Among them lives an old Sufi from the east who has been with the Berbers for over twenty years. He greets me enthusiastically as kindred brethren and encourages me to stay. We pray together and contemplate. We spend days and days sitting by a rock near his tent, talking. The Berbers good-naturedly laugh at our animated discussions. Older women come to bear food and drink. They come giggling, barefoot, and adorned in their colorful headdresses.

One day I ask this old Sufi about the Philosopher's Stone.

"It has taken you a long time to ask me the question uppermost on your mind," he says with an amused chuckle.

I am surprised at his reaction. "You know about it?"

"Yes, I know about it."

"Please, tell me," I say.

"It is not something which can be told. It must be discovered in the fertile soul of your mind."

"Can you not tell me anything?"

"Ask me a question."

I recount my experience with the old alchemist who had interpreted the three elements of sulfur, salt, and mercury.

"But if mercury is spirit, sulfur is the soul, and salt is the body, then the search is within," I conclude.

"Yes." His eyes look toward the darkening sky.

His glance slowly moves from star to star. Then he finally says, "Sulfur is nobility, greatness. Salt is learning, the spice of knowledge. Mercury is the key that opens the lock." His gaze slips from the stars to settle on me. "Also, the god Mercury is the descendant of Hermes who transcends space and time and moves faster than thought. Mercury is Divine speed."

"The combination of these three produce Light?"

"Yes, if the workplace is clear, if the soul is pure."

"Logically I understand your words. But I know that is not enough."

"You must arrive at numerous levels of understanding before these three elements will combine in your soul to reach the Light," he says.

This is the work of a lifetime! Is there always yet another form of understanding? Will I ever be able to simply sit back in comfort, sip mint tea in the sun, and dream? Is it possible to reach the end of the road?

I make my way back to Fez, treasuring the words of the old Sufi and doubtful about my ability to ever reach my goal. I settle in at Jamal's house. My brother provides me with all the solitude I need. I spend most of my time at the Karouin mosque in prayer and contemplation. At times, I listen to the lectures. Students come and go, engaged in heated discussions. I remember my student days and realize how little I knew back then. One day I join a group of students in the middle of an argument. My presence soon tickles their curiosity, and they begin to ask me questions about Sufism. They ask about the need for serenity, concentration. "Is prayer five times a day not enough to reach out to God?" they ask.

Gradually, over a period of several weeks, I find myself giving regular lectures, surrounded by a group of followers. I talk about how words can only give one level of the Truth. To attain a much higher level of Truth, we must look toward Allah; to find Him, we must first look within. "The journey to Truth is fraught with obstacles," I explain, "but unless we are prepared to do battle, we will never reach our destination."

One day an older man joins the group. As I take a closer look at him, I recognize 'Abdallah and let out a joyful cry of surprise. His still handsome features show the distinguished lines of time. His hair and beard are nearly white. Seeing my old friend and teacher again brings a flood of memories. A sudden flash of the past makes me smile. How far I have come since then!

Back at Jamal's house, the two of us cannot stop talking, exchanging experiences. 'Abdallah tells me how he has traveled to the major centers of the east, working for ruling families. His cynicism toward politics greatly amuses me. I tell him of my journey from cadi to Sufi. 'Abdallah laughs and shakes his head.

"I would never have suspected you would one day become a Sufi," he tells me between bursts of laughter.

"Yet it was you who first introduced me to Sufism."

"I?" He is totally taken aback by this revelation. Clearly, he does not remember.

"As a student, you took me to Sheykh Mundhir's hermitage," I remind him.

He is at first perplexed. Suddenly, his eyes light up.

"Of course. Of course." He pauses as he thinks back. A cloud of confusion passes across his eyes. "I did not realize the meeting had such a tremendous effect on you."

"The influence of the hermitage was at first slow."

"Now, you are a teaching Sufi."

"My lectures have come purely by chance. They are not even formal lectures."

'Abdallah rubs his beard; concern deepens the lines of his face. "The lecture I heard you give today," he says, "is it typical of your lectures?"

"Typical? I could not say. However, it was certainly not unusual."

"Sulayman, I have just arrived in Fez. I am not yet totally familiar with the political climate. I have heard that it is nothing like what Cordoba once was during the time of your student days. Freedom of curiosity is not common currency."

"What are you saying?" I have paid no attention to the political situation of Fez. The students have questions, and I feel called upon to answer to the best of my ability. Their questions indicate that their professors are not satisfying their curiosity.

"The subject of your lectures could be dangerous. Do be careful."

I laugh at 'Abdallah's warning. His cynicism has a tendency to cloud his vision.

Several months later, the mosque is filled with angry shouts. Swords flashing, the police quickly break up my lecture, roughly grab my arms, and drag me across the tiles of the mosque. I yell questions at them, but they remain silent, hauling me through the narrow stone streets. They throw me atop a donkey, tightly tie me to his stomach so I cannot move, and pull me after them.

In time, we reach a heavy iron gate. They pull the donkey into a courtyard laid with rough gray stone. By this time, I have fallen silent, ready to accept whatever the situation may present. They untie me and, with strong hands locked under my armpits, they carry me through a thick wooden door and down large stone steps built into the earth. Down and down into the dark, cold dampness. My tunic has torn, my legs are bleeding, yet I feel no pain, only a superficial sting. I am not a part of what is going on, as if this poor body did not belong to me. They carry me further and further down, toward the center of the earth. Lanterns hang on the walls, illuminating the infernal passage. Our shadows madly dance around us. At last we reach a passageway. They drag me along the floor to a thick iron door. They open it. A rattling sound echoes through the damp space. With violent strength, they throw me inside.

I land on a cold body that I think must be dead. Then the chains around his ankles begin to rattle. The guards push me against the stonewall and chain my wrists and ankles. On either side, the heavy metal chain is connected to other prisoners. Whenever I lift my hand, I pull at my neighbor's arm. A movement of my leg means moving my neighbor's leg.

The guards loudly slam the door as they leave. The stench of the place is so overwhelming that it takes a tremendous effort to control the heaving of my stomach. A very dim light comes into the cell from the lanterns on the stairway. The space is packed with at least a hundred people. Some wear dark rags, some are naked, their bodies smeared with dirt. The men are sitting in their feces. The walls are caked with dried vomit. Ants, spiders, lizards, rats freely crawl over the bodies and along the dirt floor. The chain connecting all the prisoners is constantly squealing, creaking, clanging. Sleep is not possible.

I force my eyes to focus into the distant darkness. We form a chain of men shackled to each other. It is as if the chain has made us one. Though my surroundings are more horrifying than I have ever encountered before, I feel at one with the men around me.

"Why don't they get him out?" comes an angry yell from the distance.

"His body is decomposing!" shouts another.

"Is it not enough that we are left to die in our own juices?" moans someone nearby.

The man beside me explains in a low voice and with great effort that men are simply left to die here and their dead bodies remain for a long time chained to the ones still alive.

Time passes. It is impossible to tell when the sun rises and when it sets. We exist by the dim glow of the distant lanterns. No daylight is discernible. Silently, I invoke the name of Allah. I say the verses of the Qur'an swaying back and forth.

"Allah has forgotten about us," cries a man.

"He's punishing you," roars another.

I remember the words of Sheykh Mundhir. "A true believer is always living in the physical prison of this world. Only Allah can lead us out, into the light."

I continue reciting the verses of the Qur'an. The sharp, acrid smell threatens nausea. I must concentrate to keep my stomach under control. These conditions would have filled me with terror at one time. The sounds of groaning, screaming, reminiscent of animals at slaughter, would have once chased me to the depths of mad despair. Now, I am surprised to discover tranquility, sublime peace at the mouth of hell.

The name of Allah brings light into my heart. Love glows in my soul for the men around me. I want to take them all in my arms and comfort them. Are they not all creatures of God? My love encompasses, its rays reaching outward, moving beyond the prison door and walls, reaching into the open air, toward the sky. The fear and ignorance of men have created this dungeon. Do they think oppression can wipe away knowledge? Ignorance can only kill on this physical plane. It has no power beyond. Fear and ignorance are small in their impotence. The rays of the sun bathe me in warmth. Gratitude washes over me. I thank God for giving me the test necessary to temper my soul.

At intervals, more prisoners are thrown in and shackled to the chain. Some men are called out, never to return.

In a low voice, I chant the Qur'an. I concentrate on the sound flowing from my throat, like the strings of a lyre plucked by the fingers of God. I sink into serenity. All sounds fall away. There are only the words of the Qur'an. The verses transfuse and transpose me to a place of infinite light and space. Sweet air enters my nostrils. Divine silence fills my ears.

"Sulayman ibn Ahmed ibn Idris," roars out a guard from the corridor.

I open my eyes.

"Sulayman ibn Ahmed ibn Idris," yells out the guard again.

I try to raise my hand. The chain rattles, and I pull the hand next to me into the air.

The door roars open and the guard unlocks my shackles. He pulls me up and out into the corridor, slamming the door behind him. Here another guard comes to help him. Strong palms reach under my armpit and roughly carry me up the stairs. They take me out into a courtyard where someone quickly runs over to embrace me. It takes some time for my eyes to adjust to the light. When I finally focus on the face before me, I recognize Jamal. I hug him with joy.

He hands me the clothes he is carrying in his arms.

"You are due to appear before the cadi today." He is breathless and talks quickly. "I have secured two excellent and honorable witnesses for you. I have asked the guards to allow you to wash and put on these clothes." He turns to leave.

"Are you not waiting for me?" I call after him.

"I will meet you before the cadi with the witnesses."

As I am changing into fresh clothes, I start to have doubts. What am I doing? My true place is with the other men in prison. My shared time with them made me feel close to Allah. Why am I now ready to embrace this sudden offer of physical freedom?

Appearing in court is no guarantee of safety, as I well know.

Perhaps I am going to meet my end. The cadi will judge if I deserve to be stoned to death.

I finish dressing. I will put my trust in Allah. I tell myself confidently as I walk out.

An old familiar feeling tingles within me as I stand before the cadi. The witnesses swear to the piousness of my character. I defend myself against the charge of heresy by liberally quoting the Qur'an and the Hadith. Having been a judge, I know what sections make a particularly strong impression in court. Since I am familiar with the language of the cadi, my defense is so strong and competent that, by the time my accusers stand against me, they are helpless to penetrate my mantle of piety.

A sense of elation grows within, and I search out Jamal's eyes. He vigorously nods his head in approval.

After a long, drawn-out hearing, I am set free to return home with my brother. I take a languorous, warm bath, allowing my body to bask in the clean softness of the water. A smile plays upon my lips, and I thank Allah for this moment.

Before supper, Jamal takes me into the library and tells me that while I was in prison 'Abdallah has died. He presents me with numerous books that our old friend has left specifically for me.

I sink into the cushion. My elation of the day quickly evaporates as I caress the books. Tears drop onto the binding, puckering the leather. The pain of 'Abdallah's death forces me to recall Jahm. I have now lost two precious friends. Had I not been in prison, I could have stayed by 'Abdallah's side at the time of death or could have joined him by now had the judge passed the sentence of death.

"Were you with him?" I finally ask Jamal.

"Yes. I also washed his body before burial."

I bend my head toward the books. Nausea creates a dizzying imbalance within. I rush out into the courtyard to violently disgorge supper by the trunk of a date palm. I cry miserably, hugging the palm and breathing in my own vomit, remembering the prison cell. Why did I leave it?

I spend the next few days by 'Abdallah's grave. Oppression sits heavy on my shoulders. When 'Abdallah died, I was not present to lend him comfort. Now here I am with my freedom. To what purpose? Do I deserve it? I have my freedom only because I knew how to defend myself. In addition, Jamal's choice of witnesses was truly superlative. Did I believe in my defense? How could I have, since I no longer believe in the ways of a cadi? I was not acting honestly. I should have stood up before everyone, the cadi, the counselors, the crowd, and proudly repeated what I had taught the students at the mosque. I should not have qualified my statements. I should not have been so ready to fall back on my knowledge of the Qur'an and Hadith. Have I lost my courage to be honest?

The law that had condemned Jahm to death is the very law that has now given me my liberty. Yet we had both been accused of heresy.

"I am a coward," I yell at 'Abdallah's grave. I was afraid to die. Jahm met his death with dignity. And I? Lacking the courage of my convictions, I defended myself. I did not stand up for my views. I defended myself! What a failure! I have failed in love, in law, and in the path of spirituality. My life as a Sufi has ultimately taught me nothing. All those prayers have proved useless. I am a hypocrite.

This is exactly how I felt when I condemned Jahm. I did not have the courage to stand up for him. Nor was I beside 'Abdallah at the time of his death. Am I capable of friendship? Am I even worthy to be called anyone's friend? If another human being cannot count on me, how dare I approach Allah! How dare I live!

I return to Jamal's house feeling as if I were once more in chains. I am still festering in prison. But in prison, I felt peace. In the prison of my mind, I only feel lethargy. When Jamal's children speak to me, I hardly respond. I spend my days brooding inside my room. I refuse to join the family during mealtime. A servant brings up my food. Every once in a while Jamal comes up to urge me to go with him to the shop, to go out to the mosque, to go shopping with him. I refuse.

He sends a doctor to see me. After examination, the doctor can find nothing wrong with me. He recommends a soothing herbal tea to ease my anxiety and hopelessness.

I spend my days in bed. I no longer bother to pray. I watch the light slowly give way to darkness. The days checkerboard, blending into each other until light and dark become one. I sink deeper and deeper into the well, into numbing oblivion.

One day Jamal marches into my room.

"I must go into the desert to visit some Berber tribes and buy carpets," he announces. "I want you to come with me. I insist. This is not a request but an order."

"You don't need me," I say feebly.

"I want you to come with me. I am your elder brother, and your duty is to obey."

"I can't go with you to the Berber tribes. I'm afraid I might encounter the old Sufi I once met in the mountains."

"You need not come with me to the tribes. You can stay at the caravansary in the desert as I make day trips into the mountains. You can stay and guard the merchandise."

I turn away from him, mumbling, "You give me no choice."

"No. We are leaving in two days after the first prayer. I expect you to be ready. If I find you still in bed by the time we want to leave, I will order the servants to carry you out."

I hear him march out of the room.

After breakfast, ten of us set out from Fez on camels. We head south into the desert, toward the Atlas Mountains. We move up, down, around hills, which gradually turn to sand. Vast, golden stretches of dunes undulate before us toward infinity. In the distance, the sand rolls under the Atlas mountains, holding up enormous masses of snow-capped peaks against the blue sky. The soft, rolling sensuality of the sand dunes bring to mind the hills of al-Andalus. The handiwork of God. The devastating beauty of Divine Aesthetics. I begin to breathe easier, deeper.

I am grateful Jamal has insisted I accompany him on this trip. The days upon days of moving across the beauty of God, lulled by the roll of my camel, has encouraged me to once more seek that inward glimmer of light. The words of the Qur'an begin to float before my mind.

We move up and down the dunes, up and down. Deeper and deeper into the desert. The rhythm of our caravan imitates the rhythm of the dunes; the movement blending into the stillness, becoming one.

We pass golden villages rising out of the sand, punctuated by white minarets.

"There it is," Jamal calls out, pointing into the distance.

I strain my eyes and see a round caravansary, hardly distinguishable from the round hills of sand.

"That will be our base," explains Jamal. "We sleep there and make forays into the mountains to see the tribes."

The verses of the Qur'an sing in my head.

We settle in at the caravansary, and the next day, Jamal leaves me one of the servants and heads off into the mountains. I watch Jamal and his group move across a dune with their camels. They dip down and disappear. It is midmorning and the sun promises to bloom into full brilliance by midday.

I turn away from the mountains, toward the east, and see the sand stretch to eternity. Vast bodies of golden waves shift in the breeze. The landscape beckons. The clear sky is filled with hidden promise. I tell the servant to stay at the caravansary while I explore the surroundings. I begin to walk. The wind caresses my face. The long robe, open to my waist, flutters behind me. I walk, feeling the texture of the sand beneath my feet, feeling its soft give beneath the weight of my body. To float over the sand like the birds! To float over this golden landscape and view its glory from above! Directly in front of me, the sun slowly rises, piercing the translucent blue with its clear light.

I continue walking over this vast carpet of sand, unrolling, unrolling before me in welcome.

The sun rises; its rays turning the sand to gold. At last, its full roundness is revealed; its majesty overlooks eternity. The light is too strong for the human eye. Still, I look, not averting my gaze. Walking. Walking toward its center. The name of Allah is in my heart; His lightness fills my soul. I continue walking, forever if necessary, forever toward the Light.

The dry, heavy heat presses against me. Sweat streams down my face. Without stopping, I remove my headdress and throw it away. I untie the belt from my waist, remove my robe, and give it to the dunes. I throw away my shoes and feel the softness of the hot sand flowing between my toes. I feel lighter and lighter and move faster and faster until my feet begin to run kicking up the sand. I throw off my shirt. I tear off my trousers. The rays of the sun caress my naked flesh. And I run, arms outstretched. Run ankle deep in translucent dust, kicking up clouds of illumination. Run toward the beckoning magnificence. Golden lips kiss my face. I run. Run toward the golden globe, into the arms of the sun. My limbs become lighter and lighter. My physical weight falls away.

My feet no longer touch the sand. I am floating on air toward the light, toward the center of the sun with its innumerable rays beckoning me into the Light. Toward the beginning and end of all. I am floating and floating, closer and closer to the source.

The blue sky is no more. Only the sun. Its warmth envelops me. Knowledge expands me. I am surrounded by light. I gracefully fly through golden space, toward its center. Eternity of gold. Eternity of Lightness. Purity. I am closer and closer.

Nearly there. I float now slower and slower, prolonging the anticipation, the bliss of final union.

Nearly there.

There!

At last!

I come to a soft stop. The final arrival. The golden glow illuminates eternity. I am eternity. No end. No beginning. Forever One.

I see. I see. My knowledge is touched by noble humility, kissed by the infinite depth of Divinity. My knowledge rises beyond time and space. I transmute to become Light. Gold.

"I have created everything. I have created everything for your knowledge. You are everything." I hear.

Everything.

Then, at first imperceptibly slowly, I float backward, away from the Light. Backward. Away from the center. Slowly. I grow aware of my physical body. I glimpse the now distant arms of the gold rays. I fall backward with greater speed. Further back till the blueness of the sky comes into view. I fall into an eternity of blueness, its waves foaming, curling. I taste the salt as the waves play with my body which becomes filled with water, growing heavier and heavier, falling back, sinking toward the depth, lower and lower. Sinking into the embrace of the waters, into transparent darkness, into the thick sands of the world.

A dim light in my head glimmers in the distance. My body has the heaviness of lead. With enormous difficulty, I open my lids to see a vague shape resembling Jamal sitting by my side. A number of men are standing behind him.

"God is good," I hear someone say as my lids fall closed again.

Someone shakes my shoulders. My lids open again, this time with greater ease. Jamal's face comes into focus.

"We have spent the whole day searching for you," he says. "Thank God, you are alive."

I smile remembering the golden sun and close my eyes again.

I spend several days in bed. Finally, I am strong enough to get back on my feet. A servant, Jamal has instructed to stay behind, never leaves my side. I spend a long time carefully examining the carpets the caravan brings back. I revel in their texture, their brilliant colors, and their fine workmanship. I am overcome by immense wonder at the beauty man can create—the exquisite patterns his fingers weave!

As I marvel at the intricate carpet designs of gardens, animals, fishes, and mosques and as I wonder at the subtle use of colors, a verse of the Qur'an comes into my head:

"He made for you all that lies within the earth." (2; 29)

I once more walk out into the desert, this time followed by the servant. I gaze toward the mountains, lifting my eyes to their snowy peaks. I behold the drifting sand. I breathe in, expanding my chest with the fullness of life. I turn to the servant who gives me a big smile, pleased I have at last noticed him.

Am I not negating Allah's creation by ignoring it? My absolute desire to be one with Allah, my sacrifice of everything within and without in order to attain His grace, is that not just part of the path, and in no way the end? I have shunned the physical world in favor of the spiritual. Jahm too at one time shunned the physical world. Then, later, he fully embraced it. This is what led him to proclaim that God was in everything. He knew that once you touched eternity, you had to return to teach people about pervasive Divinity. We and everything on earth contain and are touched by the grace of Allah.

At last I understand what Jahm had meant! Before, I had only an intellectual understanding of his views. Now my understanding has deepened, passed through another veil.

Am I not here in this physical body to learn about physical creation, and through physical creation know Divine Creation? As above so below. As within so without. It is all One. Now that I have glimpsed the above, I must look at what is below. I must love and respect Allah in His physical manifestation. Above is unity. Below is diversity, attempting to find itself in totality. Having walked the path of Sufism and experienced the Divine, I must now return to the physical world with my newfound knowledge.

Our caravan returns to Fez. Two camels are loaded down with freshly acquired carpets. I smile at Jamal, glance at the men riding alongside of me, and surrender to destiny.

In Fez, I go to the market and marvel at the colorful variety before my eyes. I am alive to human activity, emotions, the produce of nature exhibited in straw baskets. I bite into a fresh fig, and its sweet texture on my tongue sends a wave of pleasure through my body. I gaze down at the half-eaten fruit, and its sensual beauty with its firm green exterior and soft, moist, delicate crimson interior brings tears to my eyes. I put the rest of the fig into my mouth and slowly devour its yielding flesh. I have at last returned to my body. I rub my thighs to wipe the juice of the fig from my hands and take pleasure in the feel of my taut muscles beneath the material of my slacks. I am even proud of my red hair and now laugh when people tease me about it.

As I help Jamal out in the store and gaze with renewed admiration at the patterns of the carpets, I begin to wonder about my future. I do not need to return to the hermitage. Nor do I want to return to being a judge. I must tackle a new area that requires all my knowledge.

Carrying a number of Jamal's carpets with me, I return to Tangier and take the boat back to al-Andalus. It is a clear day. The water is calm, gently lapping the sides of the boat as it glides through the playful waves. In the distance, a land very slowly comes into view. My eyes strain until I finally detect the huge rock rising toward the sky like a back of a camel. The rock of Gibraltar. Tears rise to my eyes.

In Algeciras, I join a caravan heading to Cordoba. After two weeks of travel through landscape bursting with color, I spot the minaret of the Great Mosque, with its elliptical spheres of gold and silver, glistening in the light. Spring air fills my nostrils, and I catch a hint of sweet jasmine. The rays of the setting sun clothe the hills in slashes of transparent gold and silver. I glance toward the fiery globe.

I am home.

XIII. Home

There is no better time to return to Cordoba than in the spring. The air is filled with the sweetness of flowers opening to the coming of the summer sun. All nature is in bloom.

Returning to the family house kindles memories of the past. I feel a deep gratitude for the life I have led to date. Love and compassion blossom toward every member of the family. There is always something to smile about; shared laughter comes easily.

My father has considerably aged but is still in excellent health. Leila, now a grown woman, has married, and her husband has joined the family carpet business. Lobua, who now works for al-Mansur's court, is full of complaints about the lack of respect for true knowledge. I am amused at her outrage. She responds with agitated anger. I ask how she could expect fear and oppression to respect knowledge? I suggest she simply try to enjoy the work she is given. Ali has taken another wife beside Noeima and has several grown children by now. Mustafa and Aishah now have three children; two sons and a daughter. The daughter looks just like Aishah; beautiful and proud. Of the two sons, one, Ashraf, shows particular intelligence and a leaning toward a scholastic life.

I view people and my surroundings with fresh eyes. I take pleasure in simply walking in the market, feeling at one with those around me. I pay a visit to Sheykh Mundhir. He looks exactly as I remember from five years ago. The passing of time has hardly left an imprint on his face. Clearly pleased to see me, he leads me to the reception room with enthusiasm.

"You look very well, Sulayman, very well," he says, smiling widely.

"As you see on the outside, so it is on the inside," I reply.

The Sheykh laughs. "You are now dressed as a man of the world." His hand waves up and down.

"I am returning to the physical world."

"You have acquired knowledge faster than I could have hoped," he chuckles.

"Now I must act upon that knowledge."

"Yes, you must do what you are called upon to do."

We embrace warmly before I leave.

"I will come and visit you again," I say.

"Only if you feel a need," he replies.

As I walk back along the banks of the river and across the Roman bridge, I remember the first time 'Abdallah had brought me to the hermitage. A lifetime has passed since then; in fact, I feel as if several lifetimes have passed.

Shihab now has three wives and seven children. He has restored an old Roman house to a wonderful and spacious dwelling. In the middle courtyard, on the floor, Roman mosaics depict a charioteer whipping his horses into a frenzy while the spectators watch nearby. Shihab is very proud of the mosaic; he has spent a great deal of money to revive it.

"I am still a judge taking care of endowments," he tells me once we settle down in the courtyard for coffee and cakes. "I am not like you, Sulayman. I prefer an easy life with good food and good women and lovely children."

"You are right, my friend," I say. "We must all do what gives us joy."

"I cannot honestly say that I am practicing a Divine calling." He takes a big bite of cake and glances toward the clear sky. "I would never say such a thing. However, I can say that I like my life. Changes in political climate have forced me to adapt to circumstance. Still, I have not experienced serious hardships. Allah is generous."

"Allah is generous with everyone. But most people find it difficult to recognize the form of His generosity."

After several weeks of enjoying the family, visiting old friends, and gauging the social and political climate, my mind turns to Esther. I have not yet made contact with her since my return.

It is late afternoon. I sip mint tea in the outer courtyard and watch the servants move about. The sky is a brilliant, translucent blue; so clear, so deep. The coming heat of summer warms my bare feet. The trickling of the fountain mixes with the lazy movements of the women in the middle courtyard. A white pigeon flies down to drink from the fountain. A servant quickly runs to chase it away. It leaves behind, on the pink marble floor, the digested bright green waste of its lunch. The servant clucks in disgust and quickly wipes it off with a cloth in her hand. The small, daily activities of nature and men are filled with humor.

In the library, I search for pen and paper and write Esther a note. I fold it carefully and ask a servant to deliver it.

A reply arrives the next morning. She asks me to meet her in a week's time in the pleasure garden by the river, near the central fountain. I wonder why a week's time only.

I wait on the tiled bench by the fountain. Once more, the sun is out in its full magnificence and the white pigeons cluster around the falling water. I luxuriate in the heat and lose myself in the ripples of the river below. I feel a hand covering mine and I quickly look up to see Esther. Her smile sparkles with surprising brilliance. Her black hair is streaked with a few strands of white. Over the years her slim frame has filled out to a sensuous roundness, just enough to make her pleasantly appealing. And the deep brown darkness of her eyes! I had forgotten their immeasurable depth. We look at each other for a long time in silence. Our eyes travel over features we had half forgotten, features that now show the proud passing of time, features that hold experiences and knowledge. How I want to take her in my arms! The ardor of my youth has now been replaced by a soft desire, a gentle longing. I look toward the fountain, silently reminding myself that Esther is a married woman.

"I wanted to see you as soon as your note arrived," Esther says quietly, sitting down beside me. "I could not because I was sitting Shiva."

I quickly look back at her and notice that she is wearing black. Of course, I had forgotten. We Muslims wear white on a death. She reads the question in my eyes.

"Simeon has died. He died in his sleep. He had been complaining about chest pains for several months. Being a doctor, he tried everything to cure himself. At times, he felt better but the pain always came back. Finally, the pain won and he could no longer fight."

"Allah has taken only what he has given," I say softly.

"Yes." Her laughter is light, as the flowing water of the fountain.

I look at her silently, taking in her reaction. "You do not seem very sad."

"Sulayman, I have done my duty. I have done it to the best of my ability, without complaint. My four children are nearly all grown. My duty toward others is almost done. Soon I will have a chance once more to go back to my reading, once more to sit quietly and think, not always worry about another."

I smile. I smile at her firmness, her conviction, and her strength.

"Is Simeon's death hard on the children?" I ask.

"Of course they are sad but Simeon spent long hours at his medical practice. His patients will miss him more than the children. In addition, my brothers have played a major role in their upbringing. They have been as much a father to them as Simeon."

"Good. It seems expressions of grief are not necessary."

Again Esther laughs, throwing back her head. "No, Sulayman, no. I have been preparing myself for his death while he was still alive. Now, I am ready to begin a new phase of my life." She closes her eyes, enjoying the sun. After a short time she turns back to look at me, her face slightly flushed with warmth. "Tell me about you. You are extremely well-dressed for a Sufi."

It is my turn to laugh. "I am here to stay. I am living at my father's house."

"Have you left Sufism?"

"Once you become a Sufi, you are a Sufi. It is not something to leave. What I have learned, I will take with me no matter where I go."

"Perhaps you can say that about anything and everything. Certainly what I have learned in my marriage, I will always have. What I have learned as a mother, I will always cherish."

We both begin to laugh. Our laughter joins the singing water of the fountain. The light black shawl around Esther's head falls to her shoulders. I glance at her. A surge of warmth rises within me. Isaac is dead. Now Simeon is dead. Dare I revive a dream that is more than twenty years old?

Within days of seeing Esther, a letter arrives informing me Sebastian has died. The news produces a much greater shock than I would have expected. How often have I seen Sebastian in my life? Twice? Yet, those two times were both important periods for me. Both times our conversations had a lasting influence. Sebastian gave me that intangible needed element to help me move to a new level. Only two other men have given me that: 'Abdallah and Jahm. Both dead now. In the courtyard, I look toward the sky. Soft white clouds float over a gentle blue. I have been lucky to know such men. I am grateful for the knowledge they have passed on to me.

Recently, I have been searching for ways to give back to the world what I myself have learned. At the same time, I do not want to neglect my own development. Since I have left the desert with Jamal I have had only vague thoughts of the future. Now the answer has crystallized. I will teach. In addition, I will think. Also, I will write: about Truth, as I understand it. My time as a judge and Sufi has provided me with a variety of experiences. It is time for me to pass on what I have learned. It is also time to digest my accumulated knowledge and go one step further. I must continue to stretch, to search.

In honor of Sebastian I go to a church to pray. I enter the dark stone building, so unlike our sun-filled mosques. There are a few stained-glass windows allowing in dim streaks of light. Candles provide most of the illumination. I kneel down in a wooden pew as I see other people do around me. No longer do the statues of Jesus, Mary, and the saints shock me. My mind is calm as my eyes explore my surroundings; the elaborate frescoes, the carved columns, the enormous cross. Can God hear when one speaks to Him from here? Of course. One can speak to God from anywhere, be it a church, synagogue, mosque, or the open fields.

I pray to Sebastian in my own way, reciting a few verses from the Qur'an. My mind embraces him. In addition, I thank him for all he has given me.

Esther and I make our way up the mountain toward the Christian monastery where Sebastian had always stayed. At a short distance from the monastery, we find a flat spot under some linden trees and tie our donkeys to the trunk. Esther spreads out a blanket and unties the picnic basket from the back of the donkey. We calmly settle down to the chirping of birds and the sweet smell of summer. We both lie down and close our eyes, idly searching in the basket for fresh figs. Our hands meet reaching for the same fruit.

"We share it," announces Esther, sitting up.

She takes a bite of the fig and puts the rest in my mouth. I remember when I came back from the desert; how I felt eating that fresh fig. I reach over and caress Esther's hair and face. She moves closer and lies into my arms.

"We have each other once more," she says.

"Do we?"

"Now there is no one to stop us."

She looks up at me. My lips find hers and my arms wrap around her shoulders and waist.

"Will you marry me now?" I ask when we have disengaged.

"Must we marry? Can we not just be lovers and friends?"

"It is against Islamic law to have sexual relations with a woman other than your wife. I would be committing a crime making love to you."

Esther looks down at her hands, thinking. Finally, she takes an audible breath and looks up.

"I would still like to spend time in my own house. I do not want to move suddenly from my house to yours. I would like to have my solitude."

"You can have as much freedom as you need within our marriage."

"You would not mind if I did not stay with you every night?"

"No. As long as I know we are together, we need not be together physically all the time."

Esther throws her arms around my neck. "Oh, Sulayman, to think my love for you has not diminished after all this time."

"There is one more thing," I add. "We must promise to be always truthful to each other."

"Yes, yes," she nods eagerly.

Could it really be true? I will at last fulfill my youthful dream. Loving God, loving all, has taken me to a plane where all is possible.

My past qualification as a judge secures me a teaching post in the Great Mosque. There are very few foreign students. A great number are Berbers. They are part of families originally from the hills of North Africa. These students have had an extremely dogmatic early training. They are very uncomfortable with the questions I pose during my classes. They cannot accept that a given problem can be viewed from more than one perspective. They simply want to be taught the correct way of looking at questions and answers; the one and only way.

I patiently encourage them to examine questions and to discover the variety of ways that a question could be interpreted. Then I point out that if a question can be interpreted more than one way, then surely that question could have more than one answer.

The intellectual life of Cordoba is tightly controlled. I had received my education under al-Hakam II who himself respected knowledge. Under his reign, ideas flowed freely; questions were eagerly discussed. Now the approach to education has become highly conservative. Questions are discouraged. Doubts are suppressed. The written word is the only acceptable answer.

The other teachers look upon me with mistrust. Some take me aside and in a friendly way advise me to be careful how I teach. Often spies are known to attend lectures, they tell me. Al-Mansur does not tolerate thinking that veers from the accepted line. Orthodoxy reigns. Anything that seems to threaten this orthodoxy is immediately crushed. If I value my life, they warn me, I must be cautious. I appreciate their advice.

Does one have to be cautious about the truth? I ask myself as I am walking back home. Yes. If the Truth is presented to people who are not seeking it, they will debase it. Only those who search can find the Truth. Without the desire to know, one does not learn. I should tone down my lectures and give my students only small pieces of knowledge to tickle their curiosity.

Finding myself in a house crowded with innumerable very affectionate and helpful family members is becoming overbearing. However, I enjoy and love them, I long to be alone once more. As well, when Esther and I marry, I would like to have more privacy.

I set out to actively search for a house. I cannot decide whether I want a house in the city of Cordoba itself or a little further out. Perhaps in the hills, or near the river. I decide to look in all areas and buy the house that is appealing, that looks as if it will suit my needs. I have never looked for a house before. I have never had to define exactly what sort of an external environment I would like. This search is a new experience for me, a little like choosing my own clothes for the first time.

One day I go to look at a house standing on the side of a small hill just to the north of the city walls. Spruce and pine trees surround it.

A couple close to my age let me into the house. There is only one large courtyard laid with turquoise and blue tiles. Intermittently, there are also yellow tiles which form a five-pointed star around a central single-jet fountain rising from a round white marble pool of water built into the ground. There is a deep portico, which leads to the various rooms on the main floor. The house has two levels with a cedar gallery on the second floor. In the back of the house is a walled garden with stables for donkeys and horses. The servants' rooms open toward this garden. An arched hallway leads from the courtyard to the back.

I find the house charming. In size, it is perfect for Esther, about three servants, and myself. In addition, as I look around, I think it could even be big enough for me to hold classes here, should the need arise. The house is so enchanting that I am surprised the couple wants to sell.

They invite me to sit down and have a coffee with them in the garden, near the rose bushes. As we relax, they explain they are planning to live in Cairo. Upon further questioning, they reveal that they disapprove of al-Mansur's reign and their children have already moved to Cairo. They claim any man who usurps the rightful Caliph's power must fall. They feel that no justice can come of such a rule. I nod in agreement. Other people have expressed similar feelings. Still, I am optimistic. I like to think that after the death of al-Mansur, and the man cannot live forever, especially since he fights several campaigns a year, a rightful ruler, who is not afraid of knowledge, will take his place.

I take Esther to see the house. She is as enchanted with it as I am. I commit myself to buy it.

It takes several months to clean up the house and move everything in to make it comfortable.

When it is finished, Esther and I finally get married. We hold a modest celebration, inviting only our immediate families. For the occasion, the house is gaily decorated both inside and out. We cleared out part of the land behind the garden and opened the iron door to allow the guests to roam in the back. The servants move among the crowd with trays of fine meats, delicately marinated vegetables, sweets, and fresh fruit. We all join the singers when they burst into song. The wedding turns into a warm and intimate affair where everyone thoroughly enjoys themselves. Esther and I feel in our twenties again. No time has passed. Yet several lifetimes have passed.

My daily trip to the Great Mosque takes considerably longer from my new house. My travel through the city makes me even more aware of the expanding population of Cordoba. Increasingly Berbers are coming in from North Africa. So many have now settled in Cordoba that al-Mansur has ordered an expansion of the Great Mosque to accommodate the burgeoning population. I now teach with a construction crew constantly working behind me.

To my surprise, the new extension is finished within a year. However, al-Mansur's addition is not of the same refined quality as al-Hakam II's had been. Al-Mansur is more concerned about space for the Berbers than about aesthetics. What can be expected from a man whose sole desire is power?

The numerous fortunetellers on the street warn of a great famine to come. Storytellers sing tales of people who must pay dearly for desires that grow in bad soil. Rumors multiply in the market. The embers of people's fears are fanned. To counteract this invisible threat, the orthodox theologians grow even stricter. However, the whispering will not be muzzled.

My ability to teach, as I would like, grows even more restricted. I find my students tainted by the element of fear circulating in the city. They are more nervous; their attention span grows shorter. I decide to move my classes up to my house. I find this a much more pleasant surrounding for learning. As well, it is removed from the centre of the city, from the source of the fear. I lay the cushions out for the students in the courtyard and we have all the time we need for the lecture and subsequent discussion without having to worry about other classes. Often, after a lecture, I ask the servant to pour tea for the students, serve cake, and we sit back and talk at leisure. At times, Esther joins us.

Now that I have moved my classes to the house, Ashraf, Aishah's son, has come to attend. He is a very soft-spoken yet an eager student. He is still young, the youngest of my students, but certain inclinations are already evident. His bend is much more toward scholasticism than the family carpet business. Aishah has asked me to watch him. She has indicated that if he desires to follow scholasticism she would consider sending him to the east for further studies.

I enjoy the company of young people around me. I take pleasure in their inquisitive minds. Here, in my own house, I need not worry how I teach. I need not worry that I might offend the local authorities.

Ghaylan, one of my students, a rather bright young man with a sharp mind and an excellent future, has taken to dropping in on me between classes. At first, we discuss philosophy and law. After several visits, he veers the subject toward politics. He tells me that my political views are very clear in the way I teach. This comes as a surprise to me; I am not at all aware of taking a political stand in my lectures. I think Ghaylan has been interpreting my words to suit his own needs. Of course, I say nothing of my view to him. I simply smile.

He lowers his head, clasps his hands together, and announces, "There is a secret, a very important political secret I would like to share with you."

It seems that his father is involved in a conspiracy with a number of other Arab aristocrats to overthrow al-Mansur and put the rightful Caliph back in the seat of power. At first, I am concerned to hear him discuss such a plot in my presence.

"Your father would certainly punish you if he heard you tell me this," I say.

"No," he quickly replies. "I have spoken at great length about you to my father. He would like you to join their plans."

"You would like me to join in the overthrow of al-Mansur?"

"Yes," he says eagerly. "You would make an important addition to the group."

I look at the gently falling fountain. When I was still a judge, I had joined in the plot of putting al-Hakam's brother on the throne instead of Hisham. I had such hopes. I was devastated when the brother was murdered by al-Mansur. Now, my place is not in politics. My knowledge is not meant to serve politics.

"Thank you for the invitation, Ghaylan," I say. "But I must refuse it. I am a teacher. It is the people I must teach."

Ghaylan's eyes grow wide with disbelief. Clearly, he had expected me to be flattered by his invitation and to accept.

"Do you think these days you have the luxury to watch from the sidelines?" he accuses. "Are you naive enough to believe that politics do not affect your personal life?"

"My ability does not lie in politics," I stress.

"Your ability can be affected by politics. You might not be able to continue teaching the way you have been," he says in anger.

"Perhaps. When that time comes then I will take action. Not before."

"Then it might be too late," he cries, very upset. "You might not be able to act."

"It is always possible to act."

Ghaylan flashes me a look of hatred. "I hope you will not mention to anyone what I have said to you."

"Of course not."

After Ghaylan leaves, I wonder if it was truly wise of me to refuse an invitation to overthrow al-Mansur. Though the man fascinates me in the way he has built up his power, I believe he has done Cordoba great harm. Would it not be a better contribution to society to overthrow the man?

When Esther arrives home, I raise my doubts with her. She is very aware of the political climate. Though the Jews have lived here in peace for over three hundred years, their political sensitivity is finely tuned, aware of any change the wind might bring. They know from the past, as well as the present situation around the world, that all it takes is a whim of a new ruler to reverse the circumstances of their communities. How must the Christians feel? Al-Hakam II had tried to maintain relative peace with the northern Christian territories. Al-Mansur's chief policy has been to devastate one Christian territory after another. Could these devastations mean that one day the Christians will unite and rise up against the Muslims in revenge? Will the Arabs have to pay for the bellicose actions of al-Mansur?

"Perhaps I could better serve al-Andalus if I fought to put Hisham back on the throne," I tell Esther.

"And if you are killed and the plot fails?" she asks.

"At least the effort will have been made."

"Will a failed effort mean more to you than continuing your teaching?"

I consider her words and laugh. Of course, I must continue to teach. It might not have as great or as glorious an effect as putting Hisham back on the throne, but my teaching has the capacity to stir deep currents within the students. Then, in time, they will demand a more responsible government. Indirectly, I am serving the same cause whether I join the plot or remain a teacher. Potentially, as a teacher, I have a longer life span and can touch more people. If I join the plot, there is a great possibility I will be caught and killed.

I take Esther in my arms and thank her. It helps to have someone close to mirror one's own thoughts.

The predictions of the market fortunetellers have come true. In the Muslim year 378, 988 for the Christians, there is a terrible drought. All the crops have dried in the lands. People are making bread from whatever grain is available. Famine starts to set in. Al-Mansur opens the court granary and in no time it is emptied out. People fall sick. Innumerable die. Even Esther and our families as well as I are forced to reduce our daily food consumption.

The fortunetellers say the drought has been brought on by al-Mansur's greed for power. The Berbers claim the drought is the will of Allah and all suspicious elements must be wiped out since Allah's wrath is raging against them.

I point out to my student that just as the Qur'an and the Hadith are open to interpretation, so is the action of nature.

After one of my classes, when we are all sitting in the courtyard sipping tea, one of my Berber students accuses me of encouraging dissent because I claim that the law should be open to interpretation. Another student adds that at a time like this, a time of drought, we should all hold firmly together to the word of Allah and accept the theologians' interpretation. This is not a time to throw open the door to other perspectives. Another student adds that this drought shows Allah is clearly displeased with teachers like me who sow seeds of doubt about the Divine word in the minds of his students.

To my surprise, Ghaylan quickly jumps to my defense and accuses the Berber students of supporting a usurper in the person of al-Mansur. He yells that it is because of them Allah has brought the drought, not because of people who encourage freethinking.

"The Qur'an does not want you to believe in its teachings blindly. It encourages you to think for yourself and to interpret," Ghaylan continues, turning red in anger.

"How dare you think you can interpret the Word of God?" yells another Berber student.

"Would you think yourselves greater than Allah by questioning Him?" cries another Berber, waving a fist in the air.

At this all the Berbers storm out of the house, furiously yelling at the rest of us who remain behind.

"There is still time for you to join my invitation," says Ghaylan quietly.

"No, my role lies elsewhere."

"There is not much time left." Ghaylan gets up, ready to leave. "Do think again, carefully."

Over the next two weeks, none of my Berber students attend my classes. One day, after the third prayer of the day, Shihab shows up. I am very pleased to see him and warmly welcome him into my house. He looks good and the famine of the city hardly shows on his round frame.

As we sit down on the round leather puffs in the courtyard, it is clear that he has come to relay an important message. He does not look me in the eyes. His gaze moves around the courtyard. He praises everything. The servant brings us tea, and then departs.

"This is a very difficult visit for me," Shihab finally says, exhaling loudly.

"We are friends. You should feel comfortable to say anything to me."

Shihab shakes his head sadly. "If you do not drastically change your teaching you could lose your life. There is an accusation of heresy against you. The only reason the guards have not yet come to throw you into prison is because I vouched for you and begged them to let me first have a word with you before they acted."

I smile inwardly. This news is not a surprise. "Did my Berber students bring a charge of heresy against me?"

"I do not know if it was the students or their parents. But, yes, it was the Berbers. They want you dismissed as a teacher, preferably executed for your heretical views."

A space of silence passes between us as we sip our teas. I find it amusing to think that I could lose my life as a teacher, just as I could lose my life by joining Ghaylan's political plot. After all, was it not my teaching in Fez that got me thrown into prison and nearly killed? It seems the same situation has come back to test me the second time.

"I can only teach what I believe," I finally say. "I will not change the structure of my courses to suit the authorities."

"In that case you should consider giving up your teaching altogether. Find another way to express your views."

I remember the desert. The sun. Did I truly find the Philosopher's Stone? On the other hand, will I spend the rest of my life looking for it? Perhaps my experience in the desert was a mere tantalizing glimpse. However, now that I have committed myself to walk the path of Truth, I cannot turn back. It is impossible to turn back.

"Let me think about it." I smile kindly at Shihab's extreme discomfort.

"Remember, they are willing to execute anyone they suspect. You are now being carefully watched."

"It is not yet time for me to die," I assure him. "There are things I have yet to accomplish.

After bidding Shihab good-bye and thanking him for his warning Ashraf, Aishah's son, arrives.

"I met some of the Berber students at the Great Mosque," he says breathlessly, "and they said you have stopped teaching. When I told them I was here only two days ago for a class they became very angry and said you will die if you continue."

"Yes, Ashraf," I reply, indicating him to sit down.

"I don't understand." He sinks onto the puff Shihab just vacated.

"It seems I cannot continue teaching as I have," I explain.

"Why?"

"The people in power view curiosity as a threat."

"Are they going to kill you if you continue to teach?"

"If I continue as before, then certainly."

"What will you do?"

"Ashraf," I ruffle his dark curls and pat his cheek. *Such a simple question and so hard to answer.* I think in silence, "Yes, what will I do?"

"You can go to the east and teach there. I would follow you," Ashraf suggests.

I laugh. "Later, I might consider your proposal. As for now, I am not yet ready to travel."

"You will not let them kill you!"

"No. I suppose to stay alive I must stop teaching. But I cannot stop thinking."

"Then write down your thoughts, and I will read them."

I look at him. Of course, the writing! How could I have forgotten? Is writing not a form of teaching?

Though I have officially stopped teaching, Ghaylan and Ashraf still come to the house for discussions and to read the books in my library. One afternoon Ghaylan stays behind to have supper with Esther and me. After supper, when we are alone in the garden, I ask him about the plot to assassinate al-Mansur.

Ghaylan turns away from me. When I press him for details he finally blurts out that everyone, including his father, have been caught and imprisoned. Tears well up in his eyes. He had been ashamed to tell me. I put my arms around him in a warm embrace.

One morning Ashraf arrives early. The news he brings plunges me into the depths of sadness. Last night my father died in his sleep.

The whole family mourns as we bury him next to his wives, in the family plot. After the funeral, when we have shed all the tears possible, my brothers begin to talk about the business. They know that I have stopped teaching.

"You should think of coming to join us. It will give you extra capital," says my brother Husan.

"Perhaps. I might consider coming to help from time to time. But I must focus on writing now."

"Working with carpets could provide a good balance for writing," offers Ali.

"It could. It could. Give me time. We'll see," I reply.

We eat, drink, and exchange memories of our childhood. We review our lives in detail, recalling special events. We seem to be redefining our lives for a new beginning—a beginning without our father. We attempt to relive several decades through words. We laugh. We cry. We hold each other in tight embrace. Gradually the weight of the loss becomes easier. After all, it is not our father we are mourning but ourselves, our loss. With the death of our father, a part of ourselves has also ceased to exist. We must readjust to that missing piece within each of us. We must now make ourselves whole again.

Much to Shihab's relief, I settle down to a very quiet life of writing. At first, I spend months and months reading, taking only a few notes. Gradually, my notes grow longer and longer until I find my mornings are totally taken up with writing. I return to my reading in the late afternoons or evenings. I discover that writing is not like teaching. It requires a much tighter inner discipline. The concentration I had learned in my early Sufi days is proving to be a considerable help.

After reviewing my notes, I realize I must clearly define what I want to write. I must give my notes a specific structure. This brings up another question. Why do I want to write? It is another form of teaching. In that case, my writings must present my point of view. I must write down my perspective of law. However, Islamic law is linked to the Qur'an and the Hadith. This means I must also write down my views of these two works. In other words, I must write a commentary. However, writing a commentary on the Qur'an has preoccupied lifetimes. How, at the age of fifty-one, could I hope to begin? I am starting too late. I will never accomplish the task I am setting for myself. I spend days and days paralyzed by the enormity of my task. Esther tries to console me. She suggests I dictate to her. She offers to buy whatever supplies I need for my work. She offers to arrange the house as comfortably as possible to suit my needs.

Nothing helps to dislodge the dark cloud now stationed above my head. It is all too much. Why even bother to start? I will never be able to finish. Even if I do finish a work, it will never see the light of day, given present political circumstances. The authorities will burn whatever I have written before a bookseller could even acquire it. No one will ever be able to read what I write.

From my encircling despair, I spot a little dim light in the distance. How could you have so neglected all you have learned, says a kind voice. How could you have forgotten the sun, the trust, and the surrender?

I get up from my cushion. Push open the latticed wooden doors of the library and rush out into the courtyard where I plunge my face into the jet of the fountain. Cold water splashes over my clothes. The winter air is chilling, but the shivering brings a sharp alertness to my mind. Gray clouds cover the sky, and a light rain is falling with a promise to mature into a heavy downpour.

I remove my shoes and perform the necessary ablution by the fountain. Symbolically I cleanse my soul, my spirit, and the innermost part of my being. I cleanse my doubts, my fears, and my hopelessness and thank Allah for my place in the whole. I thank Him for my ordeals, which guide me back to the light.

How often must we travel the same road?

I am learning. I am learning.

The prayers fill me with warmth and gratitude. At the end, I sit down on the tiles, on one tip of the yellow star. I sit and dream as the pouring rain washes over my body. Darkness finds me still sitting in the courtyard. I look up at the black sky. No stars are visible. Clouds cover the moon. Yet, innumerable stars sparkle in my heart.

Slowly, painfully slowly, I begin to write. I tell myself that political systems change, as everything on this physical plane must change. Even if no one reads my works while I am alive, a time will come when my words will see the light. I am not writing for only today. I am writing for eternity. I am writing for my own development. I am writing for the development of the world. I am writing to maintain the flow, the fluidity of all through one.

I spend my days writing. I pray at home, only for the Friday prayers do I join my brothers and go to the Great Mosque. For relaxation, I take walks with Esther or wander down to the market. The slave markets have predominantly Christian slaves; the stores are selling increasingly more Christian artifacts: all booty from al-Mansur's expeditions. Bronze church bells brought back from the Holy Wars have been converted to lanterns. There are intricately worked ceremonial candleholders. All objects for which blood has been shed.

I stroll down the street of the booksellers and chat with the owners. I listen to the storytellers, the minstrels, and the Qur'an chanters. I watch the workers laying in the pebbles for the gutter. I listen to the news of the city and join in discussions of the future. I hear that one of al-Mansur's sons took refuge in Castile with Count Garcia Fernandez because his father had preferred his younger brother, Abd al-Malik. The Count, due to his fear of al-Mansur, soon returned the son to his father who, without hesitation, killed him for his betrayal. It seems desire for external power knows no bounds. Al-Mansur must live in constant fear, never fully secure in the power he had long ago stolen from Hisham. He must kill and destroy whatever threatens his personal authority.

From time to time, I also go down to the warehouse to write letters for my brothers. I spend entire afternoons gazing at the new shipment of carpets. Their colors and designs never fail to captivate me.

Through thinking, reading, and writing, I realize that, on a certain level, all the monotheistic religions require unquestioning belief. Orthodox groups claim to teach the revelation of their religion as written in the Book. In reality, they are teaching an interpretation.

Some have said that reason is not contrary to revelation, I write. Reason is needed to understand revelation. How can one understand through blind acceptance? The revelations of the Old and New Testaments and the Qur'an are often written in parables. The true meaning of these parables is hidden behind countless veils. Man must be trained to think in order to understand, in order to pull aside the veils one by one.

It is impossible to give man the Truth. It is too brilliant for the untrained eye. Its rays will blind the feeble-sighted. At first, it must be veiled in darkness, and then gradually revealed, as the eye grows accustomed to the light. Truth can harm those not strong enough to withstand its splendor. This is why the holy books talk in parables, I write.

The common people believe God is reached through the practice of concretely choreographed prayer. Few understand that there is a much more brilliant light behind these external forms of veneration. Few want to understand because understanding takes effort. It takes effort to break the habit of religious laws.

People refuse to accept different interpretations because they need to believe that they, exclusively, hold the Truth. Little do they realize that man cannot hold Truth. The eternal cannot be held by the temporal. It is Truth, which holds man, not the other way around. And man changes. His circumstance changes, civilization changes, societies change. It is inevitable that his vision of the Truth must also change. If interpretation of the Truth is not allowed fluidity, it hardens to oppression. Any religion must contain openness or else it stagnates.

Ultimately, when man travels down the road in search of Truth he will always find the same thing. Truth will never change. However, the roads leading to that Truth are infinite in number. Anything human will merely express the shadow of the Absolute, through veils of symbolism.

Interpretation must grow and evolve. Interpretation does not change the intrinsic value of that which is interpreted; the Qur'an will always be the holy book. Allah will always be Omnipotent. Only man's perspective shifts and changes as he himself shifts and changes. In addition, Allah has created all things to shift and change. Man's vision must always be subjective. Only Allah can be objective.

I put down my pen and gaze out the door of the library, at the gently falling fountain. What joy there is in writing!

Esther passes through the courtyard, glances into the library, and smiles.

My love expands to embrace Esther, to embrace Cordoba, to forgive the orthodox theologians and al-Mansur, who are all part of the One.

During one of my forays into the marketplace, I learn that al-Mansur has conferred the title of hajib on Abd al-Malik, one of his sons. This move indicates he plans to make the post hereditary. A move equal to declaring himself Caliph.

Within weeks, Hisham officially announces he is incompetent to govern. This clears the road for al-Mansur. To crown his legal acquisition of power, he longs to prove himself equal to his role. He undertakes a campaign against the Christian Mecca at Santiago in the northwestern part of the Hispanic peninsula. Santiago is a European center of pilgrimage, which houses the tomb of the Apostle, St. James the Great.

Al-Mansur triumphantly returns from his campaign carrying the bells from the Church of Santiago de Compostela through the city streets of Cordoba, to the Great Mosque, where they are hung as trophies to the victorious ruler.

According to his poets, whose poems are sung in the marketplace, al-Mansur ruthlessly sacked and burned the city but his superstition left the saint's tomb unmolested. Clearly, his conscience did not allow total desecration for fear of God's retribution.

The fortunetellers of the city are whispering the inevitable downfall of Cordoba, though commercially, the city is prospering. My brothers are doing excellent business. However, Cordoba has long lost its international attraction. Fewer travelers come through the gates of the city. The once magnificent flower is now wilting.

I have witnessed Cordoba's blossoming into the center of the world under al-Hakam II. Soon, time will erase its very existence. The eternal, cyclical change continues. Nothing physical is exempt from Divine Law.

I write with furious speed. Thoughts form and reform in my mind. I make new connections and discover new meanings. With each day, my mind becomes sharper, more alert. However, my body is starting to slow down. At times, I have trouble breathing and wake in the middle of the night gasping for breath. Esther grows concerned and calls the doctor. The doctor gives me herbs to seep in hot water. They help for a few days. Then again, my respiration grows increasingly more difficult. However, my mind races ahead, alive with the freshness of new ideas.

I compare the Torah's version of Adam and Eve with the one in the Qur'an. The tree of knowledge in the middle of the garden certainly provoked curiosity! God must have surely known that Eve would eat of the fruits of the tree, must have known that Eve's curiosity would mature to the point of breaking His law. After all, is it not curiosity, which leads to knowledge? Once man tasted the fruits, he was ready for a much larger world than the garden. He was ready to tackle a home with much wider limits. Does the Qur'an not say, "My righteous slaves will inherit the earth." (21:105)?

Another issue that draws me is the concept of heaven and hell. The Greek word Hades referred to our physical world as the lowest point of existence: hell. Is it not possible that man has it within his power to create both heaven and hell here on earth? Perhaps it is not a heaven and hell in the hereafter but in this life. It is not a heaven and hell of God's creation but of man's. And for this, man must take responsibility.

One day two guards show up at my door and insist on seeing my writings. I deny having anything.

"We have information that you spend your days writing," the big-shouldered guard says with gruff boredom in his voice.

He pushes me aside with an easy swipe of his thick arm and strolls into the courtyard. The smaller guard quickly follows him. They stroll around, looking into the open doors off the portico.

"Here," calls the smaller guard eagerly. "Here is the library."

"There is nothing in there, just books," I say a little too quickly.

"Just books?" Snickers the big guard. "Don't you know books are dangerous?"

He walks into the library and stands at the entrance, hands on hips. The smaller guard begins to search the materials on my desk. I stand behind the enormous shoulders of the guard at the door, trying to see in.

The big guard also goes to my desk and rummages around, picking up sheets of paper and reading the writing without interest. I think of the trunk hidden in the stables, filled with my writings. I silently pray that they will be satisfied with the few hundred pages on the desk and not look any further.

They pack the papers on my desk into a big jute bag and then head over to the shelves of books.

"Do you know which books are banned?" asks the smaller guard from the bigger one.

"No, just take some books at random," replies the bigger one.

They fill the jute bag with as many books as it will hold, then tie a string around it. The big guard hoists it atop his head and walks out with easy strides.

"You'll hear from us after the writing is checked," shouts the smaller guard as they leave.

I shut the door behind and collapse onto a cushion. Ignorance is frightening.

Alone, I sit in the courtyard and try to remember the contents of those few hundred pages the guards have hauled away. I will have to rewrite them. *It does not matter,* I tell myself. I will continue as if the guards had never come.

The Christians are celebrating the New Year. They now write thousand. This year has created a tremendous frenzy among their fortune-tellers. There are predictions of the inevitable Judgment Day, the end of the world. Groups of bleeding flagellants parade in the squares before bemused Muslims. Priests preach with a furious fervor, yelling that hellfire is about to erupt from the bowels of the earth, burning the very fabric of the world. It takes little time for Muslim fortunetellers to catch the fever of unequivocal horror. They now predict the downfall of al-Mansur, unprecedented chaos, and the end of Muslim rule. Fear sizzles in the marketplace. Even buying an eggplant comes with dire predictions.

The state of my health grows weaker as the ardor of the predictions become more frantic. My breathing grows increasingly more painful, while my thinking grows more and more sublime. Esther, concerned about my physical health, calls upon several doctors to help me. None can find a cure. My own concern lies less with a cure than with the masses of documents I have written over the years. If predictions of the fall of Muslim rule are correct, there is no hope my writings will see the light of day. The Christians will certainly make no effort to preserve them.

One night, during supper with my family, Aishah tells me she is sending Ashraf to Cairo for further studies. Ashraf eagerly asks me to accompany him. He tells me that in Cairo I would be able to teach again.

That night, in bed, I consider Ashraf's suggestion. Certainly, I could take all my writings to Cairo. There I would have a much greater chance to disseminate my work. Here my words are simply languishing in a trunk. In addition, I no longer want to be vulnerable to further raids. Now that the guards have taken my work, someone in authority will surely read it. My manuscript will condemn me to certain death. Though it is not death I fear. I must do everything within my power to ensure my writings will survive.

By the time I wake up in the morning, I know I must leave.

I begin to prepare for the journey. Esther will not accompany me because she wants to stay with her family right now. The Jews are fearful for their safety; the community is discussing ways of avoiding a tragedy. She assures me she will join me in six months.

I prepare my belongings. I carefully seal the trunk containing my writings. My personal clothing is relegated to another trunk. Esther and I exchange a loving farewell, certain a reunion is no more than a few months later.

I ride away on the donkey, continually turning back toward Esther and the house. I will probably never return here. Though this house has given me tremendous joy, I do not find it difficult to give up. I willingly go wherever I am guided. I smile up at the glowing sun. That is my true home.

Ashraf and I, along with two servants, head toward Pechina. It takes us two weeks to reach this southeastern port. Its harbor holds ships from Syria, Egypt and Byzantium. The naval fleet is also standing in waiting. We have a couple of days in Pechina before our boat is ready to sail. The morning we are about to board, we hear that al-Mansur has destroyed the monastery of San Millan in Castile and, on his way back home, he died at Medinaceli. The rosewood coffin that had been accompanying him for years on all his campaigns, waiting for its owner to claim it, is finally filled.

What will happen to Cordoba now?

The boat slowly moves away from the shores of al-Andalus. Ashraf's mind is already in Cairo. My eyes stay on the receding land mass as I silently say good-bye to the country of my youth, to the nurturing bosom of the rolling hills.

The ship sails smoothly along the open sea. The weather is favorable with calm waters and clear skies.

"I hope you have your work with you," says Ashraf as we look out at the playful waves.

"I have brought everything with me. It's all in the green trunk," I smile.

Sea gulls swoop close to the waves, picking up bits of food thrown to them by the passengers.

"Will you let me read something?"

"When we have settled in Cairo, you can read all you want." I laugh.

"Can't I read something now? We have more than a week before landing," Ashraf pleads.

His youthful curiosity gives me pleasure. "I don't want to open the trunk. But you are welcome to read whatever I write on the boat."

I had hoped to write during the trip but Ashraf is full of questions. I enjoy talking. I enjoy instructing. There is such pleasure in passing on knowledge.

Unfortunately, my breathing has once more started to bother me. I silently fight the pain in my chest and say nothing of it to Ashraf. The boat rocks us, cradling us over the vast expanse of water. Despite the pain, I enjoy my nights, feeling the roll of the sea under my body.

One night, as I am about to fall asleep, I look out my small window and see a clear dark sky dotted with sparkling stars. I close my eyes and inside my mind's eye, I see a blue sky splashed with the radiance of the sun. The boat rocks me. I suddenly open my eyes, quickly reach for my green trunk, and search for my writing papers and utensils. Whatever happens to me, I will leave all these papers to Ashraf. I write feverishly.

The rocking grows increasingly gentle until I no longer feel the movement of the boat. Gradually, I cease to sense the bed underneath me.

It is with great effort that I maintain my hand on the page to write this.

I am here, yet elsewhere. I begin to move gently upward, very slowly upward, until I am floating on air. A lighter, distant, part of me rolls with the clouds

In the softness of the sky, a puff obscures my clarity. I try to squeeze through two wisps. I struggle to rise higher, to join the sun.

A part of me is here, writing, another part is dissolving, rising.

I break through the clouds and see the sky again, the splendor of the sun. I arch my back and with tremendous effort try to fly upward into the embrace of the golden rays.

I write rapidly, to capture all.

Clouds once more obscure my view. I am overwhelmed by opaqueness. Once more, I struggle to break through, clawing at the grayness. Suddenly, there is an opening, a yield.

I am moving again.

At last!

Soon I will be there; I will return.

I float through space, over the fluidity of time, above the vast sea, toward the glow of the sun, toward the perfect gentleness of eternity.

I am one with All—the flowers and fruit of the earth and the beings who walk upon it.

I exhale loudly, profoundly satisfied. Done, a period is all that is needed.

This perception, the grasp of this knowledge, I leave to Ashraf and humanity.

THE END

CPSIA information can be obtained at www.ICGtesting.com
Printed in the USA
LVOW091129161011

250583LV00001B/2/P